Transactions
of the
American Philosophical Society
Held at Philadelphia
for Promoting Useful knowledge
Volume 88, Pt. 6

From *Academia* to *Amicitia*: Milton's Latin Writings and the Italian Academies

ESTELLE HAAN

American Philosophical Society
Independence Square ● Philadelphia
1998

Library of Congress Cataloging—in—Publication Data

Haan, Estelle.
    From Academia to Amicitia Milton's Latin writings and the
Italian academies / Estelle Haan.
        p.   cm. —(Transactions of the American Philosophical Society
    v. 88, Pt. 6)
    Includes bibliographical references (p.) and index.
    ISBN 0-87169-886-2 (pbk.)
        1. Milton, John, 1608—1674—Knowledge—Language and languages.
    2. Latin literature, Medieval and modern—England—Italian
influences. 3. British—Travel—Italy—History—17th century.
    4. Milton, John, 1608—1674—Knowledge—Italy. 5. Italy—
    Intellectual life—17th century. I. Title. II. Series.
PR3594.H3   1999
821' .4—dc21   99-10707
                                                            CIP

ISBN: 0-87169-886-2
US ISSN: 0065-9746

for Tony

CONTENTS

PREFACE

The origins of the present study are many and varied, as indeed are my debts of gratitude to all who have made it possible. I wish to thank the Queen's University of Belfast for granting me one semester's sabbatical leave in order to write this book, its Research and Scholarships Committee for funding trips to the British Library, London, and the Bodleian Library, Oxford, and the authorities of those institutions for permitting me to consult manuscripts and books relevant to my research. I am indebted also to the Queen's University Library, especially its special collections and inter-library loans divisions, and to the Arts Computing Unit. Thanks are also due to the authorities of the Biblioteca Nazionale Centrale of Florence for their prompt response to my numerous queries, and for the efficiency and incredible speed with which they arranged a whole series of microfilm reproductions of archive material vital to my research.

A much abridged version of part of this study appeared as "*Written encomiums*: Milton's Latin Poetry in its Italian Context," in *Milton in Italy: Contexts, Images, Contradictions*, ed. Mario A. Di Cesare (*Medieval and Renaissance Texts and Studies* vol. 90 [Binghamton, 1991]), 521-547 (Copyright Arizona Board of Regents for Arizona State University). Chapter 10 includes material that first appeared in "Milton, Manso, and Ovid's Chiron," *Classical and Modern Literature* 17.3 (1997), 251-264, "John Milton Among the Neo-Latinists: Three Notes on *Mansus*," *Notes and Queries*, n.s. 22.2 (June 1997), 172-176, and "Milton and Two Italian Humanists: Some Hitherto Unnoticed Neo-Latin Echoes in *In Obitum Procancellarii Medici* and *In Obitum Praesulis Eliensis*," *Notes and Queries*, n.s. 22.2 (June, 1997), 176-181. In all instances I am grateful for permission to reproduce the reworked material.

I first had the opportunity of studying Milton's Latin poetry in its neo-Latin and vernacular contexts as a doctoral student at Queen's University, Belfast, under the supervision of Professor Michael McGann. I wish to record my thanks to him for his wisdom and guidance both then and now.

Finally I wish to thank my family, especially my late mother, Eva, by whose example I have been inspired and encouraged in so many ways, and my sister Elga, in whose company I first traced Milton's footsteps through Florence and Rome in the scorching summer sun. To my husband Tony, Arts Computing Officer at Queen's, I am most grateful not only for his professionalism in computerising me and in facilitating network connections with the remotest parts of the globe, but also, and especially, for the constant support, good humor and unfailing care with which he continues to sustain me. It is to him that I dedicate this book.

EH
10 vi 98

ABBREVIATIONS

I   Works by Milton

Ad Pat.	*Ad Patrem*
Ad Sals.	*Ad Salsillum Poetam Romanum Aegrotantem*
DS	*Defensio Secunda*
El. 1, etc.	*Elegia Prima*, etc.
Ep. Dam.	*Epitaphium Damonis*
Ep. Fam.	*Epistolae Familiares*
Mans.	*Mansus*
PL	*Paradise Lost*
RCG	*The Reason of Church Government*

II   Editions of Milton's Works

CM	*The Works of John Milton*, ed. Frank A. Patterson, (New York: Columbia University Press, 1931-1940)

III   Periodicals and Serials

AJP	*American Journal of Philology*
CML	*Classical and Modern Literature*
CQ	*Classical Quarterly*
ELH	*A Journal of English Literary History*
ELR	*English Literary Renaissance*
ELS	*English Literary Studies*
EMLS	*Early Modern Literary Studies*
ES	*English Studies*
G&R	*Greece and Rome*
HL	*Humanistica Lovaniensia: Journal of Neo-Latin Studies*
JEGP	*Journal of English and Germanic Philology*
M&H	*Medievalia et Humanistica*
MLN	*Modern Language Notes*
MLQ	*Modern Language Quarterly*
MLR	*Modern Language Review*

Mnem.	*Mnemosyne*
MP	*Modern Philology*
MQ	*Milton Quarterly*
MS	*Milton Studies*
NA	*Nuova Antologia*
N&Q	*Notes and Queries*
PMLA	*Publications of the Modern Language Association of America*
PQ	*Philological Quarterly*
RES	*Review of English Studies*
RQ	*Renaissance Quarterly*
SB	*Studies in Bibliography*
SEL	*Studies in English Literature*
SP	*Studies in Philology*
SR	*Studies in the Renaissance*
TLS	*The Times (London) Literary Supplement*
UTQ	*University of Toronto Quarterly*

INTRODUCTION

I n a Latin letter composed in the autumn of 1637[1] Milton announced to his close friend Charles Diodati his quest for the Idea of the Good (τοῦ καλοῦ ἰδέαν)[2] — an Idea which he was seeking "through all the forms and appearances of things."[3] This remarkable expression of the artist's desire to look beyond the confines of his present, tangible world betrays an elevated concept of vocation. The theme recurs to some degree in the ensuing statement that he is contemplating a flight (*volare meditor*), although his Pegasus still possesses wings that are only slight and small.[4] But this Daedalean or quasi-Joycean idealism is balanced by Miltonic realism: juxtaposed with the desire to soar beyond the boundaries of his present existence is the indication that this artist has been reading voraciously — in Italian history no less.[5] In searching for the Idea of the

---

[1] *Ep. Fam.* 7. Although in the printed edition of the *Epistolae Familiares* in 1674 the letter is dated 23 September 1637, Gordon Campbell, *A Milton Chronology* (London and New York, 1997), 57, argues for November, pointing out that the internal evidence in the letter (where Milton in fact urges Diodati to hurry because winter is imminent) actually conflicts with the September dating in the printed edition: "It seems likely that JM dated the letter ... 23 ix.1637, and that the printer of the 1674 edition took the Roman numerals to refer to the ninth month of the year beginning in January (i.e. September) rather than the ninth month of the year beginning in March (i.e. November)."

[2] All quotations from Milton are from *The Works of John Milton*, eds. Frank A. Patterson *et al* (New York: Columbia University Press, 1931-1940), hereinafter abbreviated to *CM*. The current reference is to *CM* 12, 26. In all instances I have modernised spelling and punctuation.

[3] *CM* 12, 26: *hanc ... veluti pulcherrimam quandam imaginem per omnes rerum formas et facies.* All translations of Latin, Greek and Italian which appear in this study are mine, unless otherwise stated.

[4] *CM* 12, 26: *sed tenellis admodum adhuc pennis evehit se noster Pegasus.* Contrast *Paradise Lost* 7. 1-4, in which the speaker in following his Muse Urania is enabled to soar "above the flight of Pegasean wing" (4).

[5] *CM* 12, 28: *Italorum in obscura re diu versati sumus sub Longobardis.* Among Milton's entries in his Commonplace Book which may tentatively be dated to 1637 (by the occurrence of the Greek ε instead of the Italian *e*) are the following of Italian interest: Sigonius, *De Regno Italiae*, Dante, *Divina Comedia* (and the commentary of

Good, Milton simultaneously immerses himself in things Italian.[6] It is a juxtaposition that is hardly coincidental.

Only six months later perhaps that quest was about to be realised, at least in part, in Milton's actual journey to that country about which he had been reading so avidly — a journey which he describes in his associated Latin poems[7] by reverting once more to the imagery of flight. In his Latin scazontes to Giovanni Salzilli of Rome[8] Milton depicts himself in terms suggestive of a bird migrating from a cold to a sunny climate, leaving the "nest" of England,[9] with its cold winds and northerly gales, and arriving at last at the fertile soil of Italy.[10] The metaphor recurs in his Latin poem to the Neapolitan Giovanni Battista Manso.[11] There the speaker's self-identification with his Muse is strikingly evident in his description of her nourishment beneath the chilly Bear[12] and in his retrospective account of her audacious flight (*ausa est volitare* [*Mans*. 29]) through the cities of Italy (*Italas ... per urbes* [*Mans*. 29]). That tentative *volare meditor* enunciated in the Latin letter to Diodati has now been transformed into a daring image of a daring Muse (who is also both bird and bard),[13] leaving the confines of the cold north and flying instead to the sunny warmth of a somewhat idealised Italian landscape. There, no doubt, that search for τοῦ καλοῦ ἰδέαν would be fulfilled in a number of ways: through the first-

---

Bernardino Daniello, cited from the Venice edition of 1568), Boccaccio, *Vita di Dante*, Ariosto, *Orlando Furioso*. Cf. Campbell, *A Milton Chronology*, 56-57.

[6] For a general study of Milton's links with Italy, see F.T. Prince, *The Italian Element in Milton's Verse* (Oxford, 1954). Cf. also John Arthos, *Milton and the Italian Cities* (London, 1968), and, in particular, *Milton in Italy: Contexts, Images, Contradictions*, ed. Mario A. Di Cesare (Binghamton, 1991), *passim*. References to *Milton in Italy* will appear hereafter under the editor's surname: Di Cesare.

[7] For a discussion of Milton's Latin poems associated with the Italian journey, see Estelle Haan, *"Written encomiums*: Milton's Latin poetry in its Italian context" in Di Cesare, 521-547. For text and facing translation of these poems, see the Appendix to the present study.

[8] See 85-98; 186-187 below.

[9] *diebus hisce qui suum linquens nidum* (*Ad Sals*. 10). For a parallel in one of Salzilli's Italian sonnets, see 95-96 below.

[10] *venit feraces Itali soli ad glebas* (*Ad Sals*. 14).

[11] See 173-174 below.

[12] [*Musa*] *quae nuper gelida vix enutrita sub Arcto* (*Mans*. 28). This notion of nourishment may also underlie Milton's self-description at *Ad Sals*. 9: *alumnus ille Londini Milto*.

[13] Cf. the swan imagery at *Mans*. 30-33, on which see 165-178 below.

hand observation of the art and architecture of a world reborn,[14] a world that would subsequently function in many respects as an iconographical subtext of the blind poet's vernacular epic;[15] through the creation of a network of friendships with Italian humanists;[16] through enraptured transportation by a soprano voice;[17] through the eventual formulation of an epic language with which the speaker might move beyond the confines of his own poetic world. Hence the medium of the vernacular might rise Phoenix-like from the ashes of an erudite Latinity, a Latinity not dead, but transformed into a vibrantly unique Miltonic voice.[18] In Italy moreover Milton would witness and participate in the rebirth of a particularly Platonic Idea of the Good — the institution of the Academy.[19] And Seicento academicians prided themselves in their Platonic precedent. It was to Plato and to the ancient counterpart of the *accademia* that they frequently turned for inspiration and guidance. Thus the Florentine

---

[14] See in general Michael O' Connell, "Milton and the Art of Italy: A Revisionist View," Di Cesare, 215-236.

[15] See Roland Frye, *Milton's Imagery and the Visual Arts: Iconographic Tradition in the Epic Poems* (Princeton, 1978); Phillip Fehl, "Poetry and the Entry of the Fine Arts into England: *Ut Pictura Poesis*," in *The Age of Milton: Backgrounds to Seventeenth-Century Literature*, ed. C.A. Patrides and R.B. Waddington (Manchester, 1980), 273-306; Diane McColley, "Edenic Iconography: *Paradise Lost* and the Mosaics of San Marco," Di Cesare, 197-214; Mindele Treip, "*Descend from Heav'n Urania: Milton's Paradise Lost and Raphael's Cycle in the 'Stanza della Segnatura'*," ELS 35 (University of Victoria, 1985), *passim*, and her "'Celestial Patronage': Allegorical Ceiling Cycles of the 1630s and the Iconography of Milton's Muse," Di Cesare, 237-279.

[16] See chapters 3 and 4 below.

[17] On Leonora Baroni and Milton's associated Latin epigrams, see 99-117; 188-189 below.

[18] In *Epitaphium Damonis*, Milton's pastoral lament on the death of Charles Diodati, the apotheosis of Damon (Diodati) in a Christian Heaven (symbolised by an *ekphrasis* of the Phoenix looking back at Aurora rising from the glassy sea, and of a Platonic Amor releasing his darts upon the heavenly spheres) is mirrored by the rebirth of a Miltonic language, as the pastoral *fistula* undergoes a metamorphosis into the instrument of vernacular epic. For further discussion, see John K. Hale, *Milton's Languages: The Impact of Multilingualism on Style* (Cambridge, 1997), 57-61; Stella P. Revard, *Milton and the Tangles of Neaera's Hair: The Making of the 1645 Poems* (Columbia and London, 1997), 226-236.

[19] On Plato's academy and its "rebirth" in Renaissance Italy, see, for example, A. Field, *The Origins of the Platonic Academy of Florence* (Princeton, 1988); J. Hankins, "The myth of the Platonic Academy of Florence," *RQ* 44 (1991), 427-475; D.S. Chambers, "The earlier 'Academies' in Italy" in D.S. Chambers & F. Quiviger eds., *Italian Academies of the Sixteenth Century* (Warburg Institute: London, 1995), 1-14.

academician Benedetto Buonmattei, addressee of one of Milton's Latin letters,[20] would invoke Plato's Academy as an ideal towards which his fellow-academicians might strive.[21] Similarly Carlo Dati, perhaps Milton's closest and subsequently his most constant Florentine friend and correspondent,[22] would recommend to his fellow-academicians the Platonic Academy in general and Socratic discourse in particular as prototypes for the Accademia della Crusca and the Accademia Fiorentina.[23] Milton himself would in a sense partake of this ideal by attending Italian academies and by reciting there his own compositions. And his erudition was acknowledged in the form of "written encomiums"[24] composed in his honor by Italian academicians. In one such tribute, by the Florentine Antonio Francini,[25] this precise motivating factor of a quest for τοῦ καλοῦ ἰδέαν is attributed to Milton, who is "like a divine artist" ("fabro quasi divino"[43]) seeking to "forge the Idea of every virtue" ("per fabbricare d'ogni virtù l'Idea"[48]), and actively selecting Florentines ("quanti nacquero in Flora"[49]) "for his treasuring" ("volesti ricercar per tuo tesoro"[53]).

It was indeed in Florence, birthplace of the Italian Renaissance, that this Miltonic quest was perhaps most fully realised. In *Defensio Secunda* Milton states that he esteemed Florence "above other cities on account of the elegance both of its language and of its geniuses."[26] Although remaining in Florence for "about two months" (*ad duos circiter menses*) in 1638,[27] he would return there the following year for a further two months' sojourn. That he established contacts at a very early stage is

---

[20] *CM* 12, 30-38. See 16-19 below.

[21] Benedetto Buonmattei, "Sopra l'Ozio," *Prose Fiorentine Raccolte dallo Smarrito Accademico della Crusca*, ed. Carlo Roberto Dati (Florence, 1716-1745), pt. 2, vol 4, 276, hereafter abbreviated to *Prose Fiorentine*. See also Anna K. Nardo, "Academic Interludes in *Paradise Lost*," *MS* 27 (1991), 209-241 at 210, 237.

[22] On Dati, see David Masson, *The Life of Milton: Narrated in Connection with the Political, Ecclesiastical, and Literary History of his Time* (Cambridge, 1859-1894), I, 774-776; Guidi Andreini, *La Vita e l'Opera di Carlo Roberto Dati* (Milan, 1963); *Dizionario Biografico degli Italiani* (Rome, 1960 -), *s.v.*

[23] Carlo Dati, *Prose Fiorentine*, pt. 3, vol. 2, 152-153. See Nardo, "Academic Interludes," 210, 237.

[24] *Reason of Church Government* (*CM* 3, 235-236). See 22 below.

[25] On Francini, see G. Negri, *Istoria degli Scrittori Fiorentini* (Ferrara, 1722), 60.

[26] *CM* 8, 122: *illa in urbe quam prae ceteris propter elegantiam cum linguae tum ingeniorum semper colui ...*

[27] *CM* 8, 122.

indicated by his statement that "in that city [sc. Florence] I *immediately* made the acquaintance of many noble and learned men"[28] (*multorum et nobilium sane et doctorum hominum familiaritatem statim contraxi*).[29] In his Latin letter to Carlo Dati, written some eight years after his return to England,[30] Milton asks to be remembered to a host of academicians, whom he mentions by name. He looks back to his Florentine period as if to an idealised world, remembering the multitude of friendships he cultivated in that single city, and reflecting on his own sorrowful departure:

> Gravis admodum, ne te celem, discessus ille et mihi quoque fuit eosque meo animo aculeos infixit, qui etiam nunc altius inhaerent, quoties mecum cogito tot simul sodales atque amicos tam bonos tamque commodos una in urbe, longinqua illa quidem, sed tamen carissima, invitum me et plane divulsum reliquisse.[31]

> [Very painful to me too, so as not to conceal it from you, was that departure, and it imprinted stings upon my heart, which even now cling to it more deeply, as often as I think to myself of my reluctant departure, of my being completely wrenched away from so many companions at once, friends so good and so accommodating in a single city, far-distant indeed, but most dear nonetheless.]

For the solitary middle-aged Englishman, distracted from his studies by the horrors of a civil war, is this a retrospective glance to a paradise lost? Perhaps that *gravis ... discessus* and the associated unwillingness to suffer what is presented as a virtually enforced departure (*invitum me et plane divulsum reliquisse*) anticipate his poetic vision of another painful expulsion from a "happy seat":

> They looking back, all the eastern side beheld
> Of Paradise, so late their happy seat,
> Waved over by that flaming brand, the gate
> With dreadful faces thronged and fiery arms:
> Some natural tears they dropped, but wiped them soon;
> The world was all before them, where to choose

---

[28] Italics are mine.

[29] *CM* 8, 122.

[30] *Ep. Fam.* 10. *CM* 12, 44-52.

[31] *CM* 12, 48. Cf. Nicolas Heinsius, *Elegia* XII: *Italiae et Musis Valedicit*, 1-2: *Poscimur in patriam; patria iam vivere tempus./Ah trahor invitus, terra Latina, vale.* Text: *Poemata* (Lugd. Batav., 1653), 107-108 at 107.

> Their place of rest, and providence their guide:
> They hand in hand with wandering steps and slow,
> Through Eden took their solitary way.

(PL 12. 641-649)

But the way does not have to be solitary. The lost paradise that was Italy can perhaps be regained through the bonds of *amicitia* and through the power of memory. Dati's extant letters to Milton convey greetings not only from Dati himself, but also from other Florentine academicians.[32] It is highly probable that these friendships owed their origin at least in part to the institution of the Italian academy. This is indicated in a number of ways, not least of which is Milton's own statement in *Defensio Secunda* that he constantly frequented "private academies," and his associated acknowledgement of the fact that the academy is an excellent way of maintaining friendships:

> quorum etiam privatas academias (qui mos illic cum ad literas humaniores, tum ad amicitias conservandas laudatissimus est) assidue frequentavi.[33]
>
> [I also constantly frequented their private academies (a custom there most praiseworthy in its preservation not only of learning, but also of friendships.)]

In actual fact, the Florentine friends mentioned in the Milton/Dati correspondence and in *Defensio Secunda* belonged to two academies in particular — the Svogliati and the Apatisti, two examples of those "private academies" which he attended.[34]

By the time of Milton's Italian sojourn, the "private academy" was already a well-established institution.[35] While often finding its origins in informal conversation among friends, it had become a microcosm not only of Italian sociability, but also of formality, order and hierarchy.[36] As a rule, it was an extremely efficiently organised institution, preserving what was usually a very full charter outlining its aims and methods. For the most part the academy (and sometimes even individual academicians) possessed an

---

[32] See 60; 79-80 below.

[33] *CM* 8, 122.

[34] For incontrovertible evidence of Milton's participation in the Svogliati, see 19-22 below; for almost certain proof of his attendance at the Apatisti, see 36-37 below.

[35] See Eric W. Cochrane, *Tradition and Enlightenment in the Tuscan Academies 1690-1800* (Chicago, 1961), especially 4-27.

[36] This is nowhere more fully epitomised than by the Neapolitan Oziosi, on which see 121-125 below.

impresa and motto (agreed upon only after much internal discussion).[37] These were designed to encapsulate in iconographical and succinctly epigrammatic terms the particular character of an academy and/or the aspirations of its members. In most cases the academy would possess statutes expounding its elaborate procedures for the election of a series of office-holders, whose clearly defined titles such as "consolo" or "principe" or "secretario" were matched by equally prescriptive job-descriptions. Many such posts were designated by rota, although generally the job of secretary tended to be longer-term. It was the secretary's responsibility to keep careful records of the academy's meetings, and to note in the minute-book the names of those present at a given meeting. Sometimes he might summarize the content of that meeting's proceedings, perhaps even singling out a notable performance by one or more academicians, if it warranted such. In some academies the secretary would transcribe into a vast book for its private holdings, and indeed for future posterity, particularly meritorious compositions performed at a meeting. In some academies, most conspicuously the Neapolitan Oziosi,[38] obedience was the rule. Many scrupulously imposed a ban on certain topics: thus in a majority of cases any form of theological debate or interpretative analysis of the scriptures was forbidden. By contrast, linguistic and literary topics were recommended and endorsed on such an individual and collective level that they came to constitute standard practice. On the whole, translations from Greek and Latin into Italian were given pride of place, but the methodology advocated and practised was uniformly rigorous.[39] Debates might be held on such linguistic issues as how to improve the vernacular tongue. Prominence was given to the analysis of both ancient and modern texts. (Among the latter the sonnets of Petrarch seem to have been particularly popular). In all instances careful attention was paid to the advocation or defence of a particular textual variant. And at times such discussions in their meticulous citation of *exempla* and in their frequent digressions seem to have employed a rather labyrinthine methodology. This is also evident in the extant writings of individual members. For example, one of the foremost Italian academicians, the Florentine Jacopo Gaddi,[40] took upon himself what was surely the impossible task of compiling a huge encyclopaedia on just about every conceivable writer, both "ancient" and "modern." While the work provides a wealth of

---

[37] See, for example, 15-17 below.

[38] See 125 below.

[39] Cf. Cochrane, *Tradition and Enlightenment*, 15.

[40] On Gaddi, see Masson, *Life*, I, 773-774. See also 10-15 below.

invaluable information, it is hardly surprising that it remains incomplete, although the author did manage to reach the letter "S".[41] Many academies, most notably the Florentine Apatisti,[42] seem to have thrived in witty repartee, jokes, anagrams, and in what were often rather absurd etymological games. As noted below, most academies observed a meticulously rigorous procedure for admitting new members. And when original compositions were performed, a piece of prose or verse would be read or recited by its author. Then, in response to comments or questions from fellow-academicians, who participated in a line-by-line critique of the whole, that author would present what amounted to a viva voce *defensio*. But hand in hand with the academy's apparently prescriptive formality was its essentially social role. Many academies were very well-connected, possessing a princely, as well as a celestial, patron figure;[43] many were attended by the nobility and leading members of the church.[44] But besides functioning as a forum for erudite discussion, they also constituted a weekly meeting-place for friends. Some, like the Florentine Svogliati, founded and hosted by Milton's friend Jacopo Gaddi,[45] were noted for their particularly convivial atmosphere, manifested, for example, in sumptuous banquets. And the Platonic title of symposium was hereby adopted and adapted to suit a seventeenth-century context. These symposia were hosted often by rota, courtesy of an academy's leading members. Indeed in the case of the Accademia degli Affidati of S. Miniato, the organisation of symposia was accomplished in accordance with an actual statute written c. 1636: "Ordini del Simposio dei Sei Della Nostra Illustrissima Comunita."[46] The symposium's social function is indicated by the statute's recommendation that it act as a means of enticing people to come together ("... affinché coloro che erano traviati dal bene operare s'abbiano con quell' allettamento a riunire per concorrer poi ad esercitarsi unitamente con gli altri").[47] And among the organisers of such symposia, and indeed as two of the six authors of the statutes are some

---

[41] See 10-11, 157 below.

[42] See 29-37 below.

[43] Cf. Cochrane, *Tradition and Enlightenment*, 4.

[44] Cf. the Apatisti and Fantastici members listed below at 36 and 82 respectively.

[45] See note 40 above.

[46] Biblioteca Riccardiana Fiorentina Cod. Riccardiano 1949, 85r-88r, transcribed in Allessandro Lazzeri, *Intellettuali e Consenso nella Toscana del Seicento: L'Accademia degli Apatisti* (Milan, 1983), 21-24.

[47] Biblioteca Riccardiana Fiorentina Cod. Riccardiano 1949, f. 85r; Lazzeri, *Intellettuali*, 21.

further Florentine academicians known to Milton: Agostino Coltellini and Benedetto Buonmattei (referred to under their anagrammatic names as "l'eccellentissimo signor Auditore Ostilio Contalgeni, e col signor Boemonte Battidente ...").[48] It is evident then that the "private academy" was certainly a *mos ... ad amicitias conservandas laudatissimus*. Milton himself, in that Latin letter to Dati, would remember his Florentine acquaintances as *tot simul sodales atque amicos*.[49] The juxtaposition of *sodales* "(Fellow) members of a fraternity meeting for religious or social purposes"[50] and *amici* is hardly coincidental. Indeed it was precisely on account of this felicitous co-existence of both scholarship and friendship that the seicento *accademia* had become virtually synonymous with *amicitia*.

---

[48] Biblioteca Riccardiana Fiorentina Cod. Riccardiano 1949, f. 88ʳ; Lazzeri, *Intellettuali*, 21, 24. The statutes spell out the importance of the rota, and this works on a number of levels: each of the six organisers should have his turn at being proprietor and symposiarch until the end of the cycle (Statute III: "Che ciascuno de' detti sei debba la sua volta essere Provveditore e Simposiarcha fino che si termini il circolo"); at each symposium there should be an indication of where the next one will be held (Statute IV); as for the symposium itself: the symposiarch together with the chancellor should appear one hour before in order to make the necessary preparations (VII); the symposiarch should sit on a chair and propose the subject-matter for discussion after they have eaten (VIII). (Lazzeri, *Intellettuali*, 22).

[49] *CM* 12, 48.

[50] See *Oxford Latin Dictionary*, Fascicle VII, ed. P.G.W. Glare (Oxford, 1980), 1780. The noun occurs twice in *Epitaphium Damonis*: *omnes unanimi secum sibi lege sodales* (95); *ut te tam dulci possem caruisse sodale* (118). Cf. Revard, *Milton and the Tangles of Neaera's Hair*, 227.

CHAPTER 1

Milton and the Accademia degli Svogliati

The Florentine Accademia degli Svogliati or "Academy of the Will-less"[1] traced its origins to a conversation held at the house of the Italian scholar and poet, Jacopo Gaddi.[2] Gaddi's role as founder and prime force behind this erudite body[3] is evident from the prominence given him in the title of its statutes: "Statuti dell' Accademia degli Svogliati sotto il Principato dell' Illustrissimo Signore Jacopo Gaddi, suo Primo Principe e Promotore Stabiliti,"[4] and from the numerous manuscripts of Gaddi's own works among the holdings of the Biblioteca Nazionale Centrale in Florence.[5] A Florentine of a respectable family, Gaddi, although still less than forty at the time of Milton's visits in 1638-1639, had already seen four of his major works published, earning him a not insignificant reputation as a writer of both prose and verse.[6] But it was not only for his

---

[1] Mistranslated by Masson, *Life*, I, 773, as "Academy of the Disgusted."

[2] Michele Maylender, *Storia delle Accademie d'Italia* (Bologna, 1926-1930), V, 287.

[3] Maylender, *Storia*, V, 288, cites as evidence of the erudition of the Svogliati the numerous references in its archive marginalia to classical authors, myths and ancient history.

[4] Biblioteca Nazionale Centrale, Florence, MS Cl. VI, 163. Cf. Maylender, *Storia*, V, 287.

[5] MS Cl. VI, 94: Iacopo Gaddi, *Esercitazioni Retoriche*; Cl. VII, 694: *Iacobi Gadii Carmina* (autogr.); Cl. VII, 696: *Iacobi Gaddii Patricii Fiorentini Carminum Libri Duo* (autogr.); Cl. VII, 697: *Poeticus Hortus ab Jacopo Gaddio non Alienis Flosculis Gemmatus* (autogr.); Cl. VII, 698: *Esemplare a Stampa dei Carmi di Jacopo Gaddi, con Riere Giunte e Correzioni* (autogr.); Cl. VII, 699: *Annotationes ex Martiale et Aliis Poetis Epigrammaticis Depromptae* [a Jacopo Gaddio].

[6] Prior to Milton's visit and undoubtedly accessible to him in the course of his sojourns in Florence were Gaddi's *Poematum Libri Duo* (Patavii, 1628), *Adlocutiones et Elogia, Exemplaria, Cabalistica, Oratoria, Mixta Sepulcralia* (Florence, 1636), *J. Gadii Corollarium Poeticum, scil. Poematia, Notae, Explicationes Allegoricae Olim Conscriptae* (Florence, 1636), *J. Gadii Elogia Historica Tum Soluta Cum Vincta Numeris Oratione Perscripta et Notis Illustrata* (Florence, 1637). Among the various

scholarship that Gaddi was noted. He was also celebrated for his personal qualities, in particular, his endearing hospitality, especially towards foreigners. A volume published in 1647[7] in honor of the Venetian Accademia degli Incogniti (of which Gaddi [like the Dutch Nicolas Heinsius][8] was a member) includes a brief *vita*[9] of Gaddi, in which he is presented very much as a celebrity of his own age,[10] and as one of the leading luminaries of Florence, particularly receptive to foreigners newly arrived in the city: it is to his house (in the Via del Giglio, and home of the academy)[11] that all nationalities, including Italians, French, English and Germans, converge as though to an oracular font of wisdom:

> e tutti i virtuosi Italiani, Francesi, Inglesi, Tedeschi, e d'ogni altra natione Oltramontana, che per godere delle bellezze di quella augusta Città concorrono in Firenze; ricorrono parimente alla sua Casa, per riportare dalla Sublimità del suo ingegno gli Oracoli della Sapienza.[12]

> [And all the talented — Italians, French, English, Germans and those from every other transalpine nation who converge in Florence to enjoy the beauties of this august city, turn likewise to his house to receive from the sublimity of his genius the Oracles of Wisdom.]

Gaddian works post-dating Milton's Florentine sojourns is his vast encyclopaedic *De Scriptoribus non Ecclesiasticis, Graecis, Latinis, Italicis Primorum Graduum in Quinque Theatris, scilicet, Philosophico, Poetico, Historico, Oratorico, Critico*: 2 vol. (Florence, 1648), on which see 157 below.

[7] *Le Glorie degli Incogniti O Vero gli Huomini Illustri dell' Accademia de' Signori Incogniti di Venetia* (Venice, 1647).

[8] On Heinsius, see 62-71 below.

[9] The *vita* of Gaddi occurs at *Le Glorie degli Incogniti*, 180-182. Beneath a portrait of Gaddi (180) is the distich: *Quamvis et genere et patria clarissimus iste,/carmine clarescit nobiliore tamen.* Other Florentine academicians who, like Gaddi, were also members of the Venetian Incogniti and are included in this volume are Alessandro Adimari (14) and Gabriello Chiabrera (64).

[10] *Le Glorie degli Incogniti*, 182: "Cosi hà egli potuto per la solitaria e faticosa via della Gloria arrivare felicemente al Tempio dell' immortalità, dove con eterni encomi viene il suo nome altamente celebrato dall' età presente, e verrà da' posteri incessantemente honorato."

[11] Now the Hotel Astoria. The Paradiso Gaddi with the adjacent gardens on the Via Melarancio was one of two splendid locations provided by Gaddi for meetings of the Svogliati; the other was the Villa Camerata near Fiesole. See Arthos, *Italian Cities*, 19. Campbell, *A Milton Chronology*, 61-62, notes: "the census of 1632 places *Iacopo Gaddi e fratelli* in Via del Giglio (Biblioteca Nazionale Centrale, MS Palatina E.B. 15, 2, Striscia 1406)."

[12] *Le Glorie degli Incogniti*, 182.

But admission depended on merit. The Academy's statutes were very specific in their proviso that only visitors of distinction be admitted.[13] Upon proof of such merit, however, the Svogliati, like its sister Florentine academy, the Apatisti,[14] welcomed foreigners with open arms. There is indeed a tradition that Milton actually stayed at Gaddi's house.[15] Was he then among those unnamed "Inglesi" so hospitably received? Very probably. But evidence of Milton's possible links with Gaddi and of his involvement in the Svogliati is much more conclusive than this. The minutes of at least four of the academy's meetings prove that he not only attended, but also actively participated in, its sessions. At least one way in which he contributed to its proceedings was through reading his own compositions. In so doing he earned himself not a few admirers among the Svogliati's membership, for in response to his performance they joined with other Italian academicians in composing in his honor those "written encomiums" mentioned above. And Milton was to demonstrate a justifiable pride in this acclaim by prefixing these to the 1645 edition of his *Poems of Mr John Milton, Both English and Latin.*[16] An Englishman, having travelled to Italy *animi causa,*[17] had thus assumed upon his arrival a rightful place among leading Florentine *litterati*. It is indeed very likely that Milton was actually elected a member of the Svogliati. Before examining such evidence, it should be noted that in the prose works which he wrote subsequent to the Italian journey Milton actually mentions not only Gaddi individually, but the Gaddian academy collectively. In *Defensio Secunda* when referring to, but not naming, the "private academies"[18] which he visited, he invokes the memory of Gaddi along with such other academicians as Dati, Frescobaldi, Coltellini, Buonmattei,

---

[13] Article X of the academy's statutes states: " ... non però s'accetti in Accademia, fuora, ò di qua dall' Alpi suggetto si sangue, o virtù, o scienza chiarissima, non sia notabile." See Arthos, *Italian Cities*, 46.

[14] On the Apatisti, see 29-37 below.

[15] Cf. Piero Rebora, "Milton a Firenze" in *Interpretazioni Anglo-Italiane: Saggi e Ricerche* (Adriatica editrice, 1961), 139-157 at 149: "Milton dovette alloggiare, con molto fondata probabilità, nelle case dei Gaddi, in via del Giglio, presso i giardini gaddiani o 'paradiso dei Gaddi.'"

[16] For this customary practice, see F.B. Williams, *Index of Dedications and Commendatory Verse in English Books Before 1649* (London, 1962).

[17] The phrase is Milton's: from the prose preface to *Ep. Dam.*: *Thyrsis animi causa profectus*; cf. *DS*: *me animi causa otiose peregrinari* (*CM* 8, 124); *Ep. Dam.* 12-13: *pastorem scilicet illum/dulcis amor musae Thusca retinebat in urbe.*

[18] Milton repeats this phrase "private academies" in the *Reason of Church Government*: "In the private academies of Italy ..." (*CM* 3, 235).

Chimentelli and Francini,[19] while in a letter to Carlo Dati, discussed below,[20] he asks to be remembered to the entire Gaddian academy (*toti denique Gaddianae Academiae*).[21] Milton obviously saw himself as part of a Florentine academic circle under Gaddi's directorship.

Further evidence of his involvement in the Svogliati is provided by the archives and minutes of its weekly meetings. An examination of these may even suggest the possibility that he was in Florence by as early as 28 June/8 July 1638. The register of the Svogliati on that day records the presence of "an English man of letters who wanted to enter the academy":

> Il Signor Bartolommei et il Signor Buonmattei recitarono lero sonetti e ci furono presenti li Signori Alessandro e Giulio Pitti, il Signor Marchese Vincenzio Capponi, il Signor Canoneo Vincenzio Bardi, il Signor Lettor Silvestri, L'Abate D. Eusebio, il Gaddi, *e un letterato Inglese che desiderava d'entrar nell' Accademia.*[22]

> [Mr Bartholommei and Mr Buonmattei recited their sonnets, and there were present Messrs. Alessandro and Giulio Pitti, Marchese Vincenzio Capponi, Canon Vincenzio Bardi, Reader Silvestri, Abate Eusebio, Gaddi, *and an English man of letters who wished to enter the Academy.*][23]

It is just possible that this "English man of letters" seeking admission to the Svogliati is Milton newly arrived in the city. His own account of his travels in *Defensio Secunda* does seem to suggest a rather hasty progression through France:[24] after his reception by Thomas Scudamore in Paris and his introduction to Hugo Grotius, it is only after a few days that he left for Italy (*discedenti post dies aliquot Italiam versus*).[25] He proceeds to state that he stayed in Florence "about two months" (*ad duos*

---

[19] *CM* 8, 122: *Tui enim Jacobe Gaddi, Carole Dati, Frescobalde, Cultelline, Bonmatthaei, Clementille, Francine, aliorumque plurium memoriam apud me semper gratam atque iucundam nulla dies delebit.*

[20] See 53-60 below.

[21] *CM* 12, 52.

[22] Biblioteca Nazionale Centrale, Florence, Magliabecchiana MSS., Cl.IX, cod 60, f. 46ᵛ. Cf. J.M. French, *The Life Records of John Milton* (Rutgers Studies in English, 7 [1949-1958]), V, 385; Campbell, *A Milton Chronology*, 61. Italics here and elsewhere are mine unless otherwise stated.

[23] I have adapted the translation of French, *Life Records*, V, 385.

[24] As noted by Neil Harris,"Galileo as Symbol: the 'Tuscan artist' in *Paradise Lost*," *Annali dell' Istituto e Museo di Storia della Scienza di Firenze* 10 (1985), 3-29 at 6.

[25] *CM* 8, 122.

circiter menses)[26] but, as Harris observes,[27] this figure, written over ten years later, is probably not exact.[28] It is also possible that one week later Milton was one of two people proposed for election to the academy's membership, for in the minutes of the next meeting on 5/15 July 1638 Jacopo Gaddi writes:

> A di 15
> Nell' Accademia, nella quale si trovarono li Signori Alessandro Adimari, Alessandro e Giulio Pitti, Bacchio Valori, Benedetto Buonmattei, Feliciano Silvestri, Francesco Rovai, Frescobaldi, Gaddi, Girolamo Bartolommei, Don Vincenzo della Rena, *furono proposti l'Abate D. Eusebio, e il Signor ... per Academici li quali vinsero nonostante una fava bianca.*[29]

> [Minutes of 15
> In the Academy, at which were found Messrs. Alessandro Adimari, Alessandro and Giulio Pitti, Baccio Valori, Benedetto Buonmattei, Feliciano Silvestri, Francesco Rovai, Frescobaldi, Gaddi, Girolamo Bartolommei, Don Vincenzo della Rena, *there were proposed the Abate Don Eusebio and Mr ... as members of the Academy, who won notwithstanding a white bean* (i.e. blackball)]

Harris poses some interesting questions about the blank space in the minutes at this point and suggests that "il Signor ..." may indeed refer to the "letterato Inglese" (i.e. Milton), but that Gaddi had not yet been able to catch the newcomer's name, which he intended to fill in at a later date.[30] And this is an attractive suggestion. A blank in the minutes is surely more likely to be evidence of an as yet unrecognised (hence perhaps foreign?) name than of carelessness on the part of the secretary. So perhaps in the previous week Milton wished to be admitted to the academy, and now one week later that wish has been granted. The possibility may be strengthened by the juxtaposition of "Abate Eusebio" and "il Sr ..." in the current entry (in Gaddi's hand), given the fact that in the minutes of the previous week "Abate Eusebio" and "un letterato Inglese" are separated only by the name

---

[26] *CM* 8, 122.

[27] Harris, "Galileo as Symbol," 6.

[28] French includes this possibility at *Life Records*, V, 385: "June 28, 1638 Milton visits Svogliati Academy (?)".

[29] Biblioteca Nazionale Centrale, Florence, Magliabecchiana MSS., Cl.IX, cod. 60, f. 47; cf. French, *Life Records*, V, 386; Campbell, *A Milton Chronology*, 62. Italics are mine.

[30] Harris, "Galileo as Symbol," 6.

of Gaddi himself. And as Harris points out,[31] it would have been most unusual if the Svogliati had actually failed to elect to its membership someone who, as seems to have been the case, may have attended a total of five, if not more, of its meetings. It surely could not have overlooked this particular "English man of letters," who is recorded as having performed his own Latin poetry in at least three separate meetings, and whose recitations earned particular mention ("particolarmente")[32] in the academy's minutes. If so, then the admission of "il Signor Miltonio," like that of any other new member of an Italian academy, would probably have been preceded by formal proposals (usually two or three) and a speech of thanks.[33] But if the blank in the minutes is indeed a reference to Milton, newly proposed to the academy, a hitherto unnoticed element of interest is provided. The minutes continue as follows:

> si strinse dal Gaddi la cosa dei lezioni, siche si concluse, che il Signor Rovai avanti passare il presente mese ne facesse una e non molte giorni doppo il Signor Buonmattei. Si discusse di varie imprese facendosi, e rifacendosi varie obbiezioni e difficoltà, le quali risolute si ratificò a voce quasi comune l'elezione già fatta della pianta de capperi. Furon' letti dal Signor Adimari due nobili sonetti, e dal Signor Buonmattei un piacevole Prologo d'un suo Dramma.

> [The matter of readings was pressed by Gaddi so that it was concluded that Mr Rovai, before the present month had passed, should give one, and not many days afterwards Mr Buonmattei also. The creation of various *imprese* was discussed, and various objections and difficulties were rehashed, upon the resolution of which the choice already made of the caper plant was ratified almost unanimously. Two noble sonnets were read by Mr Adimari, and by Mr Buonmattei a pleasant prologue from one of his dramas.]

French mistranslates "Si discusse di varie imprese facendosi" as "Various activities were discussed."[34] The phrase refers in fact to a discussion of *imprese*[35] for the academy, and should be translated "the creation of

---

[31] Harris, "Galileo as Symbol," 6. An example of an "outsider" elected to the Svogliati is the Venetian Francesco Loredano (9/19 June 1637), on whom see 175 below.

[32] See 19 below.

[33] See Cochrane, *Tradition and Enlightenment*, 4.

[34] French, *Life Records*, V, 386.

[35] On academic *imprese*, see Jennifer Montagu, *An Index of Emblems of the Italian Academies* (Warburg Institute, 1988); Roberto P. Ciardi, "A Knot of Words and Things: Some Clues for Interpreting the *Imprese* of Academies and Academicians," *Italian Academies*, eds. Chambers & Quiviger, 37-66.

various *imprese* was discussed." The minutes continue to highlight the ratified choice of a "caper plant" as the academy's official *impresa*. Italian academies were much given to learned discussion and debate about the most intricate and obscure subjects, and this often led to internal conflict. The Svogliati seems to have been no exception to this general rule — at least when the question of *impresa* (and indeed title of the academy) arose. As Maylender has shown, it seems that for a period of at least sixteen years(!) the Svogliati could not even decide on its own name, rules or *impresa*.[36] For example, as late as 1636 the minutes of a 27 October/ 6 November meeting refer to general discussion about the academy's name and *impresa*.[37] Among possible *imprese* proposed was that of Mount Tmolus of Lydia,[38] together with the motto *separare nefas*, with *Lydii lapidis* as the academy's name.[39] Another proposal was that of a flowery meadow together with the motto: *efficient seu florebunt*, with *Imperfetti* as the academy's title.[40] It was not until 10/20 August 1637 that its membership agreed to assume the title Svogliati,[41] but they still did not have an *impresa*. In this regard Ristoro Antinori proposed a caper plant with the motto *Hinc pergit orexis*.[42] Finally, the matter seems to have been resolved on 5/15 April 1638 (only *three* [or at most five] months before Milton's visit) as Antinori's *impresa* of the caper plant (but not his motto) was adopted by members of the academy. The motto eventually agreed upon was the Petrarchan "Per chi m'invoglie."[43] Indeed Benedetto Buonmattei, addressee of a Latin letter from Milton written in Florence in September 1638,[44] delivered to the academy no fewer than two lectures on this precise subject. These are usefully summarised by Buonmattei's

---

[36] Maylender, *Storia*, V, 288.

[37] Maylender, *Storia*, V, 288.

[38] Proposed by the academician Roveri. Worthy of comparison is Milton's statement in a letter to Alexander Gill. Expressing his delight in being asked to judge one of Gill's compositions, Milton compares the honor of so doing to that of the god Tmolus on mount Lydia (when he had to judge the gods competing in a musical contest) (*CM* 12, 8).

[39] Maylender, *Storia*, V, 288.

[40] As proposed by the academician Giovanni Bartolomei. For other examples, see Maylender, *Storia*, V, 288.

[41] Maylender, *Storia*, V, 289.

[42] Maylender, *Storia*, V, 289.

[43] Maylender, *Storia*, V, 289.

[44] *CM* 12, 30-38.

biographer Giovanni Battista Casotti.[45] The first outlines in general terms the origins of *imprese*: an academy's *impresa* is like the body; its motto is like the soul;[46] the second examines in some detail the general *impresa* and motto of the Svogliati. The rationale behind the specific choice of caper plant and of the Petrarchan motto is analysed by Casotti as follows:

> Elessero una pianta di Capperi per loro impresa, col motto PERCHÈ M'INVOGLIE, il quale procedendo per via di contrapposto col nome di Svogliati riesce non meno vago, che artifizioso. Il Cappero è preso per l'Accademia, il nome per se medesimi, e'l motto per lo desiderio loco. L'applicazione è fondata su la simiglianza, che l'accademia ha col cappero, che è di far tornar l'appetito, a chi è svogliato ...[47]

> [They chose a caper plant for their *impresa* with the motto "In order to allure me," which by advancing along a route contrasting with the name Svogliati, proved to be no less vague than artificial. The caper plant was adopted for the Academy, the name for themselves, and the motto for their fixed desire. The analogy is founded upon a resemblance that the academy has with a caper plant in that it has the power to whet the appetite of the will-less ...]

It is evident then that one of Milton's Florentine fellow-academicians and correspondents showed a particular interest in the Svogliati's *impresa*, an *impresa* formally ratified: "le quali risolute si ratifico a voce quasi comune l'elezione già fatta della pianta de capperi,"[48] at that very meeting on 5/15 July 1638 at which Milton, by a strange coincidence, may have been nominated for election to the academy. Did he even witness this discussion about the academy's *impresa*?[49] In his Latin letter to Buonmattei (31 Aug./10 Sept.), Milton seems to indicate that he has already established important links with the academy's membership. It is evident, for example,

---

[45] Giovanni Battista Casotti [ps. Dalisto Narceate], *Vita* of Buonmattei prefixed to *Della Lingua Toscana di Benedetto Buommattei Libri Due* (Milan, 1807), 50: "Di quest' Accademia fù censore, e come tale prese a spiegarne e a difenderne in due dottissime lezioni l'Impresa generale, poichè dopo lunghi e vari discorsi, dopo molte e spessissime conferenze, non senza dottissime e ingegnosissime opposizioni da risposte seguite, parimente ingegnose e dotte, ebbero alla fine gli accademici accettata la figura della pianta del Cappero, come al nome di Svogliati, e al motto Perchè m'invoglie, sopra tutte l'altre conveniente." Cf. Maylender, *Storia*, V, 289.

[46] Casotti, *Vita*, 51.

[47] Casotti, *Vita*, 51.

[48] French, *Life Records*, V, 386.

[49] The intricacies of such labyrinthine discussions may even underlie the convoluted debates in the "hellish academy" of *Paradise Lost*. See Nardo, "Academic Interludes," 218-219.

that he has met Buonmattei on numerous occasions and has discussed many literary topics with him. Milton in asking his addressee to include in his forthcoming work on the Tuscan dialect a guide to pronunciation for foreigners,[50] states that he has already made this request to him in conversation (*atque haec ego tametsi videor mihi abs te [nisi me animus fallit] iam primo impetrasse*) whenever they have discussed the matter (*quoties in istius rei mentionem incidimus*).[51] That *quoties* seems to suggest frequent conversations. On these grounds French posits a date of 1 September (i.e. 22 August) for their meeting,[52] a date that could actually go back much further. Apart from the occasion on 5/15 July discussed above, the Svogliati met on the following dates: 19/29 July,[53] 26 July/5 August,[54] 3/13 August,[55] two unspecified dates probably in August,[56] and 30 August/9 September.[57] There is no record of attendance for any of these occasions, but it is highly likely that Milton would have been present at some, if not all, of these meetings.[58] In any case, the fact that he has already made important contacts seems to argue in favor of much earlier dates than the extant evidence would suggest for the commencement of what was at least an oral network of communication between Milton and

---

[50] *CM* 12, 34: *Quo magis merito potes meminisse quid ego tanto opere abs te contendere soleam, uti iam inchoatis, maiori etiam ex parte absolutis, velles quanta maxima facilitate res ipsa tulerit in nostram exterorum gratiam de recta linguae pronuntiatione adhuc paululum quiddam adiicere.*

[51] *CM* 12, 36.

[52] French, *Life Records*, I, 382: "c. Sept 1: Meets and talks with Benedetto Buonmattei."

[53] Biblioteca Nazionale Centrale, Florence, Magliabecchiana MSS. Cl.IX, cod. 60, f. 47.

[54] Biblioteca Nazionale Centrale, Florence, Magliabecchiana MSS. Cl.IX, cod. 60, f. 47.

[55] Biblioteca Nazionale Centrale, Florence, Magliabecchiana MSS. Cl.IX, cod. 60, f 7ᵛ.

[56] Biblioteca Nazionale Centrale, Florence, Magliabecchiana MSS. Cl.IX, cod. 60, f. 47ᵛ.

[57] Biblioteca Nazionale Centrale, Florence, Magliabecchiana MSS. Cl.IX, cod. 60, f. 48.

[58] Cf. Campbell, *A Milton Chronology*, 62.

such Florentine, or more specifically Svogliatine, academicians as Buonmattei.[59] This in turn lends support to the argument that the "letterato Inglese" of the July meeting is indeed John Milton.[60]

There are still more precise indications of Milton's participation in the Svogliati. Only six days after writing that letter to Buonmattei, he certainly attended one of its meetings, at which he read a Latin poem. The minutes of Thursday 6/16 September 1638 seem to single him out from the other participants (as if to highlight the outstanding performance of this Englishman) for having read to the academy "a very erudite Latin poem of hexameter verses":

> A di 16 di Settembro
> furono lett' alcune compositioni *e particolarmente il Giovanni Miltone Inglese lesse una poesia Latina di versi esametri molto erudita.*[61]

> [Minutes of 16 September
> Some compositions were read *and in particular John Milton, Englishman, read a very erudite Latin poem of hexameter verses.*]

That "particolarmente" is important — a youthful Englishman abroad doing much more than simply being "in attendance" at the academy. Rather, in using the universal language of Latin and in reviving that language through his own verse-composition, Milton excels among fellow neo-Latin and vernacular poets. Even the fact that his poems were granted a performance is in itself a tribute to their author's erudition, for as Cochrane's analysis has indicated, the methods by which academic officers selected individual contributions for performance were extremely rigorous. The following procedure would have been typical of most Seicento academies:

> From two to six censors in each academy met secretly every fortnight or so to examine the contributions deposited, usually anonymously, in a locked box known as the *tramoggia* or the *zucca*. The best were those selected for a formal line-by-line criticism (*critica*) and then an equally detailed defense

---

[59] Buonmattei was also a member of the Accademia degli Apatisti, and is included by Anton Francesco Gori, (Manoscritto Marucelliano di Firenze A. 36, f. 44[r], [on whom see 29 below]), along with his anagrammatic Boemonte Buttidente, for the years 1631-1634 of the Apatisti's membership and history. See 31 below.

[60] Noteworthy in this regard is Milton's own comment in *Defensio Secunda*, noted above, that he contracted the friendships of Florentines immediately (*statim*). *CM* 8, 122.

[61] Biblioteca Nazionale Centrale, Florence, MSS Magliabecchiana, MSS. Cl. IX, cod. 60, f. 48; cf. French, *Life Records*, I, 389; Campbell, *A Milton Chronology*, 62.

(*difesa*) ... Finally a vote of the assembly decided either to return them to the authors for appropriate correction or to transcribe them into one of the permanent books.[62]

Evidence would suggest that original verse for recitation at a meeting was particularly welcome and, very probably, subject to careful scrutiny:

The writing of original verse ... was intended not as mere entertainment. It was rather a means of stimulating creativity.[63]

There is no reason to suppose that the Svogliati was an exception to these general academic rules. And Milton not only passed the test, but did so with flying colors. Before analysing the relevant minutes in their context, it is important to note that Milton's presence at the Svogliati is attested on three further occasions, this time on his return visit to Florence c. March 1639.[64] He certainly read "noble Latin verses" at a meeting of the academy on 7/17 March of that year. The minutes are as follows:

A di 17 di Mar.
Nell' Accademia si trovarono *li signori* ... *Miltonio* ... Furon portati dal sesto, dal X e dall' undecimo, e *letti alcune nobili versi latini*.[65]

[Minutes of 17 March
In the Academy there were Messrs. Milton etc. ... By the sixth, tenth and eleventh there were brought and *read some noble Latin verses*.]

"Furon portati" is interesting, indicating that Milton and his fellow-participants personally brought their own compositions to the meeting of the academy in the hope perhaps of being granted a performance. And obviously this hope was subsequently fulfilled. Indeed among the participants on this occasion was Alessandro Adimari, who read a "moral sonnet."[66] Milton once again seems to be attending on a weekly basis, for

---

[62] Cochrane, *Tradition and Enlightenment*, 19.

[63] Cochrane, *Tradition and Enlightenment*, 19.

[64] French, *Life Records*, I, 408; Campbell, *A Milton Chronology*, 65-66.

[65] Biblioteca Nazionale Centrale, Florence, Magliabecchiana, MSS. Cl. IX, cod. 60, f. 52. Cf. French, *Life Records*, I, 408. French interprets the entry as follows: "Milton's name is 10th on the list of those present at the meeting. The meaning seems to be that three of the spectators or guests, 6, 10 and 11 read poems." Cf. Campbell, *A Milton Chronology*, 65.

[66] Biblioteca Nazionale Centrale, Florence, Magliabecchiana, MSS. Cl. IX, cod. 60, f. 52[v].

one week later the minutes of the 14/24 March meeting attest to the presence of *Miltonio*, recording that he read "diverse Latin poems":

> A di 24 Mar.
> Furon recitate oltre un elogio et un sonetto dal Signor Cavalcanti diverse poesie Toscane delli signori Bartolommei, Buommattei e Doni, che lesse una scena della sua Tragedia, *e diversi poesie latine del Signor Miltonio* e un epigrama dal Signor Girolami.[67]

> [Minutes of 24 March
> There were recited, besides a eulogy and a sonnet of Mr Cavalcanti, various Tuscan poems of the Messrs. Bartolommei, Buonmattei and Doni, who read a scene from his Tragedy, *and various Latin poems of Mr Milton*, and an epigram of Mr Girolami.]

Andrea Cavalcanti, recitor of the eulogy and sonnet on this occasion, was a learned teacher and charter member of the Svogliati.[68] The Doni mentioned in these minutes is very probably not Giovanni Battista Doni, who, as would appear from Milton's letter to Lucas Hostenius (19/29 March 1639), was still in Rome or at most en route from Rome to Florence.[69] Rather the reference is to a certain Nicolo Doni, likewise a member of the academy from as early as 1637 and referred to in other Svogliati minutes simply as "Doni."[70]

Again, one week later on 21/31 March Milton's presence is attested:

> A di 31
> Nell Accademia si trovarono li signori ... *G. Miltonio*[71]
> [Minutes of 31
> In the academy are found the Mssrs. ... *G. Milton*.]

---

[67] Biblioteca Nazionale Centrale, Florence, Magliabecchiana, MSS. Cl IX, cod. 60, ff. 52-52ᵛ; French, *Life Records*, I, 408-409; Campbell, *A Milton Chronology*, 65.

[68] On Cavalcanti, see *DBI s.v.* On his attending Apatisti symposia, see Maylender, *Storia*, V, 288-289.

[69] *CM* 12, 42: *esse tamen aiunt Romae Ioannem Baptistam Donium, is ad legendas publice Graecas Literas Florentiam vocatus indies exspectatur ...* See in general L. Schleiner, "Milton, G.B. Doni and the dating of Doni's works," *MQ* 16 (1982), 36-42.

[70] Cf. Edith Hubbard, *N & Q*, n.s. 8 (1961), 171-172, who corrects J.H. Hanford, *A Milton Handbook* (New York, 1946), 408; cf. also J.H. Hanford, *John Milton Englishman* (New York, 1949), 95; Piero Rebora, "Milton a Firenze," *NA* 88 (1953), 157.

[71] Biblioteca Nazionale Centrale, Florence, Magliabecchiana MSS. Cl.IX, cod. 60, f. 52ᵛ. See French, *Life Records*, I, 414, who correctly observes that "Although this entry is not dated as to the month, there is little doubt about its being March, since the last previous entry is for March 24." Cf. Campbell, *A Milton Chronology*, 66.

   In summary, the evidence when viewed as a whole seems to suggest
that Milton attended a *minimum* of four of the weekly Thursday meetings
of the Accademia degli Svogliati: certainly one (and possibly three) in
1638 (at one of which he read an "erudite Latin hexameter poem"), and
three in 1639 (at two of which he read "diverse" and "noble" Latin poems
respectively). It is actually very probable that he attended many more than
these. His constant involvement in the Svogliati and indeed in other
academies (*privatas academias ... assidue frequentavi*)[72] seems to set
Milton apart from other seventeenth-century English travellers abroad,
exemplifying, in the words of Stoye, an "almost solitary instance of an
English traveller who assiduously attended Italian literary societies."[73]   In
the *Reason of Church Government* Milton refers to his participation in
Italian academies as follows:

> But much latelier in the privat Academies of Italy, whither I was favoured
> to resort, perceiving that some trifles which I had in memory, composed at
> under twenty or thereabout (for the manner is, that everyone must give
> some proof of his wit and reading there), met with acceptance above what
> was looked for; and other things which I had shifted in scarcity of books
> and conveniences to patch up amongst them, were received with written
> encomiums, which the Italian is not forward to bestow on men of this side
> the Alps ....[74]

Despite its assumed modesty *topos*, the passage soars from the
conventional (participation in such meetings and the usual demonstration
of "wit and reading") to the unconventional (a reception that was quite
unusual, and tributes which Italians do not normally bestow upon
Englishmen or other such northerners). Milton does not identify the
language in which these "trifles" were composed, nor does he state
whether they were prose or verse. But given the fact that it is as a reader
or recitor of *Latin* poetry that he is recorded in the minutes, it seems likely
that Latin was the language he most frequently used, and that verse was
his most popular medium. Moreover he surpassed normal expectations.
Did he read *only* Latin poems? Probably not. In view of the acclaim he
received from Italian academicians as a polyglot,[75] it is very likely that he
familiarised them with some of his Italian, English or even Greek poetry.
For by the time of the Italian journey Milton had in fact composed in at

---

[72] Milton, *DS, CM* 8, 122.

[73] J.W. Stoye, *English Travellers Abroad, 1604-1667* (London, 1952), 223.

[74] *CM* 3, 235-236.

[75] See 40, 43, 47, 84 below.

least four languages (His six Italian sonnets, for example, can probably be dated to c. 1629).[76] Is it possible to identify at least in a general sense the works, or more precisely, the Latin poems that he may have read at these meetings? With one exception, probably not. Although French sounds a cautionary note,[77] he does venture to suggest as the likeliest possibilities "some of [Milton's] college Latin poems on the deaths of officials, his Greek translations, or possibly his Italian verses,"[78] and continues "It is, however, not impossible that his 'under twenty' may be slightly exaggerated."[79] Certainly when minutes refer to "noble verses" or "diverse Latin poems" nothing more than speculation seems possible. Did he recite perhaps some of the Latin elegies, especially nos. 1 and 6 — his verse epistles to Charles Diodati, himself descended from a noble Italian family?[80] Evidence elsewhere may indeed suggest that such academicians as Dati and Francini knew of (and composed poems on?) Milton's great friendship with Diodati. In *Epitaphium Damonis*, Milton's pastoral lament on the premature death of his friend, written after his Italian trip, a poem of

---

[76] In both the 1645 and 1673 editions the Italian sonnets are printed as a group before Sonnet VII (Dec. 1631). Cf. John Carey, "The Date of Milton's Italian Poems," *RES*, 14 (1963), 383-386; cf. also John Carey, ed., *Milton: Complete Shorter Poems* (Longman: London and New York; 2nd ed., 1997), 94, where he dates them to 1629, stating "The Italian sonnets are so closely related in subject that they are probably of similar date." Likewise Campbell, *A Milton Chronology*, 38. In 1762 according to Warton (*Poems Upon Several Occasions, English, Italian and Latin* [London, 1785], 338) "the late Mr Thomas Hollis examined the Laurentian library at Florence for six Italian sonnets of Milton, addressed to his friend Chimentelli, and, for other Italian and Latin compositions and various original letters, said to be remaining in manuscript at Florence." There is no evidence to support any of this, but in view of the fact that the reference is to *six* Italian sonnets supposedly addressed by Milton to Chimentelli, it is not impossible that rather than pieces "patched up" while in Italy, these constitute the six Italian sonnets which Milton had already composed prior to his Italian journey. It is possible moreover that Francini's encomium of Milton discussed at 38-43 below echoes aspects of Milton's English and Italian sonnets.

[77] French, *Life Records*, I, 373: "One would hesitate to venture to identify the early poems which Milton read to his Italian acquaintances if they were any which still survive." Contrast Revard, *Milton and the Tangles of Neaera's Hair*, 3, who asserts (without any evidence): "When Milton went to Italy in 1638 and 1639 he was hailed as the writer of the elegies and odes of the *Poemata*, not as the writer of the *Mask at Ludlow* and *Lycidas*."

[78] French, *Life Records*, I, 374.

[79] French, *Life Records*, I, 374.

[80] Donald C. Dorian, *The English Diodatis* (New Brunswick, 1950), 5, states: "In the sixteenth century, the Diodatis were already honored as one of the oldest patrician families in the flourishing little north-Italian republic of Lucca."

which he was subsequently to arrange in London a separate printing, possibly for the precise purpose of sending to Italian academicians,[81] Milton in an allegorical passage makes the somewhat puzzling comment that "Dati and Francini have taught their beech trees our names" (*Quin et nostra suas docuerunt nomina fagos/et Datis et Francinus* [136-137]). John Hale in an interesting interpretation of these lines paraphrases: "He did well, moreover, for the Florentine poets (*Pastores Thusci*, 126 and 134) gave him gifts (134-135) — including poems recording his friendship with Damon (136-138)."[82] In support of this reading of the lines is the plural *nostra ... nomina* in a poem which frequently apostrophises Diodati, in contrast to *ipse ego*, thereby suggesting that Milton is referring not simply (by way of a poetic plural) to his own name, but also to the name of Diodati. Bearing this in mind, in association with the fact that Milton chose to send the *Epitaphium Damonis* to Italian academicians, and that in his subsequent letter to Dati drew his attention precisely to an "emblematic" passage in that poem (intended no doubt as an allegory of the academy and of its participants),[83] it is tempting to speculate that these academicians knew of the Milton/Diodati friendship not merely through day-to-day conversation with Milton, but perhaps also through reading or indeed hearing such works as Elegy 1 and 6 (or perhaps the fourth Italian sonnet addressed to Diodati). Further speculation is possible: were they to witness Milton's grief on his return visit to Florence (if by that time he had indeed heard of Diodati's death)?[84] Perhaps then or on some other occasion Milton familiarised his fellow-academicians with his own Latin (or Italian) poems to Diodati. Or more generally, would it not seem logical that he would have introduced to such academicians (at least by reputation) his own closest friend at home, descended from a reputable Italian family,[85] and like such academicians, composer of Latin and Greek works?[86] If Hale's interpretation is correct, it raises two important

---

[81] See 55-56 below.

[82] Hale, *Milton's Languages*, 58.

[83] See 56 below.

[84] Cf. 74-75 below.

[85] Cf. Milton's identification of Diodati (Damon) as *Tuscus tu quoque Damon/antiqua genus unde petis Lucumonis ab urbe* (*Ep. Dam*. 127-128) in a passage in which Italian academicians are likewise allegorised as *Tusci: pastores Tusci* (126).

[86] Diodati, at the age of only 15, contributed a Latin poem to the *Camdeni Insignia* (Oxford, 1624). Two undated Greek letters from Diodati to Milton are among the holdings of the British Museum: BM Add. MS 5016, ff. 5 and 71. (*CM* 12, 292 [1625]; *CM* 12, 294 [1626]). These are also printed in French, *Life Records*, I, 98-99 and 104-105. Both letters are written in very colorful Greek and contain vibrant descriptions of

questions: 1) Exactly *how* did these academicians learn of the Milton/Diodati friendship? Through conversation, undoubtedly, but perhaps also through knowledge of Milton's compositions; 2) Precisely *where* did they record it? Perhaps on now lost gifts of their own works which they presented to Milton, and which he in turn was to describe in pastoral terms as *munera vestra/fiscellae, calathique et cerea vincla cicutae* (*Ep. Dam.* 134-135). Milton's description of the works he pieced together in the course of his Italian trip "other things [as opposed to 'some trifles ... under twenty or thereabouts'] which I had shifted in scarcity of books and conveniences to patch up amongst them,"[87] would seem to embrace *Ad Salsillum, Mansus* and the Leonora epigrams, all of which were indeed composed in the course of his Italian sojourn.

While French's overall caution in attempting to identify the Latin poems actually recited by Milton at the Svogliati is prudent, it may be possible, in one instance at least, to be slightly more specific. As noted above, the minutes of the meeting of the 6/16 September 1638 record that Milton read a "very erudite Latin poem in hexameter verses." The reference to meter is helpful here since, as far as we know, Milton had composed only three hexameter poems prior to the Italian journey. There is of course always the possibility that the minutes refer to a now lost piece "patched up" in Italy. But Milton was generally very scrupulous about gathering for publication all the works (especially Latin works) which he had composed.[88] For example, even the early school exercise in Latin (*Apologus de Rustico et Hero*)[89] not printed in the 1645 edition, was indeed included in that of 1673. It might not be unreasonable to assume that the hexameter poem referred to in the minutes is among Milton's extant works and was included in the 1645 volume. This assumption is strengthened perhaps by the fact that Milton was to prefix to that edition the very "written encomiums" which he had received from members of the Svogliati and other Italian academicians in appreciation of his performances. Would it not be rather odd to print the tributes which he had

nature. In the first, Diodati anticipates sharing a holiday amid the beauties of nature: sunlight, birdsong, rivers and trees. In the second letter, to which Milton's *Elegia Prima* replies, he extols the beauties of the countryside.

[87] *RCG, CM* 3, 234-236.

[88] Cf. Masson, *Life*, I, 783: "as Milton seems to have destroyed little of what he wrote, I should not wonder if we have now among his works every scrap of what he 'patched up' in Italy."

[89] For a discussion of this poem, see Harris F. Fletcher, "Milton's *Apologus* and its Mantuan Model," *JEGP*, 55 (1956), 230-233; Estelle Haan, "Milton, Manso and the Fruit of That Forbidden Tree," *MH*, n.s. 25, forthcoming 1998.

received, while failing to include the Latin poems which had helped to inspire their composition? These factors, together with Milton's own statement that the poems he recited were "composed at under twenty or thereabout," offer the possibility of only three contenders (of which only two are serious) among Milton's Latin poems composed prior to the Italian trip:

1) the hexameter poem *In Quintum Novembris Anno Aetatis 17*, which can immediately be dismissed in view of its anti-papal content, certainly liable to cause offence in Catholic Italy (especially in academies which as a general rule forbade theological discussion). Further proof of this is Milton's own stated hesitation in forwarding to his Florentine friend and fellow-academician Carlo Dati the Latin section of the 1645 poems. This, he says, is on account of the fact that certain anti-papal comments in a few of its pages (obviously the [hitherto unseen/unheard] *In Quintum Novembris*) might cause offence. Interestingly, however, he does state that Dati used to excuse his former freedom of speech concerning the topic of religion.[90]

2) the hexameter poem *Naturam Non Pati Senium*. Although undated by Milton, this was probably composed between 1628-1632, either for the Cambridge commencement (and thus constituting perhaps the *leviculas ... nugas* mentioned by Milton in his letter to Alexander Gill, dated 2 July 1628)[91] or, as I have argued elsewhere, in response to Hakewill's *Apologie* (either the first [1627], or second [1630] editions).[92] As a learned hexameter poem composed when Milton was between 20 and 24 years of age, this must be a serious contender.

3) the hexameter poem *Ad Patrem*, which although preceding the Italian trip, is probably to be dated no earlier than c. 1631/2 (when Milton was 23/4).[93]

---

[90] See his letter to Dati (*CM* 12, 44-52, at 50), discussed at 57-60 below. Milton's luck does not seem to have stretched so far with Manso in Naples. See 125-127 below.

[91] *CM* 12, 8-10 at 10. An interesting description paralleling perhaps his reference to "some trifles" in the *Reason of Church Government* (*CM* 3, 235).

[92] Estelle Haan, "Milton's *Naturam non Pati Senium* and Hakewill," *MH*, n.s. 24 (1997), 147-167. Campbell, *A Milton Chronology*, 43, following Shawcross, "The Date of Certain Poems, Letters, and Prolusions Written by Milton," *ELN* 2, 261-266, suggests June 1631.

[93] W.R. Parker, "Notes on the Chronology of Milton's Latin Poems," in A. Williams, ed., *A Tribute to George Coffin Taylor* (Carolina, 1955), 113-131, dates *Ad Patrem* to

Milton's own phrase "under twenty or thereabout" is sufficiently vague to
validate the inclusion of *Naturam* and possibly *Ad Patrem* as candidates
for this "poesia Latina di versi esametri molto erudita." And a case can be
made for both of these poems, although arguments would seem to favor
the *Naturam*: the probability of its slightly earlier date (hence more closely
approximating Milton's age-description), its erudite treatment of the theme
of nature's decay, its dramatic use of the rhetoric of persuasion, all
embraced by a methodology that would certainly have found a home in the
debating forum of the Italian academy. These characteristics do indeed
seem to fit the description of "multo erudita" quite neatly. It may also be
worth noting that the "written encomium" composed by Carlo Dati[94]
praises Milton as one who "with Philosophy as teacher selects the marks
of *Natura's* wondrous deeds, through which the greatness of God is
shown."[95] On the other hand, *Ad Patrem*, although probably later than
Naturam and certainly more personal, is equally erudite, albeit in a less
abstract way, and would have served as an excellent form of self-
introduction to Italian academicians. It is in many respects a defence of
poetry,[96] outlining an ideal education. Thus Milton expresses gratitude
towards a parent for the gift of education, but at the same time advertises
himself as a polyglot. It is in this poem that he thanks his father for
enabling him to learn Latin, Greek, French, Italian, and Hebrew (79-85).[97]
Some of those "written encomiums" do indeed praise Milton as a polyglot.
While it is more likely that the authors of these tributes witnessed this

---

early autumn 1634. In reply, J.T. Shawcross, "The Date of Milton's *Ad Patrem*," *N &
Q* n.s., 6 (1959), 358-359, dates it to 1638. E. Sirluck, *Milton Studies in Honour of
Harris Francis Fletcher* (Urbana, 1961), 176-177, dates the poem to 1637 or 1638.
Douglas Bush, "The Date of Milton's *Ad Patrem*," *MP* 61 (1963-64), 204-208, argues
for 1631 or 1632; John Spencer Hill, "Poet-Priest: Vocational Tension in Milton's
Early Development," *MS* 8 (1975), 41-69 at 60-62, argues for 1637 or 1638. See also
Carey, ed., *Milton: Complete Shorter Poems*, 153. Campbell, *A Milton Chronology*,
59, following Shawcross, *John Milton: The Self and the World* (Lexington, 1993),
suggests March 1638.

[94] See 46-52 below.

[95] See 47 below.

[96] For Milton's poem as a defence of poetry, and for points of contact with Vida's *De
Arte Poetica*, see Estelle Haan, "Milton's Latin poetry and Vida," *HL* 44 (1995), 282-
304 at 283-293.

[97] *cum mihi Romuleae patuit facundia linguae,/et Latii veneres et quae Iovis ora
decebant/grandia magniloquis elata vocabula Graiis,/addere suasisti quos iactat
Gallia flores,/et quam degeneri novus Italus ore loquelam/fundit, barbaricos testatus
voce tumultus,/quaeque Palaestinus loquitur mysteria vates. (Ad Patrem 79-85),
discussed by Hale, *Milton's Languages*, 52-53.

linguistic versatility first-hand, it is just possible that they are responding to Milton's self-description in *Ad Patrem*.

However, weighing up the evidence in relation to the wording of the minutes, the content of the respective poems, and Milton's own statement, and given the likeliest dating of the respective contenders, it might not be unreasonable to suggest that on Thursday 6/16 September 1638 John Milton read his *Naturam Non Pati Senium* before the Accademia degli Svogliati. His audience was clearly impressed.

CHAPTER 2

Milton and the Accademia degli Apatisti

It is very likely that Milton's participation in Florentine academic life was not confined to the Svogliati. Many of the academicians mentioned in the Milton/Dati correspondence (including Dati himself) belonged not only to the Svogliati, but also to the Accademia degli Apatisti, the "Academy of the Dispassionates."[1] Unlike the Svogliati, there are no extant Apatisti minutes to confirm Milton's attendance on a particular date (or dates)/year (or years).[2] Lazzeri's illuminating study of the academy has greatly advanced research into the Apatisti's membership and practices. Crucial to this research is a manuscript of a later Apatisti member, the erudite scholar Anton Francesco Gori (1691-1757), founder of the Accademia Colombaria (1729). This manuscript now usefully transcribed,[3] constitutes a vital source hitherto neglected by Milton scholars.

In 1631/2, only six or seven years prior to Milton's Florentine sojourn, Agostino Coltellini,[4] mentioned in Milton's prose works in a way that suggests that they were on familiar terms,[5] was beginning to organise at his home meetings of his learned friends.[6] It was as a result of a

---

[1] On the Apatisti, see E. Benvenuti, *Agostino Coltellini e l'Accademia degli Apatisti a Firenze nel Secolo XVII* (Pistoia, 1910), now superseded by Lazzeri, *Intellettuali*. Cf. Maylender, *Storia* I, 219-222.

[2] Anton Francesco Gori, writing a century later, speculated that some of the archives, statutes and institutes of the academy may have been burnt in a fire. Cf. Lazzeri, *Intellettuali*, 19, 53.

[3] Lazzeri, *Intellettuali*, 57-121.

[4] On Coltellini, see *DBI s.v.*; Masson, *Life*, I, 776-778.

[5] See 60 below.

[6] Gori, Manoscritto Marucelliano A. 36, f. 11r: "cominciò ad introdurre in casa sua gente letterata e così diede principio l'anno 1632, al tempo della peste all' accademia degli Apatisti in casa propria"; Lazzeri, *Intellettuali*, 5, 57; Gregorio Leti, *L'Itala Regnante* (Valenza, 1676), III, 377. Salvino Salvini, *Fasti Consolari dell' Accademia Fiorentina* (Florence, 1717), 607, locates Coltellini's abode as follows: "Stava egli in via dell' Oriolo, nella casa chiamata degli sporti che rierce in via Sant' Egidio presso all' volta di San Piero." This location is confirmed by Gori, BMF., Ms. A.36, f.15v. See Lazzeri, *Intellettuali*, 38, 59.

"virtuosa conversazione"[7] on one such occasion that the Academy of the Apatisti came to birth. Gori in his chronological survey of the Apatisti includes Agostino Coltellini (along with his anagrammatic Ostilio Contalgeni) under the years 1631-1634.[8] The Apatisti was to adopt as its *impresa* the sun, and as its motto a line borrowed from Tasso: "Oltre i confini ancor del mondo nostro" (*Gerusalemme Liberata* 14. 35).[9] This motto was intended no doubt to convey the world-wide fame and glory which might accrue to the academy's learned membership,[10] but perhaps also to hint at the fact that this academy in particular would readily embrace members from all parts of the globe.[11] By 1/11 November 1635 the academy was introducing lectures on Boccaccio's *Decameron*;[12] in 1637 Coltellini recited an oration on the death of Raffaello Gherardi.[13] It was not until 1637 that the academy actually decided upon its name,[14] the "Apatisti"/ "Dispassionates," a name intended to denote freedom from passion and thus perhaps an absolutely firm stylistic control.[15] The president of the Apatisti was known as the *Apatista Reggente*, who had at his service a secretary.[16] The first president was Benedetto Fioretti, its first secretary was none other than Carlo Dati, foremost among those Apatisti members with whom Milton corresponded. Other Apatisti academicians mentioned by Milton are: Valerio Chimentelli, Benedetto Buonmattei, Antonio Francini, Piero Frescobaldi[17] and Andrea Cavalcanti. The name

[7] BMF, Ms A. 36; A.F. Gori, f. 15r; Lazzeri, *Intellettuali*, 59.

[8] Gori, f. 44r; Lazzeri, *Intellettuali*, 67.

[9] Gori, f. 11r: "coll' impresa del sole col verso *Oltre i confini ancor del mondo nostro.*" Cf. f. 15r, Lazzeri, *Intellettuali*, 59.

[10] The entire Tasso stanza from which the Apatisti motto is borrowed is significantly addressed to "amici": "Amici, dura e faticosa inchiesta/seguite; e d'uopo e ben ch'altri vi guidi,/ché, 'l cercato guerrier lunge è da questa/terra in paesi incogniti ed infidi./Quanto, oh quanto de l'opra anco vi resta!/quanti mar correrete e quanti lidi!/E convien che si stenda il carcar vostro/oltre i confini ancor del mondo nostro."

[11] Cf. Lazzeri, *Intellettuali*, 17.

[12] Gori f. 15v; Lazzeri, *Intellettuali*, 59.

[13] Gori, f. 16v; Lazzeri, *Intellettuali*, 61.

[14] Benedetto Fioretti, *Osservazioni di Creanza* (Florence, 1675); A.M. Salvini, *Discorsi Accademici* (Florence, 1725); Lazzeri, *Intellettuali*, 6.

[15] Maylender, *Storia*, I, 219; Lazzeri, *Intellettuali*, 14. For a full discussion of the Apatisti's *impresa* and its significance, see Lazzeri, *Intellettuali*, 31-36.

[16] Lazzeri, *Intellettuali*, 20.

[17] See Masson, *Life*, I, 779-780.

of another Apatisti member, Franceso Rovai,[18] crops up in a letter from Dati to Milton, in which Dati states he believes Rovai was well known to Milton.[19]

One strikingly innovative feature of this academy in particular was the fact that most of its members concealed their identity by means of an anagram.[20] As Lazzeri states: "L'anagramma costituisce una novità ed è peculiare dell' Accademia degli Apatisti."[21] But such were not always "anagrams" in the strictest sense of the word. Very frequently members assumed rather a pseudonym, a sort of fictitious secular identity by which they were known, and under which some of them published.[22] Of the academicians named by Milton or occurring in the Milton/Dati correspondence, some possessed *only* anagrams; others had *both* anagrams and pseudonyms. Agostino Coltellini, as noted above, was known by the anagrammatic Ostilio Contalgeni; Carlo Roberto Dati became Currado Bartoletti (but he also assumed the non-anagrammatic pseudonym, Timauro Antiate); Benedetto Buonmattei was Boemonte Battidente;[23] Piero Frescobaldi was Bali Scoprifode[24] while Andrea Cavalcanti was Lucano da Recanati.[25] Benedetto Fioretti, the academy's president, unmentioned by Milton, published under the name of Udeno Nisieli. Such pervasive use of anagrams or pseudonyms is but one indication of this particular academy's obsession with etymology, and of its quasi-baroque interest in wordplay. It would later introduce (in 1649),[26] a game known as the *Sibilla* in which a young blindfolded boy would utter meaningless syllables, which were then picked up and interpreted by members of the

---

[18] Lazzeri, *Intellettuali*, 15. Francesco Rovai was known by the anagram Rainero Fucasco.

[19] *CM* 12, 296. Discussed at 61-71 below.

[20] Lazzeri, *Intellettuali*, 14.

[21] Lazzeri, *Intellettuali*, 14.

[22] Lazzeri, *Intellettuali*, 14: "La scelta del nome anagrammato mi sembra riconducibile, pur nella sua peculiarità, a quella più generale tendenza propria di tutte le accademie del tempo, di assumere un nome fantasioso, una sorta di identità fittizia che diviene quasi la maschera con cui si recita, lontani dalla realtà nella 'non-realtà' delle microsocietà accademiche."

[23] Lazzeri, *Intellettuali*, 15.

[24] Gori, f. 44v includes Piero Frescobaldi and his anagram noted above as a member of the Apatisti between 1631-1634; see Lazzeri, *Intellettuali*, 68.

[25] Lazzeri, *Intellettuali*, 15.

[26] Lazzeri, *Intellettuali*, 26.

academy![27] Another striking methodological practice introduced by Coltellini to the academy was that of *dubbi* or "doubtful sayings," a sort of intellectual joke. These could comprise any genre, whether sacred or profane, whether literary or scientific. The president might posit such *dubbi*, which the members would take up and debate in turn.[28] In its literary output too the academy drew its inspiration from a wide range of sources. Among the manuscripts of the Biblioteca Nazionale Centrale of Florence are two virtually identical mini-anthologies of Italian poetry by Apatisti members: 1) Ms. cl. II, IV 17 containing the *Poesie* of Domenico Poltri, which includes on folios 214r-219r *Poesie di Alcuni Accademici Apatisti.*[29] In fact, this is an unfinished compilation (in the hand of Francisco Cionacci) of poems by subsequent Apatisti members, which had been included in volume three of the *Prosinnasmi Poetici* of Udeno Nisieli (i.e. Benedetto Fioretti), published at Florence in 1627 by Pietro Cecconcelli; 2) Ms. cl. VII 623, another, fuller, version of the *Poesie di Alcuni Accademici Apatisti*, again extracted from the 1627 volume. Although these collections obviously precede Milton's Italian sojourn by at least a decade, they constitute nonetheless a very useful and illustrative example of the sheer range of talent demonstrated by some of those *litterati* who were subsequently to participate in the Apatisti. It is evident that their interests are not only classical, but also religious and indeed contemporary. Foremost among classical influences is Ovid. Many of the poems are in fact vernacular reworkings and at times close translations of selected myths from the *Metamorphoses*. That Ovid is the source is indicated by authors signposting in the actual title of their poem the relevant book of the *Metamorphoses* upon which they have drawn. Among Ovidian myths reworked in the *Poesie di Alcuni Apatisti* are Polyphemus and Galatea;[30] Europa;[31] Pomona;[32] Alpheus and Arethusa;[33] Pan.[34] The

---

[27] Gori, ff. 124r -125v "Del giuoco del Sibillone"; Lazzeri, *Intellettuali*, 26-27; 103-105.

[28] Gori, ff. 134r-142v. See Lazzeri, *Intellettuali*, 24-25; 107-121.

[29] All subsequent quotations are from this manuscript, which is much more legible than its equivalent Ms. cl. VII 623.

[30] Ms cl. II, IV 17, ff 214r-215v: "Polifemo Innamorato di Galatea Ovidio."

[31] *Poesie di Alcuni Apatisti*, 215v - 216r: "Europa in Mare."

[32] *Poesie di Alcuni Apatisti*, 216r: "Versunno in Lode di Pomona."

[33] *Poesie di Alcuni Apatisti*, 217r: "Alfeo ad Aretusa ... al Signor Giovannio Nardi, Medico, e Filosofo eccellentissimo."

[34] *Poesie di Alcuni Apatisti*, ff. 217r-218r: "Pan Acceso di Siringa ... a Monsignor del Poro."

youthful Milton had himself reworked Ovidian subject-matter in, for example, his first Latin elegy where by a clever "cross-comparison" with Ovid, he had depicted his rustication from Cambridge in London as the very antithesis to Ovid's exile in Tomis.[35] Also evident in the Apatisti collection is a certain philosophical influence. The precedent of Plato is felt in, for example, such poems as no. I, entitled "All' Amor Divino,"[36] and no. VI.[37] But if these future Apatisti academicians turned back to a pagan classical past, they also looked to an essentially Christian present. This is exemplified by the religious content of such poems as "S. Pietro penitente,"[38] and "A Santa Caterina Martire."[39] Links with the "modern" world are also apparent, and this works on at least two levels: a) the inclusion of poems inspired by passages in the works of Tasso;[40] b) poems addressed to, or in praise of, Seicento academicians. Thus, for example, the adaptation of Ovid's Polyphemus/Galatea myth, noted above, is addressed to the Accademia degli Umoristi of Rome,[41] while the poem in praise of Ovid's Pomona is addressed to Giovanni Battista Doni at Rome.[42] Perhaps most striking is an encomium of fellow-academician and poet Gabriello Chiabrera.[43] Entitled "Al signor Gabbriello Chiabrera in sua lode," the piece depicts him as a second Pindar: "Tu di lei faune un bel pregio/al gran Pindaro Toscano" (7-8).[44]

Even in its earliest years the Apatisti was rapidly increasing in size. Lazzeri's analysis of the Gori manuscript indicates that between 1632 and 1634 there were 63 names; in 1635 a further 86 had joined; in 1636 another 36. But particularly indicative in this respect is the year preceding

---

[35] See in general, Ralph W. Condee, "Ovid's Exile and Milton's Rustication," *PQ* 37 (1958), 498-502 reworked in his *Structure in Milton's Poetry: From the Foundation to the Pinnacles* (Pennsylvania, 1974), 22-27.

[36] *Poesie di Alcuni Apatisti*, f. 214^r.

[37] *Poesie di Alcuni Apatisti*, f. 216^r.

[38] *Poesie di Alcuni Apatisti*, f. 216^v.

[39] *Poesie di Alcuni Apatisti*, f. 216^v.

[40] *Poesie di Alcuni Apatisti*, f. 216^v: "Eustazio ad Arnida, Tasso *Gerusal. cant.* 4"; f. 218^r: "Espresso Sopra Aminto Tasso *Gerusal.*"

[41] *Poesie di Alcuni Apatisti*, ff. 214^r-215^v at f. 214^r: "... all' Accademia degli Umoristi in Roma."

[42] *Poesie di Alcuni Apatisti*, f. 216^r: "... Al Signor Giovambattista Doni in Roma." For Milton's possible links with Doni, see 21 above and 102 below.

[43] *Poesie di Alcuni Apatisti*, ff. 216^v - 217^r.

[44] *Poesie di Alcuni Apatisti*, f. 216^v. For Chiabrera as a second Pindar, cf. Carlo Dati's comment in his first letter to Milton, discussed at 65; 71-75 below.

Milton's Florentine sojourn: it is in 1637, Lazzeri points out, that the names of many *foreigners* are to be found, in particular Poles, English, Germans, French and Flemish.[45] Such an international dimension is indeed hardly surprising in an academy which seems to have surpassed even its sister academy the Svogliati in embracing foreign *litterati*. Coltellini himself was to boast:

> "L'Università da me fondata in casa mia più di 30 anni sono, ha per fine l'istituzione della gioventù nelle cose civili ... ed il servigio de' forestieri massime oltramontani".[46]

> [The university founded by me in my home more than thirty years ago has as its aim the instruction of youth in civil affairs ... and the service of strangers from far across the Alps.]

It is not an exaggeration to say that the Apatisti was motivated by an essentially positive aim to receive and indeed to recruit foreign scholars. There was indeed a precise means of receiving such foreigners:

> ut, cum Florentiam venerint, sciant se non in alium terrarum orbem delatos, sed quasi ad federatam amoris vinculo urbem confugerint, a concivibus suis humanissime excipiantur.[47]

> [so that when they come to Florence they may know they have not been borne into another world, but that they have as it were fled to a city allied by a bond of love and that they may be received most humanely by their fellow citizens.]

Apatisti members were permitted moreover to deliver orations in their own language.[48] In fact, the academy actually encouraged multilingual participation.[49] On the occasion of the funeral of Ferdinand II, for example, commemorative verses were recited before the academy in four different languages (besides the normal Italian) — Latin, English, German and French.[50]

---

[45] Lazzeri, *Intellettuali*, 16: "Nel 1637 troviamo già molti stranieri, principalmente polacchi, inglesi, tedeschi, francesi, fiamminghi."

[46] Biblioteca Riccardiana Fiorentina Cod. Riccardiano 1949, f. 20r. Cf. Lazzeri, *Intellettuali*, 17.

[47] Gori, f. 80r. Cf. Lazzeri *Intellettuali*, 17-18.

[48] Lazzeri, *Intellettuali*, 18.

[49] Cf. Maylender, *Storia*, I, 222.

[50] Lazzeri, *Intellettuali*, 18.

What then of *Giovanni Milton Inglese*? Did he participate in this academy, particularly receptive to foreigners, an academy moreover that was flourishing precisely at the time of his visit? Did the polyglot Milton find a place in this multilinguistic forum? Surely the fact that some of the Florentine academicians either mentioned by Milton himself or referred to by Dati in his correspondence with Milton actually belonged to the Apatisti would strengthen this possibility. Hitherto scholars, while viewing Milton's participation as a likely occurrence, have tended to stand back by way of generalising comments. Thus Masson, who does indeed discuss the Apatisti,[51] could do no more than speculate that "Milton seems to have spent his pleasantest hours among Gaddi's Svogliati and Coltellini's Apatisti."[52] Parker thought Milton's participation in the Apatisti likely, but was inconclusive because of the fact that the academicians mentioned in the *Defensio Secunda* belonged also to the Svogliati.[53] Arthos could only generalise that "Most of the friends Milton made in Florence belonged to two academies: the Svogliati and the Apatisti."[54] Even Anna Nardo's excellent analysis of *Paradise Lost* in its possible academic context,[55] which was brave enough to suggest that the names of such academies as the "Apatisti" are echoed in the description of the apathetic demons in the "hellish academy" of *Paradise Lost* 1-2, had generalised: "No records confirm our speculations, but scholars have thought it probable that Milton also visited other academies: ... the Apatisti ..."[56] More recently, Campbell, in discussing Milton's Florentine years, states that he participated "in the meetings of at least two Florentine academies,"[57] but does not cite any evidence of Milton's Apatisti involvement, obviously inferring such from the Florentine acquaintances mentioned in the *Defensio Secunda*. Unnoticed by Milton scholars however is what amounts to almost certain proof of his participation in the Apatisti, at least for the year 1638. This proof is provided by the Gori manuscript itself, which lists the members of the academy under a given year, together with their respective

---

[51] Masson, *Life*, I, 776-777.

[52] Masson, *Life*, I, 782.

[53] W.R. Parker, *Milton: A Biography* (Oxford, 1968), II, 824, states: "Although no records have been found proving Milton's attendance at meetings of the Apatisti, his mention of six of its members in the *Defensio Secunda* would seem to be proof enough; most of all these people however belonged also to Gaddi's Svogliati."

[54] Arthos, *Italian Cities*, 12.

[55] Nardo, "Academic Interludes," *passim*.

[56] Nardo, "Academic Interludes," 215.

[57] Campbell, *A Milton Chronology*, 60.

anagrams/pseudonyms (if indeed they had one). On Folio 53ʳ under the
year 1638 there does indeed occur the name "Giovanni Milton Inglese"
(but with no equivalent anagram or pseudonym). It is a list that merits full
quotation not only because of its exciting inclusion of Milton, but also as
an example of that multi-national, multilingual and even interdenom-
inational nature of the Apatisti's membership at the time of Milton's
Florentine sojourn:

1638

dr. Adamo da Rovezzano	Bartolommeo Gherardini
an. Jeonardo da Modane	dr. Baccio Morali
P. Antonio de Velasco gesuita	an. Amilcaro Cibo
Alessandro Lucri	Benedatto Rigogli segretario
D. Andrea Borghi	mons. Alessandro Venturi arc.
Bernardo da Magnale	Alessandro Verrazzani
an. Leandro Bandanegra	sen. Andrea Pitti
Bastiano Bordoni	an. Pindaro Fedi
don Ariosto Bandi	march. Alberto Altoviti
Cosimo Venturi	Alessandro Visconti
Cosimo degli Assiori	can. Alessandro Ridolfi
Pio Diego Baldovinetti	an. Don Flonsel de Aras
Filippo Capponi	R. Almanno Moronti
Francesco Niccolini	Alessandro di Carlo di
	Luigi Strozzi
Filippo Aureliani	can. F. Andrea Minerbetti
Giulio Veterani	Averardo Ambrogi
dv. Giuliano Pacioni	sen. Andrea Arrighetti
an. Gaio Ulpanio Fini	Decano Antonio de' Ricci
Giovanni Ricasoli	Annibal Donara sen. Antonio
	Quaratesi
Giovanni Milton inglese	sen. Antonio Serristori
Bernardino Lorini	
an. Bali Neri Rondoni	
dv. Bassiano Galeotti[58]	

The manuscript is a reliable source. Lazzeri is correct in his assessment of
its tone and content as essentially free of the non-critical or encomiastic
jargon that characterise others.[59] Surprisingly however he makes no
reference whatsoever to the significance of the inclusion of Milton's name
in a document written by an academician who undoubtedly would have
had access to invaluable material now lost or lying buried among the

---

[58] Gori, f. 53ʳ; Lazzeri, *Intellettuali*, 73-74. Highlighting is mine.

[59] Lazzeri, *Intellettuali*, 19.

archives of Florentine libraries. The important point is that an Apatisti member noted for his scholarly precision and writing only one century after Milton's Italian sojourn, seems to have possessed sufficiently conclusive evidence (whether from now lost minutes or from internal correspondence) to be able to include among the Apatisti's membership for the year 1638 the name *Giovanni Milton Inglese*. Milton does not seem to have had a corresponding anagram or pseudonym, but he *was* there.

CHAPTER 3

Florentine "Written Encomiums"

Among the "written encomiums" prefixed to Milton's 1645 volume are two by Apatisti members (Antonio Francini and Carlo Dati respectively). These merit close examination not only in their own right, but also in terms of the light that they may shed upon Milton's academic practice in general, and in particular his possible contribution to the Apatisti's multilingualism.

Before discussing Francini's encomium, it should be noted that in the so-called "emblematic" passage in *Epitaphium Damonis* discussed above,[1] in which academic practice is depicted in pastoral guise, Milton specifically mentions Francini and Dati by name (137); also, in a letter from Dati to Milton discussed below,[2] Dati concludes by conveying greetings to Milton from Francini (and indeed from other Apatisti members): "I Signori Frescobaldi, Coltellini, Francini, Galilei et altri infiniti unitamente le inviano affetuosi saluti ..."[3]

(i)   Antonio Francini

Francini's "written encomium" in Milton's honor constitutes the most substantial evidence of their acquaintance. It is certainly the longest and most informative of those encomia prefixed to the 1645 volume. The poem merits full quotation since the terms in which it describes Milton and its possible riddling references to some of his works, portray one who in himself seems to embody that multilingualism in which the Apatisti prided itself.

---

[1] See 24 above and 56 below.

[2] See 79-80 below.

[3] *CM* 12, 314.

Al Signor Gio. Miltoni Nobile Inglese

ODE

Ergimi all' Etra ò Clio
Perche di stelle intreccierò corona
Non più del Biondo Dio
La Fronde eterna in Pindo, e in Elicona,
Diensi a merto maggior, maggiori i fregi,   5
A celeste virtù celesti pregi.

Non può del tempo edace
Rimaner preda eterno alto valore,
Non può l'oblio rapace
Furar dalle memorie eccelso onore,   10
Su l'arco di mia cetra un dardo forte
Virtù m'adatti, e ferirò la Morte.

Del Ocean profundo
Cinta dagli ampi gorghi Anglia risiede
Separata dal mondo,   15
Però che il suo valor l'umano eccede:
Questa feconda sà produrre Eroi,
Ch'hanno a ragion del souvruman tra noi.

Alla virtù sbandita
Danno nei petti lor fido ricetto,   20
Quella gli è sol gradita,
Perche in lei san trovar gioia e diletto;
Ridillo tu, Giovanni, e mostra in tanto
Con tua vera virtù, vero il mio Canto.

Lungi dal Patrio lido   25
Spinse Zeusi l'industre ardente brama,
Ch'udio d'Helena il grido
Con aurea tromba rimbombar la fama,
E per poterla effigiare al paro
Dalle più belle Idee trasse il più raro.   30

Così l'Ape Ingegnosa
Trae con industria il suo liquor pregiato
Dal giglio e dalla rosa,
E quanti vaghi fiori ornano il prato;
Formano un dolce suon diverse Corde,   35
Fan varie voci melodia concorde.

Di bella gloria amante
Milton dal Ciel natio per varie parti
Le peregrine piante

Volgesti a ricercar scienze ed arti;   40
Del Gallo regnator vedesti i Regni,
E dell' Italia ancor gl'Eroi più degni.

Fabro quasi divino,
Sol virtù rintracciando, il tuo pensiero
Vide in ogni confino   45
Chi di nobil valor calca il sentiero;
L'ottimo dal miglior dopo scegliea
Per fabbricar d'ogni virtù l'Idea.

Quanti nacquero in Flora
O in lei del parlar Tosco appreser l'arte,   50
La cui memoria onora
Il mondo fatta eterna in dotte carte,
Volesti ricercar per tuo tesoro,
E parlasti con lor nell'opre loro.

Nell'altera Babelle   55
Per te il parlar confuse Giove in vano,
Che per varie favelle
Di se stessa trofeo cadde su'l piano:
Ch'ode oltr'all' Anglia il suo più degno Idioma
Spagna, Francia, Toscana, e Grecia e Roma.   60

I più profondi arcani
Ch'occulta la Natura e in cielo e in terra
Ch'a Ingegni sovrumani
Troppo avara tal'hor gli chiude, e serra,
Chiaramente conosci, e giungi al fine   65
Della moral virtude al gran confine.

Non batta il Tempo l'ale
Fermisi immoto, e in un ferminsi gl'anni,
Che di virtù immortale
Scorron di troppo ingiuriosi ai danni;   70
Chè s'opre degne di Poema e storia
Furon già, l'hai presenti alla memoria.

Dammi tua dolce Cetra
Se vuoi ch'io dica del tuo dolce canto,
Ch'inalzandoti all' Etra   75
Di farti huomo celeste ottiene il vanto,
Il Tamigi il dirà che gl' è concesso
Per te suo cigno pareggiar Permesso.

Io che in riva del Arno
Tento spiegar tuo merto alto e preclaro   80
So che fatico indarno,

E ad ammirar, non a lodarlo imparo;
Freno dunque la lingua, e ascolto il core
Che ti prende a lodar con lo stupore.

Del sig. Antonio Francini gentilhuomo Fiorentino.

Francini begins by invoking Clio, Muse of history, in his quest for elevation to the skies as he aims to plait for Apollo a wreath not of foliage, but of stars. But hand in hand with this concept of celestial glory and immortality is the underlying motif of the ravaging force of Time. Francini is eager that eternal worth such as Milton's should not be left a prey to "devouring time" ("Non può del tempo edace/Rimaner preda eterno alto valore" [7-8]). The theme recurs in stanza 12 as he hopes that Time will cease to beat his wings; instead he should stand still here and now ("Non batta il Tempo l'ale/Fermisi immoto, e in un ferminsi gl'anni,/Che di virtù immortale/Scorron di troppo ingiuriosi ai danni." [67-70]). While the destructive force of Time is obviously a commonplace, it is tempting to speculate that Francini is reacting to, say, Milton's vernacular poem *On Time* (c. 1632/1633?).[4] Perhaps his wish that Time should stand still and that the years which insult virtue should stop may recall and even invert Milton's injunction "Fly envious Time, till thou run out thy race" (1). More specifically, Francini's juxtaposition of the two contrasting concepts of a garland of stars ("di stelle intreccierò corona" [2]) and gnawing Time ("tempo edace" [7]) may owe something to the closing lines of Milton's poem, in which "Attired with stars, we shall for ever sit,/Triumphing over Death, and Chance, and thee O Time" (21-23). Is Francini paying an additional compliment to Milton by echoing Milton's own English poetry? He proceeds to state that Milton has penetrated the deepest mysteries which Nature hides in heaven and on earth, too frequently concealing them in her avarice from superhuman minds ("I più profondi arcani/Ch'occulta la Natura e in cielo e in terra/Ch'a Ingegni sovrumani/Troppo avara tal'hor gli chiude, e serra,/Chiaramente conosci" [61-65]). Again there is a possible link with one of Milton's own works. In the opening lines of *Naturam Non Pati Senium* he had indeed bewailed the vain attempts of mortals to ascertain divine mysteries which lie hidden (*quae vesana suis metiri facta deorum/audet* [4-5]); and one such mystery was the fate of *Natura* herself. Other aspects of the tribute may suggest that Francini had even heard or read Milton's Latin poem *Mansus*. If this is so, the

---

[4] For arguments on the dating of *On Time*, see Carey ed., *Milton: Complete Shorter Poems*, 170. The important point vis-à-vis the present argument is that in all instances the dates proposed precede Milton's Italian journey.

encomium would, of course, have to be dated to Milton's second (i.e. post-Neapolitan) sojourn in Florence. Francini depicts Britain as remote in virtue of her being surrounded by water and thus separated from the whole world ("Cinta dagli ampi gorghi Anglia risiede/separata dal mondo" [14-15]). Later he states that Milton has left his native clime, turning his "peregrine piante" (39) to other countries in search of knowledge and arts. In *Mansus* Milton had likewise stressed the geographical remoteness of Britain, describing himself as a *iuvenis peregrinus* (26) sent from the Hyperborean axis; his Muse moreover has only with difficulty been nurtured beneath the frozen Bear. Francini describes Milton as the swan of the Thames, through whom that river will proclaim equality with Permessus ("Il Tamigi il dirà che gl' è concesso/per te suo cigno pareggiar Permesso" [77-78]). In *Mansus* Milton had proclaimed his ability to hear swans (fellow-poets) upon his native river the Thames (*Nos etiam in nostro modulantes flumine cygnos/credimus obscuras noctis sensisse per umbras,/qua Thamesis late puris argenteus urnis/oceani glaucos perfundit gurgite crines.* [30-33]). Is Francini reacting perhaps to this allegory and going one stage further by including Milton himself among such swans? Moreover, his reference to "Permessus" may, as Gordon Campbell suggests, constitute a subtle acknowledgement of Milton's accomplishment as an elegiac poet, thus indicating perhaps his knowledge of Milton's Latin elegies (whether through formal recitation in an academy or through informal scholarly discussion).[5] The encomium is permeated by the theme of "virtue" ("virtù"), a noun which occurs no fewer than eight times. It is divine virtue that deserves heavenly rewards ("a celeste virtù celesti pregi" [6]); the speaker prays that virtue may fit a strong arrow to the bow of his harp, thereby enabling him to wound death ("su l'arco di mia cetra un dardo forte/virtù m'adatti, e ferirò la Morte" [11-12]); banished virtue finds a refuge in the breasts of heroes ("alla virtù sbandita/danno nei petti lor fido ricetto" [19-20]); such is reiterated by Milton, by whose true virtue is revealed the truth of the speaker's song ("ridillo tu, Giovanni, e mostra in tanto/con tua vera virtù, vero il mio canto" [23-24]) etc. It is not impossible that the recurrence of this theme reflects Francini's knowledge of Milton's sonnets.[6] In Sonnet 2, for example, Milton had indeed praised the blossoming virtue "là onde l'alta

---

[5] See Gordon Campbell, "Francini's Permesso," *MQ* 15 (1981), 122-133.

[6] Cf. Revard, *Milton and the Tangles of Neaera's Hair*, 29, who rather overstates the issue: "Virtue is the beginning point not only of the sonnets Milton wrote for the young Lady and to Margaret Ley, but also of every other sonnet he wrote for an individual — male or female." See in general Anna K. Nardo, "Milton and the Academic Sonnet," Di Cesare, 489-503.

tua virtù s'infiora" (8) of his "donna leggiadra" (1). Or had Francini read *Comus*?

But the encomium is interesting for a number of other reasons also. It is here we discover that Milton while in Florence sought out not only native Florentines, but also those who had learned there the art of speaking the Tuscan tongue ("quanti nacquero in Flora/o in lei del parlar Tosco appreser l'arte" [49-50]);[7] it is here we learn of Milton's knowledge of Spanish (60),[8] unattested both in the other tributes (which do praise his multilingualism), and in Milton's own account in *Ad Patrem* of the languages which he has acquired.[9]

(ii) Carlo Dati

Foremost among those academicians who participated in both the Svogliati and the Apatisti[10] was Carlo Roberto Dati.[11] Milton's friendship with Dati, only eighteen years of age at the time of Milton's visit to Florence, is attested in numerous ways: by the "written encomium" in Latin prose which the Florentine academician wrote in his honor and which, like Francini's and others, was subsequently prefixed to the 1645 volume; by Milton's reference to Dati (along with Francini) in the "emblematic lines" of *Epitaphium Damonis* when describing in allegorical terms his experiences in Italian academies;[12] by Milton's Latin letter addressed to Dati (dated 21 April 1647);[13] by two Italian letters addressed by Dati to Milton (dated 22 October/1 November 1647 and 24 November/4 December 1648 respectively).[14] And the network of communication between these two *amici* was obviously much more extensive than the extant evidence would suggest. For this was a friendship that was to cross national, linguistic and even temporal barriers. Although

---

[7] For his possible parallel practice in Rome, cf. Milton's links with David Codner discussed at 48 below.

[8] See Hale, *Milton's Languages*, 7, 209; Gordon Campbell, "Milton's Spanish," *MQ* (1997), 127-132.

[9] See *Ad Patrem* 79-85; Hale, *Milton's Languages*, 52-53.

[10] Gori, f. 46ᵛ includes Carlo Ruberto Dati and his anagram Currado Bartoletti under the year 1635; cf. Lazzeri, *Intellettuali*, 69.

[11] On Dati, see *DBI, s.v.*

[12] See 56 below.

[13] *CM* 12, 44-52.

[14] *CM* 12, 296-312 and 312-314.

some ten years Milton's junior, Dati had similar interests, not least of which was a devotion to, and expertise in, the classics, and a love of erudite discussion on the *minutiae* of scholarship.[15] From his earliest years he had shown outstanding talent in this field. Dati moreover had been taught by Galileo Galilei (whom he was later to remember with much fondness),[16] just as Milton would recall "the famous Galileo ... grown old."[17] If Milton did indeed meet Galileo,[18] it is possible that he did so through the agency of either Dati himself or perhaps Vincenzo Galileo, son of the great astronomer, who is included in a letter from Dati to Milton as among those academicians who send him their regards.[19] At the time of Milton's Florentine sojourn, Galileo was indeed residing (for the purposes of medical treatment) at Vincenzo's home on the Costa San Gorgio.[20] It was in the fields of humanism and science that Dati won acclaim in the academies.[21] He seems moreover to have possessed a maturity and open-mindedness far beyond his years. In his Latin letter to Dati Milton displays his confidence that Dati at least should be inclined to excuse his own anti-papal sayings in a few pages of his poetry.[22] And his social skills were no less impressive. At a time when academies were springing up in Florence and in many other cities, Dati, like Gaddi, seems to have forged permanent links with many important ones. What is certain is that he participated in both the Svogliati and the Apatisti. Not long after Milton's departure from Florence Dati would become secretary to the Apatisti (1640),[23] while in 1645 he was to be inscribed in that academy with the anagrammatic pseudonym of "Currado Bartoletti."[24] Then, on 3/13 October 1649, he would earn the honor of being fully elected *apatista reggente* with the

---

[15] See his scholarly discussion of Venus's birth from the sea in his first letter to Milton (*CM* 12, 300-310), discussed at 77-79 below.

[16] On Dati's fond reminiscences of Galileo, see his *Esortazione allo Studio della Geometria* (Florence, 1814); Arthos, *Italian Cities*, 41.

[17] *Areopagitica* (*CM* 4, 330).

[18] For an excellent survey, see Harris, "Galileo as Symbol," *passim*.

[19] *CM* 12, 314. See 80 below.

[20] See Harris, "Galileo as Symbol," 7.

[21] See, for example, Masson, *Life*, I, 775.

[22] *CM* 12, 50. See 59 below.

[23] Lazzeri, *Intellettuali*, 20.

[24] Gori, f. 129r: "3 Settembre 1649 Carlo Dati Ardaclito avendo proposto un dubbio come Apat. regg. e risoluto;" Lazzeri, *Intellettuali*, 105.

pseudonym of "Ardaclito."[25] But while very much a man of his time with his feet set very firmly in the world of the seicento academy, Dati was also an expert classicist. It was thus in recognition of his classical talents that in 1648 he would be appointed as successor to Giovanni Battista Doni[26] to the chair of classical languages in the University of Florence. And, as discussed below,[27] Dati was to inform Milton of this honor in the second of his two extant letters.[28] While it is for his *Lives of the Painters* ("Vite de' Pittori Antichi" [Florence, 1667]) that he is chiefly remembered today, he was author of several other works.[29] Although all of these post-date Milton's Italian sojourn, at least one (and quite probably many more) was read by Milton. And we know this from Milton's own testimony. In his Latin letter to Dati discussed below,[30] Milton states that he has been reading with pleasure Dati's funeral oration on King Louis XIII of France.[31] This is a reference to the *Esequie della Maesta Christianiss. di Luigi XIII Descritte da Carlo Dati* which had been published at Florence in 1644. Milton praises Dati's eloquence in this work.[32] In Dati's second letter to Milton, discussed below,[33] he promises to send him (when it is

---

[25] Gori, f. 131[r]; Lazzeri, *Intellettuali*, 107. Dati also figures among the members of the Academy of the Percossi. His major contribution however was to the Accademia della Crusca, of which he became a member on 19/29 November 1640; on 21/31 December he was elected "castaldo," and on 13/23 March 1647 he was elevated to the grade of archconsul. The Diary of the Academy attests the work of "Smaritto" (the "bewildered"), another pseudonym assumed by Dati.

[26] On Doni, see *DBI*, *s.v.* Cf. Milton's reference to Doni in his letter to Lucas Holstenius, Florence, 20/30 March, 1639 (*CM* 12, 42).

[27] See 79-80 below.

[28] *CM* 12, 314.

[29] Among Dati's other published works are: 1) *Discorso dell'Obbligio di Ben Parlare la Propria Lingua di C. D. con la Declinazioni de' Verbi de Benedetto Buommattei* (Florence, 1657); 2) *Prose Fiorentine Raccolte dallo Smarrito Accademico della Crusca,* (Florence, 1661), volume I of which was edited by Dati; 3) *Lettera a Filaleti di Timauro Antiate della Vera Storia della Cicloide e della Famosissima Esperienza dell' Argento Vivo* (Florence, 1663); 4) *Delle Lodi del Commendatore Cassiano del Pozzo* (Florence, 1664). Dati also wrote poetry — *Sylva*, an epithalamium entitled *La Pace* (Florence, 1660) on the occasion of the marriage of Louis XIV with Maria Teresa of Austria.

[30] See 56-57 below.

[31] *CM* 12, 50: *Exequias Ludovici Regis a te descriptas libenter lego.*

[32] *CM* 12, 52: *facundum illum, Musis acceptum, et Mercurialium virorum praesidem, agnosco.*

[33] See 79-80 below.

published) his recently delivered funeral oration on Prince Lorenzo of Tuscany.[34] Like Milton, Dati was interested in the purity of language, and was involved in what was almost an academic obsession with enhancing and improving the Tuscan tongue. He betrays his linguistic puritanism in the introduction which he provided for Buonmattei's *Declinazione de' verbi*.[35] Milton's love of Italian and his interest in academic works on the purity of the Tuscan tongue are attested in his extant letter to Buonmattei.[36]

But for the youthful Dati of 1638/9, the years of Milton's Florentine sojourn, all of these achievements lay very far in the future.[37] For the thirty-year old English poet too there were still in store those major vernacular works for which he is generally acclaimed today. In Italy however Milton's projected self-image seems to have been for the most part that of a budding neo-Latinist. As noted above, it is for his erudite <u>Latin</u> poems that he earns particular mention in the minutes of Italian academies, and in response to which (although probably not exclusively so) he received those "written encomiums," including one by Dati himself (appropriately in Latin). Dati's is the only prose tribute,[38] and it merits close analysis both in its own right and also in terms of the possible light that it may shed on Milton's Florentine sojourn in general, and his academic practice in particular:

IOANNI MILTONI
LONDINIENSI
Iuveni patria, virtutibus eximio,
Viro qui multa peregrinatione, studio cuncta orbis terrarum loca
perspexit ut novus Ulysses omnia ubique ab omnibus apprehenderet;

---

[34] *CM* 12, 314: "La passata settimana per la morte del Serenissimo Principe Lorenzo di Toscana zio del Granduca Regnante feci l'orazione funerale, come ella sia publicata sarà mia cura inviarne copia a V.S. illustrissima."

[35] *Discorso dell' Obbligo di Ben Parlare*, 9: "Ah, che la licenza del nostro secolo, e i corrotti costumi son quelli, che adulterano la purità, ed offuscano il candore di nostra lingua; l'ozio non coltivando gl' ingegni lascia imboschire i guardini dell' eloquenza Toscana, e l'ignoranza a' giusti depravati fa parer belli vocabilo barbari e mostruosi."

[36] *CM* 12, 30-38. Cf. in particular his statement: *possum tamen nonnumquam ad illum Dantem et Petrarcham aliosque vestros complusculos libenter et cupide commessatum ire; nec me tam ipsae Athenae Atticae cum illo suo pellucido Ilisso nec illa vetus Roma sua Tiberis ripa retinere valuerunt quin saepe Arnum vestrum et Faesulanos illos colles invisere amem. (CM 12, 34).*

[37] Dati died in Florence, 11 Jan 1676. His body was buried in the cloister of the church of San Spirito. His posthumous publications include *Veglie Inedite* (F. Grazzini, Florence, 1814).

[38] Cedric Brown, *John Milton: A Literary Life* (Macmillan, 1995), 60, incorrectly states that Dati wrote a poem to Milton.

polyglotto in cuius ore linguae iam deperditae sic revivescunt ut idiomata omnia sint in eius laudibus infacunda, et iure ea percallet ut admirationes et plausus populorum ab propria sapientia excitatos, intelligat;

illi, cuius animi dotes corporisque sensus ad admirationem commovent, et per ipsam motum cuique auferunt; cuius opera ad plausus hortantur, sed venustate vocem laudatoribus adimunt;

cui in memoria totus orbis, in intellectu sapientia, in voluntate ardor gloriae, in ore eloquentia, harmonicos caelestium sphaerarum sonitus astronomia duce audienti, characteres mirabilium naturae per quos Dei magnitudo describitur magistra philosophia legenti, antiquitatum latebras, vetustatis excidia, eruditionis ambages, comite assidua auctorum lectione,

exquirenti, restauranti, percurrenti.

At cur nitor in arduum?

illi in cuius virtutibus evulgandis ora Famae non sufficiant, nec hominum stupor in laudandis satis est, reverentiae et amoris ergo hoc eius meritis debitum admirationis tributum offert Carolus Datus Patricius Florentinus,

Tanto homini servus, tantae virtutis amator.

The extravagant nature of this piece has led Masson to suggest that Dati must have sent it as a companion to some gift,[39] but this is probably unnecessary speculation. Although, as Masson notes, Milton does refer in *Ep. Dam.* 135 in an allegorical way to certain gifts which he had received from his Italian friends, there is no evidence to support the suggestion that the Dati encomium was inscribed on one of these. It is just as likely that it was composed as a genuine compliment (albeit over-exploiting the encomiastic nature of the genre) by a young Florentine, impressed by a Londoner's *opera* recited (from memory?)[40] in those very academies in which he himself participated. Perhaps it was initiated also by conversations which he must have had with Milton, in the course of which his elder no doubt displayed his erudition. The encomium may simply reflect the admiration and affection of one who, subsequent to Milton's return to England, would after all write three letters to his English friend (which were lost in the post) and would later write a further three, and

---

[39] Masson, *Life*, I, 785: "Surely the enthusiastic Dati sent this extravagance as a companion to some gift, — inscribed, say, on the blank page of a valuable folio! Such an epistle *alone*, from so young a man, even if on vellum and in gold letters, would hardly have justified itself. Moreover, Milton seems to allude to certain gifts from his Florentine friends as still in his possession after his return to England (*Epitaph. Damon.* line 135)."

[40] The tribute praises Milton's memory: *cui in memoria totus orbis*. Cf. Francini's encomium discussed at 38-43 above.

perhaps more.[41] What is undeniable is that fellow-academicians Carlo Roberto Dati and Giovanni Miltoni shared a genuine bond of *amicitia*.

In the heading of the tribute Milton is given the title *Londiniensis*, a feature which finds a parallel in Dati's letter to Milton dated 24 November/4 December 1648: "Il Signor Giovanni Miltoni, Londra."[42] The encomium proper begins by describing Milton as distinguished for his native land and his virtues. This sense of nationality occurs also in other encomia, which refer either to the fact that Milton is an *Anglus* (Manso; Salzilli)[43] or "Inglese" (Francini)[44] or even to *Anglia* herself (Selvaggi).[45] And this is probably to be expected.[46] Dati presents Milton as a seeker of knowledge on both an academic and a geographical scale. The encomium strikes a parallel between Milton's literal *peregrinatio*[47] and his studies (*studium*). Both go hand in hand. Thus, like Ulysses, through his travels he has beheld many regions, but through his studies he has perceived all areas of the world (*cuncta orbis terrarum loca perspexit*). This is developed later as Dati admires the way in which Milton explores the *antiquitatum latebras* and the *vetustatis excidia* through his assiduous reading. It is just possible that Dati, both here and in a subsequent reference discussed below,[48] is reacting to certain details from one of Milton's Latin prose prolusions, addressed significantly to Cambridge *academici*, but perhaps revived and indeed revised for oral performance in Italy. Now fellow-students (*academici*) have become fully-fledged Italian academicians! In one such prolusion entitled *Contra Philosophiam Scholasticam* Milton had

---

[41] See 53 below.

[42] *CM* 12, 314.

[43] Manso: *Joannes Baptista Mansus, Marchio Villensis Neapolitanus ad Ioannem Miltonium Anglum* (see 130-136 below for a discussion of his pun on *Anglus*); Salzilli: *Ad Ioannem Miltonem Anglum*.

[44] Francini: "Al Signor Gio. Miltoni Nobile Inglese."

[45] Selvaggi: *Graecia Maeonidem, iactet sibi Roma Maronem,/Anglia Miltonum iactat utrique parem*. For the possible identity of Selvaggi as the English Benedictine monk, David Codner, known in Italy as Matteo Selvaggi, see Edward Chaney, *The Grand Tour and the Great Rebellion* (Geneva, 1985), 244-248.

[46] Dati's representation of Milton as *patria ... eximius* introduces a theme that recurs in subsequent Dati/Milton correspondence. In his extant Italian letters to Milton, Dati takes pleasure in the fact that Milton holds Italy, his *patria*, in high regard. In return, Italy counts it among its treasures that Milton magnifies its glories. See 59 below.

[47] Cf. *Mansus* 26, where Milton describes himself as a *iuvenis peregrinus*. For a parallel phrase in an Italian tribute to Manso, see 142-143 below.

[48] See 50-51 below.

indeed emphasised the importance of acquiring practical geographical as well as academic knowledge:

> Ah quanto satius esset, Academici, quantoque dignius vestro nomine nunc descriptas chartula terras universas quasi oculis perambulare et calcata vetustis heroibus inspectare loca, bellis, triumphis et etiam illustrium poetarum fabulis nobilitatas Regiones percurrere, nunc aestuantem transmittere Adriam, nunc ad Aetnam flammigantem impune accedere, dein mores hominum speculari et ordinatas pulchre gentium respublicas.[49]

> [Ah how much better it would be, fellow academics, and how much more worthy of your name, now to traverse as if with your eyes all lands depicted on the map and to observe places trodden by ancient heroes, to hasten through regions made renowned by the stories of illustrious poets, now to cross the seething Adriatic, now to approach flame-bearing Aetna without getting hurt, next to view the customs of men and the finely organised governments of nations.]

Dati, like most of the other academicians who wrote in Milton's honor, praises Milton's linguistic skills. Unlike Francini, however, he does not specify the languages, but that the reference is to Latin and Greek is suggested by the plural *linguae iam deperditae sic revivescunt*. Milton can thus revive dead languages. Dati was later to make the same point in his letter to Milton discussed below.[50] Milton's reputation in Italy as a Latinist is unquestionable, but Dati's possible reference to Greek as well as to Latin finds an interesting parallel in Francini's encomium.[51] Speculation is possible: had Milton familiarised these Italian academicians (either publicly or privately) with his two Greek poems (the Greek epigram *Philosophus ad regem* [c. 1624?][52] and a Greek version of Psalm cxiv [1634]),[53] both of which do seem to precede the Italian trip? Were there even some Greek verses among those things "patched up" by Milton in the

---

[49] *CM* 12, 168-170.

[50] *CM* 12, 296: "di cui è dote singularissima ravivare le lingue morte." See 64 below.

[51] Cf. Salzilli's encomium of Milton, discussed at 82-85 below: Milton surpasses Homer, Virgil and Tasso.

[52] Donald C. Clark, *John Milton at St Paul's School* (New York, 1948; rpt. Hamden, 1964), 206, suggests that this is a school exercise practised by the young Milton at St Paul's. If not, and even if one accepts Parker's later date (between 1634 and 1638 on the assumption that the order of poems in the 1645 volume reflects the order of composition), there is a very strong likelihood that this Greek poem *preceded* Milton's Italian journey.

[53] It is likely that this is the *hanc oden* referred to in Milton's letter dated December 1634 addressed to Alexander Gill, and sent to his friend in return for some verses of his (*CM* 12, 14-16).

course of his Italian sojourn? That these are original compositions may be suggested by the verb *revivescunt*. Milton does not simply recite ancient Greek and Latin; rather on his lips those dead languages undergo a renaissance. The implication is that his compositions bring these languages back to life. Dati, like Manso,[54] praises Milton's physical as well as his intellectual attributes, and proceeds to state that Milton's works (*opera*) inspire applause, and that through their charm they deprive his eulogizers of speech. Like Francini, he praises Milton's memory, thereby suggesting perhaps that some of his recitations to the academies were indeed from memory. This suggestion is supported by Milton's own comment that "some trifles which I had *in memory*, composed at under twenty or thereabout ... met with acceptance above what was looked for."[55] However it is worth pointing out that the minutes of the Svogliati on two separate occasions state that Milton "recited"/"recitarano" and "read"/"lesse" Latin poems. Dati refers to Milton's intellectual wisdom, his passion for glory, his eloquence, and then asserts that "with astronomy as a guide he hears the harmonious sounds of the heavenly spheres" (*harmonicos caelestium sphaerarum sonitus astronomia duce audienti*). To what does this refer? Perhaps "the guiding force of astronomy" reflects discussions on the subject between Milton and Dati, who, after all, had been a pupil of the famous Galileo himself? Perhaps "listening to the harmonious sounds of the heavenly spheres" indicates that Milton had familiarised Dati in particular or the academies in general with, for example, his "At a Solemn Music" (1633?)[56] which celebrates *inter alia* the "Sphere-borne harmonious sisters, Voice, and Verse" (2)? Perhaps on his return visit to Florence he had recited the first Leonora epigram, which may include a reference to this theme.[57] But surely the most likely candidate among Milton's works to fit Dati's description is not a poem at all, but another of Milton's Latin prose prolusions — the *De Sphaerarum Concentu*,[58] devoted entirely to the *harmonicos caelestium sphaerarum sonitus*. Composed while Milton was still at Cambridge, this learned piece, addressed to *academici*, would certainly have been appropriate for recitation in an Italian academy. And even if the circumstances were not those of the formal academy, is it not quite probable that Milton would have familiarised his friend Dati with his own Latin prose- as well as verse-compositions? Dati confidently

---

[54] For a discussion of Manso's encomium in its context, see 130-136 below.

[55] *RCG, CM* 3, 234-236.

[56] For the dating, see Carey ed., *Milton: Complete Shorter Poems*, 167.

[57] See 108-110 below.

[58] *CM* 12, 148-156.

announces that Milton has the ability to "hear" this heavenly music, a theme that recurs throughout the prolusion: Milton states that the melody of the sky does not go unheard (*sed nec plane inaudita est haec coeli melodia*);[59] Pythagoras is said to have heard it;[60] one of reasons why we hear so little of this harmony is on account of the boldness of the thieving Prometheus;[61] if we had hearts as pure as Pythagoras, then indeed our ears would be pervaded by this music and in effect it would be as though the golden age had returned.[62] Dati's tribute in accrediting Milton with actually *hearing* the harmony of the spheres, is bestowing upon its English addressee that honor which Milton's prolusion had reserved for Pythagoras alone. A compliment indeed. Dati proceeds to state that "with philosophy as a teacher Milton selects the marks of the wonderful deeds of *Natura* through which the magnitude of God is described." Perhaps (like Francini?) Dati knew the *Naturam Non Pati Senium*, which argues for the permanence of nature and celebrates her many facets. In that poem the *Dei magnitudo* is indeed vindicated, for in response to the suggestion of nature's decay (8-12) Milton had proclaimed the *pater omnipotens* (33) taking thought for the entire universe (33ff.).[63] Dati continues by presenting Milton very much as the erudite scholar, who with the constant reading of writers as his companion, investigates, restores and traverses the hiding places of antiquity's history, the ruins of former times, and the "wandering mazes of erudition," the *eruditionis ambages*. Such lie precisely at the heart of academic practice in Italy — that ability to tease a scholarly problem to its furthest conclusion through discussion of the most obscure, yet learned, points whereby participants became "in wandring mazes lost,"[64] as the blind epic poet of *Paradise Lost* was to state, perhaps not without a retrospective glance to the Italian academies.[65] The Milton of Dati's tribute is a worthy academician, and more than that. Even the

---

[59] *CM* 12, 154.

[60] *CM* 12, 154-156.

[61] *CM* 12, 156.

[62] *CM* 12, 156: *At si pura, si casta, si nivea gestaremus pectora, ut olim Pythagoras, tum quidem suavissima illa stellarum circumeuntium musica personarent aures nostrae et opplerentur; atque dein cuncta illico tanquam in aureum illud saeculum redirent; nosque tum demum miseriarum immunes, beatum et vel diis invidendum degeremus otium.* Cf. *On the Morning of Christ's Nativity* 133-135: "For if such holy song/Enwrap our fancy long,/Time will run back, and fetch the age of gold."

[63] See Estelle Haan, "Milton's *Naturam*," 162-163.

[64] *PL* 2. 561.

[65] See Nardo, "Academic Interludes," 218-219.

tongues of *Fama* would be incapable of proclaiming his virtues. Dati concludes by describing himself as *Carolus Datus Patricius Florentinus, tanto homini servus, tantae virtutis amator*. This conventional note of servility as concluding the tribute likewise occurs at the end of Dati's subsequent letters to Milton: for example, Dati signs off the 22 Oct./1 Nov., 1647 letter with "Di V.S. Illustrissimo *Ser.* Devotissimo Carlo Dati," while the phrase *Carolus Datus Patricius Florentinus* may be picked up by Milton in the terms of his address to Dati in his Latin letter of 21 April 1647: *Carolo Dato Patricio Fiorentino*, a letter that merits close scrutiny.

CHAPTER 4

Patterns of *Amicitia:*
The Milton/Dati Correspondence

If, in Milton's words, the *academia* constituted a *mos ... ad amicitias conservandas laudatissimus*,[1] his friendship with Dati certainly survived long after he had said his farewells to the academies of Florence. That this particular *amicitia* extended beyond the immediate period of his Italian sojourn is evident from the correspondence (or at times attempted correspondence, given the postal service) subsequent to Milton's return to England. Initially, this was one-sided (Dati sending no fewer than three letters, which Milton says he did not receive), but then it developed into the normal two-way communication. And it is likely too that they exchanged published works. As noted above, in his extant Latin letter to Dati, Milton states that he has been reading Dati's Funeral Oration on King Louis delivered in 1644. While Milton may have been able to purchase this work in England,[2] it is just possible that Dati had indeed sent him a copy,[3] perhaps along with that now lost epistle which we know Milton did in fact receive, because, as illustrated below, he answered it in his own Latin letter to Dati. What is certain is that Milton promised to send Dati the Latin part of the 1645 volume (*Poematum quidem quae pars Latina est*).[4] And he fulfilled this promise, because Dati in a subsequent

---

[1] *DS, CM* 8, 122.

[2] See, in general, Elizabeth S. Leedham-Green, *Books in Cambridge Inventories: Book-lists From Vice-Chancellors' Court Probate Inventories in the Tudor and Stuart Periods* (Cambridge, 1986) and her *Private Libraries in Renaissance England* (*Medieval and Renaissance Texts and Studies* [New York, Binghamton, 1994]).

[3] Cf. his promise in his second letter to Milton to send him (when published) his funeral speech on Prince Lorenzo (*CM* 12, 314).

[4] *CM* 12, 50. The 1645 poems were in two parts and, as Fletcher has illustrated, "The Seventeenth-Century Separate Printing of Milton's *Epitaphium Damonis*," *JEGP* 61 (1962), 788-796 at 793, sold in three different forms: the English poems and the Latin *Poemata* together; the English poems separately, and the Latin poems separately.

letter acknowledges receipt of not one, but "two copies of [Milton's] most erudite poetry, which although small, contain infinite value."[5] It is clear then that at least three letters from Dati to Milton were lost in the post (Milton mentions this with great regret in his own Latin letter to Dati),[6] and that Dati sent a fourth which Milton received (but is now lost) and to which his own extant Latin letter replies. Milton's letter conveys his esteem and affection for his Italian addressee, invoking him in the personal phrase "mi Carole." As Hale comments, "he does not address even Charles Diodati like this."[7]

(i)   Reconstructing a Lost Dati Epistle to Milton

A reading of Milton's letter helps to reconstruct, at least in a general sense, the contents of that now lost fourth Dati epistle. It seems to have included the following points:

1) Dati (near the beginning of the letter)[8] probably makes some generalising comments on the importance of friendship. This is evident from Milton's reference in the Latin reply to the fact that he can see that Dati is taking particular pains that friendship should conquer.[9]

2) Dati expresses his concern for Milton's health and tells him that he has been on his mind. This is evident from Milton's reference to Dati as *mea de salute sollicitum, semperque mei memorem fuisse.*[10]

3) Dati tells Milton that he has written to him on three previous occasions. This is evident from Milton's comment: *statim vero cum incido in illud quod scribis, ternas te iam olim ad me dedisse quas ego periisse scio.*[11]

---

[5] *CM* 12, 312: "due copie delle sue eruditissime Poesie ... perche quantunque piccolo racchiude in se valore infinito."

[6] *CM* 12, 46: *statim vero cum incido in illud quod scribis ternas te iam olim ad me dedisse quas ego periisse scio.*

[7] Hale, *Milton's Languages*, 91. See in general his analysis at 89-91 of the overall tone of this "fascinating, unexpected, unguarded letter" (91).

[8] Cf. *CM* 12, 46: *dum enim illa tua prima percurro, in quibus elegantia cum amicitia pulchre sane contendit.*

[9] *CM* 12, 46: *praesertim cum uti vincat amicitia operam te dare videam.*

[10] *CM* 12, 46.

[11] *CM* 12, 46.

4) Dati informs Milton that they (fellow-academicians, Dati included) have received the copy of *Epitaphium Damonis* which Milton had sent. This is evident from Milton's reference to that fact that now he has heard for the first time that <u>they</u> did receive it: *Id quod ipse iamdiu legisse debes, siquidem ad vos carmen illud pervenit, quod ex te nunc primum audio.*[12] This poem was printed separately in England, as has been proven by Bradner's important discovery[13] of "an apparently unique copy of a previously unknown anonymous undated edition"[14] in the British Museum.[15] Bradner dates this "probably 1640." Fletcher, on the other hand, on an examination of the poem's type and format suggests as late a date as 1646.[16] In reply to Fletcher, Shawcross suggests either 1639 or 1640 on the grounds that the printer seems to be that of *Comus.*[17] In support of Fletcher's thesis however is the possibility that it may well have been one such copy, separately printed, that Milton chose to send to his Italian friends (*ad vos*),[18] and which has since been lost or lies buried among Italian archives, and will some day come to light.[19] Fletcher thus dates it after the *Poemata* of 1645, suggesting early 1646. He argues convincingly that the poem was first printed in the 1645 *Poemata*, and that thereafter Milton arranged the printing of "a single quarto sheet that would fold to four leaves or eight pages, and did so expressly to send a copy to his friends, or at least to Dati, in Italy."[20] But it is clear that it was to the academy as a whole rather than to Dati personally, as has generally been assumed hitherto, that Milton sent the separate *Epitaphium Damonis*. This is indicated by a number of factors: his use of the plural *vos* in this passage (as opposed to *te* and *tu* elsewhere in the letter when referring to Dati alone).[21] Thus he speculates *siquidem ad vos carmen illud pervenit*, refers

---

[12] *CM* 12, 48.

[13] Leicester Bradner, "Milton's *Epitaphium Damonis*," *TLS* 18 Aug 1932, 581.

[14] As described by Carey, ed., *Milton: Complete Shorter Poems*, 271.

[15] BM ms C.57, d. 48.

[16] H.F. Fletcher, "Milton's *Epitaphium Damonis*," *passim*.

[17] John T. Shawcross, "The Date of the Separate Edition of Milton's *Epitaphium Damonis*," *SB* 18 (1965), 262-265.

[18] *CM* 12, 48.

[19] Parker, *Biography*, II, 822, states that there are almost certainly presentation copies of the anonymously printed *Epitaphium Damonis* to be found in Italian libraries.

[20] Fletcher, "Milton's *Epitaphium Damonis*," 796.

[21] *CM* 12, 48: *quod ex te nunc primum audio.*

to the *Epitaphium Damonis* as proof of his regard for you (pl.) (= academicians) (*amoris autem <u>adversum vos</u> mei ... testimonium haudquaquam obscurum*)[22] — a regard which, he says, is particularly evident by his inclusion of lines which emblematically refer to the academy (*vel illis paucis versiculis, emblematis ad morem inclusis*).[23] Indeed he explicitly points out that by sending the poem, he was hoping to elicit either you (sing.) [i.e. Dati] or someone else [from the academy referred to emblematically in that poem] to write to him (*existimabam etiam fore hoc modo, ut <u>vel te vel alium</u> ad scribendum allicerem*).[24] Conclusive evidence is finally provided by his comment that he was afraid that had he written first to any of them individually, he would have shown a preference for one, and this might have offended the others.[25] As it is, Dati has been the first of them all to reply (*nunc tu omnium primus ...*).[26] Irrespective of dating, the sending of this separate *Epitaphium Damonis* seems then to have been the initial means by which Milton (in ignorance of the fact that Dati had written to him three times already) sought *inter alia* to re-establish contact in a general sense with those "private academies," in the hope that it would entice one of their members to write to him.[27] And this hope was fulfilled in the form of Dati himself.

5) Dati asks Milton about his studies.
This is evident from Milton's comment *quoniam de studiis meis certior fieri postulas.*[28]

6) Dati tells Milton that he has been practising a style which is more suited to the mercantile concerns of street bazaars. This is evident from Milton's reference at the end of his letter to the fact that he has been reading with pleasure Dati's funeral oration on King Louis which is of a

---

[22] *CM* 12, 48.

[23] *CM* 12, 48.

[24] *CM* 12, 48.

[25] *CM* 12, 48: *mihi enim si prior scriberem, necesse erat ut vel ad omnes vel si quem aliis praetulissem, verebar ne in ceterorum qui id rescissent offensionem incurrerem; cum permultos adhuc superesse istic sperem, qui hoc a me officium vendicare certe potuerint.*

[26] *CM* 12, 48.

[27] For the plural, cf. his later statement in the letter that if the poems he had published had not been in English he would have sent them *ad vos, ... quorum iudiciis plurimum tribuo.* (*CM* 12, 50).

[28] *CM* 12, 50.

style very different to that of bazaars and mercantile concerns which recently, Dati jokes, he has been practising.[29]

(ii)   The Dati Epistles of 1647-1648

That Milton's Latin letter reached Dati is evident from Dati's extant reply written over six months later.[30] A comparative analysis of both letters is fruitful in that it reveals an Italian academician answering one by one a series of points which his downhearted English friend had made. It is likely, moreover, that the Latin letter was the very first personal communication that Dati had received from Milton since the latter's return to England. This is indicated by Dati's express joy upon hearing from his long-lost friend.[31] Thus he exclaims that all hope of his receiving a letter from Milton was dead,[32] refers to the length of time that has elapsed "che dopo si lungo tempo,"[33] emphasises the great distance between England and Italy "da si remota provincia,"[34] and begs his friend to excuse his transgression of the bounds of letter-writing, stating that he has done so because he has been so long a time without him.[35] All of these factors when combined support the suggestion that this is in fact the first time that Dati has heard from his English friend in eight years![36]

---

[29] *CM* 12, 50-52: *Exequias Ludovici Regis a te descriptas libenter lego, in quibus Mercurium tuum, non compitalem illum et mercimoniis addictum, quem tu nuper colere iocaris, sed facundum illum, Musis acceptum, et Mercurialium virorum praesidem, agnosco.*

[30] Masson, *Life*, III, 680, suggests that Dati's letter may not have reached Milton until January 1648 or even later.

[31] Perhaps this is further proof that the *Epitaphium Damonis* was sent to the academy as a whole rather than to Dati personally, because had Milton sent it to Dati personally, he would surely have included a covering letter.

[32] *CM* 12, 296: "Quando era morta in me ogni speranza, benche vivissimo il desiderio di ricever lettere di V.S." Fletcher, "Milton's *Epitaphium Damonis*," 795, erroneously attributes this statement to Milton.

[33] *CM* 12, 296.

[34] *CM* 12, 296.

[35] *CM* 12, 310: "l'essere stato si lungo tempo senza sue."

[36] Dati had obviously been worried by Milton's failure to reply to the other three letters. It is only upon reading this letter that he will discover that his three were lost in the post. Milton, at the end of the letter, attempts to rectify the situation by establishing a more reliable means of communication. For an interesting discussion of the letter's

Dati's Italian letter was obviously written as a reply to Milton's extant Latin epistle, as it picks up one by one points made therein.[37] Milton betrays a deep unhappiness (*vicem meam dolere persaepe soleo*)[38] and loneliness (*ut in perpetua fere solitudine versari mihi necesse sit*).[39] And Dati seems to acknowledge this pervasively melancholic tone as he prays for his friend's happiness "Frà tanto mentre io prege il Cielo che la faccia e conservi felice."[40] Milton speaks of his great sorrow upon leaving Florence,[41] reflecting on the numerous friendships he had cultivated there.[42] Indeed the few verses in *Epitaphium Damonis*, he says, were intended to convey his love for his Italian friends.[43] Dati in response states that he is pleased that Milton has "remembered him": "e mi accertò che di me *si manteneva memoria* tanto fresca, e si amorevole nell' animo gentilissimo del Signore Gio. Miltoni."[44] He realises [from the letter] the esteem in

---

conclusion, see Fletcher, "Milton's *Epitaphium Damonis*," 791-792; Hale, *Milton's Languages*, 90.

[37] The manuscript of Dati's Italian letter is preserved along with the holograph of Milton's Latin letter to Dati in a volume of Milton family papers, derived from the sale of the library of John Fitchett Marsh (see *CM* 12, 383), and now in the New York Public Library. Dati's letter has generally been regarded as a draft since it contains several corrections, but perhaps the fact that it actually bears Dati's signature suggests that it may indeed be the original sent to Milton. The Columbia editors state "since we do not know the early history of the mss, which Marsh seems to have acquired between 1825 and 1849, we must consider the possibility that this is a veritable letter and no draft," although they do "admit the probability that the document is a draft" (*CM* 12, 395).

[38] *CM* 12, 46.

[39] *CM* 12, 46.

[40] *CM* 12, 310.

[41] *CM* 12, 48: *gravis admodum, ne te celem, discessus ille et mihi quoque fuit.* Cf. 5 above.

[42] *CM* 12, 48: *quoties mecum cogito tot simul sodales atque amicos tam bonos, tamque commodos una in urbe, longinqua illa quidem, sed tamen carissima.*

[43] *CM* 12, 48: *amoris autem adversum vos mei, vel illis paucis versiculis emblematis ad morem inclusis, testimonium haudquaquam obscurum.*

[44] *CM* 12, 296. Italics are mine.

which Milton holds Italy.[45] Milton had complained that his studies were interrupted by the turbulent state of England, its civil war and slaughter (*turbulentissimus iste ... Britanniae nostrae status, qui animum meum paulo post ab studiis excolendis ad vitam et fortunas quoque modo tuendas necessario convertit*).[46] Dati picks this up as he regrets the fact: "duolmi in estremo che *le turbolenze* del Regno abbiano *turbati i suoi studi*."[47] Milton states that in spite of this he has published some works, and that had these not been in English, he would have sent them to his Italian friends, whose judgement he values. He promises to send the part that is in Latin, and would have done so already had he not feared that the anti-papal content in a few pages might not be too pleasing to their ears.[48] He hopes that his Italian friends will pardon his freedom of speech as indeed they were accustomed to do (he is pretty sure that at least Dati will).[49] Dati replies by stating that he is anxiously awaiting Milton's poems and anticipates his being afforded a large field for admiration of the fineness of his wit. Then he picks up Milton's acknowledgement of the anti-papal content of a few of the pages by excepting from his anticipated general admiration those which show contempt for his own religion "eccetto però in quelle che sono in disprezzo della mia Religione."[50] He will indeed excuse but not applaud these even though uttered from the lips of a friend. In any case, they will not be an obstacle to his reception of the others, if Milton excuses his (Dati's) liberty of expression "scusando la

---

[45] *CM* 12, 296: "Conobbi ancora in quale stima fosse appresso de Lei la mia Patria". As if to return the compliment, he says that Italy counts it among her greatest treasures that in England there is one who magnifies their glories, loves their citizens and celebrates their writers: "[la mia Patria] che frà suoi pregi annovera d'aver nella grande Inghilterra (come disse quel Poeta divisa dal nostro Mondo) chi le sue glorie magnifica, ama i suoi Cittadini, celebra i suoi Scrittori."

[46] *CM* 12, 50.

[47] *CM* 12, 310.

[48] *CM* 12, 50: *sermone patrio haud pauca in lucem dedimus ... poematum quidem quae pars Latina est, quoniam expetis, brevi mittam; atque id sponte iamdudum fecissem, nisi quod propter ea quae in pontificem Romanum aliquot paginis asperius dicta sunt, suspicabar vestris auribus fore minus grata.*

[49] *CM* 12, 50: *nunc abs te peto, ut quam veniam, non dico Aligerio, et Petrarchae vestro eadem in causa, sed meae, ut scis, olim apud vos loquendi libertati, singulari cum humanitate dare consuevistis, eandem impetres (nam de te mihi persuasum est) ab ceteris amicis, quoties de vestris ritibus nostro more loquendum erit.*

[50] *CM* 12, 310.

mia zelante libertà."[51] The reference to liberty here seems to pick up Milton's phrase *loquendi libertas* when referring to his own freedom of speech — possibly in the academies themselves.[52] Dati, here, like Milton there, wishes a certain "liberty" of expression to be excused. Finally where Milton had sent his good wishes to Dati himself and Coltellini, Francini, Frescobaldi, Malatesti, and Chimentelli,[53] and had asked Dati to send greetings "in his name" to the entire Gaddian academy: *toti denique Gaddianae Academiae salutem meo nomine plurimam dices*,[54] Dati replies by saying that he has done so "in Milton's name" and by returning their greetings "Tutti li amici da me *in nome di V.S. salutati* affettuosamente la riveriscono."[55]

(iii) A Paradise Regained?

But if Dati's letter is a detailed reply to Milton's, it is also much more than that. It is not an overstatement to say that in its own way it reflects on a number of levels the entire thought-world of the Seicento Italian academy. And it does so on both an explicit and an implicit level:

1) Dati explicitly refers to two academicians: a) Francesco Rovai, whom Milton probably met; b) Gabriello Chiabrera, whom he could not have met since Chiabrera had in fact just died by the time of Milton's visit. It is highly likely however that the works of this famous sonneteer and academician were discussed by Dati and Milton in private conversation, and possibly by the Svogliati and Apatisti academies collectively; 2) the methodology employed by Dati in the most substantial part of the letter seems to mirror implicitly those *eruditionis ambages* in which academicians thrived.

---

[51] *CM* 12, 310: "le quali benchè proferite da bocca amica possono esser ben compatite, mà non lodate; questo tuttavia non mi sia d'impedimento a ricever l'altre, scusando la mia zelante libertà."

[52] *CM* 12, 50.

[53] *CM* 12, 52: *Tu interim, mi Carole, valebis, et Cultellino, Francino, Frescobaldo, Malatestae, Clementillo minori, et si quem alium nostri amantiorem novisti.*

[54] *CM* 12, 52.

[55] *CM* 12, 312.

Francesco Rovai

Firstly, the explicit references: included in this epistle is Dati's statement that he has been asked to deliver the funeral oration for a recently deceased fellow-academician Francesco Rovai, who was, he believes, well-known to Milton ("per quanto io credo da lei ben conosciuto").[56] Dati's request is that Milton supply him with a poem on Rovai. Rovai's reputation in the Svogliati is attested from as early as 1626. In the minutes of the 14/24 January meeting of that year he is said to have read an academic discourse on a sonnet of Petrarch, and to have been universally acclaimed.[57] His name occurs in the minutes of that Svogliati meeting of 5/15 July 1638 in the course of which "il signor ... (Miltoni?)" may have been proposed for election to the academy's membership.[58] There it was proposed that Rovai, before the present month had elapsed, should give a lecture.[59] Whether on this or on some another occasion, Milton presumably would have had ample opportunity to meet this learned fellow-academician. Rovai, who was to become consul of the academy in 1645,[60] was also a member of the Apatisti, where he was known by the anagrammatic name of Rainero Fucasco;[61] he also participated in the Florentine Accademia degli Alterati.[62] It is hardly surprising then that he was posthumously celebrated in verse. The academic chronicler Jacopo Rilli, in his *Notizie* (Florence, 1700) selects among the many authors who wrote poems on the death of this academician: Jacopo Salviati, Nicolo Strozzi, Alessandro Adimari, Cammillo Lenzoni and Piero Salvetti,[63] the

---

[56] *CM* 12, 296.

[57] "Il Sig. Francesco di Paolo Rovai lesse pubblicamente nella solita Stanza dell' Accademia sopra il Sonetto del Petrarca, che comincia: 'Fera stella, se'l Cielo ha forza in noi', e fù universalmente commendato il suo dire, come assai erudito, giustoso, ed elegante." (*Atti dell' Accademia*, bk 5). As quoted by Jacopo Rilli, *Notizie Letterarie ed Istoriche agli Uomini Illustri dell' Accademia Fiorentina* (Florence, 1700), 335.

[58] See 14 above. Biblioteca Nazionale Centrale, Florence CLVII 357 includes Rovai; *In Morte di Raffaello Gherardo Orazione* (Florence, 1638) includes poems by Adimari, Rovai and Francini.

[59] "che il Signor Rovai avanti passare il presente mese ne facesse una." See 15 above.

[60] Rilli, *Notizie* under the year 1620, has a brief record of Rovai. He refers (331) to a manuscript *Vita* of Rovai which Cavalcanti had given to the secretary of the academy, but which he was unable to find.

[61] Gori, f. 44r; Lazzeri, *Intellettuali*, 15, 68.

[62] Rilli, *Notizie*, 331.

[63] Rilli, *Notizie*, 332.

last four cited perhaps in the order of the appearance of their respective elegies prefixed to the 1652 posthumous edition of Rovai's *Poesie*.[64] And it is in relation to the composition of *epicedia* on Rovai (or at least requests for such) that Milton comes into view.

In the current letter,[65] Dati in asking Milton to honor Rovai's memory with some verses,[66] cites the Dutch scholars Nicolas Heinsius and Isaac Vossius respectively, as having already done so at his request: "Lo stesso hanno fatto a mia petizione i Signori Niccolò Einsio, e Isac Vossio Olandesi miei Amici, e Padroni singolarissimi, e Letterati famosi dell' età nostra."[67] That Dati did in fact make such requests is attested by two of his extant letters conveniently accessible in Francesco Fontani's *Elogio di Carlo Roberto Dati* (Florence, 1794).[68] In a letter to Heinsius dated Florence 1/10 September 1647 Dati had entreated Heinsius somewhat urgently (*rogo, et iterum enixe rogo ...*)[69] to compose a poem on Rovai's premature death (*... ut tuorum carminum eligas argumentum, obitum immaturum eximii Poetae, et Nobilis Fiorentini Francisci Rovai*).[70] Likewise in a letter dated Florence 27 September/7 October Dati had written to Vossius on the same subject. Having informed Vossius that Heinsius had already written such an elegy (*Heinsius elegantissimis Elegis nostri vatis Manibus parentavit*),[71] an elegy which Dati had obviously

---

[64] *Poesie di Francesco Rovai*, ed. N. Rovai (Florence, 1652). These prefatory elegies make use of conventional panegyrical and encomiastic *topoi*. Niccolo Strozzi (f. 5ᵛ) reverts to pathetic fallacy to convey the detrimental effect of Rovai's death upon the mythical and natural world; Alessandro Adimari (6ʳ) states that those who wish to read Rovai's poetry will see a phoenix rising from his ashes and the sun rising from his night: "Francesco i versi tuoi legga chi vuole/veder del cener tuo l'alta Fenice,/e datta notte tua sorgere il sole" (12-14); Camillo Lenzoni (6ᵛ) likens him to Petrarch and Dante, while Piero Salvetti (1) sees him as a swan of the Arno: "chiude un Cigno dell' Arno il più canoro" (2).

[65] *CM* 12, 296-312.

[66] *CM* 12, 296: "Per la stessa cagione piglierò ardire di pregarla a volere onorare cò suoi versi la gloriosa memoria del Sigr. Francesco Rovai egregio Poeta Fiorentino immaturamente defunto e per quanto io credo da lei ben conosciuto."

[67] *CM* 12, 296.

[68] *Elogio di Carlo Roberto Dati Recitato Nella Reale Accademia Fiorentina nell' Adunanza del Di 30. di Settembre 1790 dall' Abate Francesco Fontani Bibliotecario della Riccardiana* (Florence, 1794).

[69] Fontani, *Elogio di Carlo Roberto Dati*, 62.

[70] Fontani, *Elogio di Carlo Roberto Dati*, 62.

[71] Fontani, *Elogio di Carlo Roberto Dati*, 63.

received by this time),[72] he now entreats him to do the same (*Tu quoque, doctissime Vossi, amici eruditissimi vestigiis inhaerens ex istius virtutibus materiam sume*).[73] If in the letter to Vossius, Dati could cite the precedent of Heinsius, now in the letter to Milton he can go one stage further by including as possible *suasoriae* the precedent of both Heinsius and Vossius. Such is the rhetoric of persuasion, and more than that. For these are reputable neo-Latinists who in themselves had in a sense followed in Milton's footsteps. They too had travelled to Italy; they too had been hospitably welcomed by academicians, who had admitted them into Florentine academies.[74] Implicit perhaps is Dati's sense of pride in what was for the Italian a network of communication that extended beyond the confines of Italy to embrace the Low Countries and now England. This letter is the first of two occasions on which Dati writes to "foreign" neo-Latin ex-academicians (including Milton) and almost contemporaneously on a virtually identical topic.[75] But from a closer comparative examination of the three Dati epistles some hitherto unnoticed points of interest emerge, which would indicate that the Italian academician is in fact remoulding aspects of his topic to suit the particular addressee. In this instance all three letters were written and sent from Florence in the autumn of 1647. As already noted, earliest is the letter to Heinsius, dated 1/10 September (*IV. Id. Septembr.*) 1647, followed by the letter to Vossius dated 27 September/7 October (*Non. Octobr.*) 1647, and finally the letter to Milton dated 22 October/1 November 1647. Of the three epistles, the one to Milton is the exception in that it is written in Italian as opposed to Latin, the medium employed in the other two. At first sight this may seem surprising. Why should Dati, who is after all replying to a *Latin* letter by Milton and who chose Latin as the medium of his prose "written

---

[72] Heinsius sent his poem from Venice to Dati with an accompanying Latin letter dated 17/27 September 1647 (Fontani, *Elogio di Carlo Roberto Dati*, 64-66).

[73] Fontani, *Elogio di Carlo Roberto Dati*, 63.

[74] For Heinsius's description of such hospitality, see his dedicatory epistle prefixed to his second book of Elegies (*Poemata* [Lugd., 1653], 172-174), in which he describes his admission *in sacra et penitiora Academiae utriusque penetralia* (172) and fondly recalls Doni, Frescobaldi, Cavalcanti, Gaddi and Coltellini (173). Cf. Masson, *Life*, I, 771-772. Biblioteca Nazionale Centrale, Florence, MSS. Cl. IX, 5; Cl.VII, 483 and 583 contain Giovanni Guidacci's *Orazione in Lode di Benedetto Fioretti* (1ff.) and a series of autographed epigrams by Nicolas Heinsius: *Epigramma in Laudem Eiusdem Orationis*.

[75] For another example of this practice, see the parallel letters sent by Dati to Milton and Heinsius, discussed at 79-80 below.

encomium" in Milton's honor,[76] write in Italian at this point? And is this a conscious choice? The answer is conveniently provided by Dati himself, for quite early in the letter he draws attention to his choice of the vernacular on this occasion. This is his personal response to Milton's love of things Italian (as expressed in his Latin letter) and more specifically, his tribute to Milton's own ability to write and speak in so polished a manner "e nel suo bello Idioma si propriamente e si politamente scrive, e ragiona."[77] And great indeed is this tribute, for while Milton is singularly gifted to revive dead languages "di cui è dote singularissima ravivare le lingue morte,"[78] he can also make foreign tongues his own "e le straniere far proprie." Dati's hope is that his addressee will find pleasure in the sound of a language which he himself speaks and possesses so well "sperando che le sia per esser grati il suono di quella che si ben parla, e possiede." Milton's Latin letter had indeed conveyed his love of Italy. At a time of civil war and distractions from study, his memories of Italy and of the academicians he met there are for the friendless and solitary Englishman perhaps memories of a paradise lost. But what if that paradise can be regained through the sound of a beautiful language or through the quasi-therapeutic recollection of a friend's voice? This is perhaps the subtext to the linguistic medium employed and, as argued below, the methodology exhibited in a letter which also seems to be a form of *consolatio*. For if Milton can bring to life the ancient tongues ("ravivare le lingue morte") so perhaps Dati, through employing the Italian language, can resurrect for his disconsolate addressee a "modern" tongue; perhaps also, later in the letter, through an extensive presentation, albeit on paper, of what is in essence an academic debate, and through his citation of passages which are not unrelated to Milton's personal suffering (and indeed to the marital problems which seem to be hinted at in Milton's own letter),[79] he can not only reintroduce his English addressee to that Italian *accademia* that once was his, but also by means of this *consolatio* rekindle memories of Italian *amicitia* — of a network of supportive and encouraging continental *litterati*. And the use of language is only one of the many ways in which Dati's letter to Milton stands out from its counterparts to Heinsius and Vossius. It is also much lengthier, betraying

---

[76] See 46-47 above.

[77] *CM* 12, 296. Compare Dati's comment in his second letter to Milton that he is writing in Italian "sapendo che la mia lingua è a lei si cara e familiare che nella sua bocca non apparisce straniera." (*CM* 12, 312).

[78] *CM* 12, 296.

[79] See 75-76 below.

what is in effect a literary intimacy between speaker and addressee, especially in the readiness with which the request for the Rovai elegy dovetails into an academic discussion of the sonneteer Chiabrera and, in particular, his adaptation of Horace.[80] So in this broader sense it is very different. However, even in the brief synopsis of Rovai's character, life and works which Dati provides for Milton, as he had done for Heinsius and Vossius, points of contact and contrast are discernible. Thus parallels in the letters to Heinsius and Vossius can be found for Dati's references (in the letter to Milton) to 1) Rovai's nobility ("era ... nobile di nascita");[81] 2) his genius ("dotato della Natura d'ingegno elevatissimo")[82] — although this is much more elaborate than the simple *maior ingenio* (to Heinsius)[83] or *nobilior ingenio* (to Vossius);[84] 3) his vast studies ("arricchito dall' arte e dallo studio indefesso delle scienze più belle");[85] 4) his compositions in the fields of tragedy "cantò tragedie"[86] and lyric poetry, "valse nelle canzoni liriche";[87] 5) his praise of heroes "nelle quali lodò gli' eroi."[88] It is noteworthy that whereas in the letter to Heinsius Dati accredits Rovai with a pindaric style (*more Pindarico*),[89] this is omitted in the letter to Milton, perhaps because he is reserving that honor for Chiabrera himself, later in the letter ("suscitatore della Poesia Pindarica").[90] Dati tells Milton that

---

[80] See 71-79 below.

[81] *CM* 12, 296. Cf. *nobilis Fiorentini* (to Heinsius [Fontani, *Elogio di Carlo Roberto Dati*, 62]); *nobilis fuit genere* (to Vossius [Fontani, *Elogio di Carlo Roberto Dati*, 63]).

[82] *CM* 12, 296-298.

[83] Fontani, *Elogio di Carlo Roberto Dati*, 62.

[84] Fontani, *Elogio di Carlo Roberto Dati*, 63.

[85] *CM* 12, 298. Cf. *multiplici lectione et studio magnus* (to Heinsius [Fontani, *Elogio di Carlo Roberto Dati*, 62]); *in omni encyclopaedia versatissimus, litterarum amore flagrans* (to Vossius [Fontani, *Elogio di Carlo Roberto Dati*, 63]).

[86] *CM* 12, 298. Cf. *poeta praeclarus innumera scripsit. Tragoedias .... politissimo carmine exaravit* (to Heinsius [Fontani, *Elogio di Carlo Roberto Dati*, 62]); *Tragoedias cecinit* (to Vossius [Fontani, *Elogio di Carlo Roberto Dati*, 63]).

[87] *CM* 12, 298. Cf. *Odas suavissimo et sublimi stylo cecinit* (to Heinsius [Fontani, *Elogio di Carlo Roberto Dati*, 62]); *in lyrico carmine excelluit* (to Vossius, [Fontani, *Elogio di Carlo Roberto Dati*, 63]).

[88] *CM* 12, 298. Cf. *more Pindarico heroum virtutes extulit* (to Heinsius [Fontani, *Elogio di Carlo Roberto Dati*, 62]); *heroum laudator praeclarus* (to Vossius [Fontani, *Elogio di Carlo Roberto Dati*, 63]).

[89] Fontani, *Elogio di Carlo Roberto Dati*, 62.

[90] *CM* 12, 300: "... suscitatore della Poesia Pindarica e Anacreontica Gabbriello Chiabrera ..." Cf. *Poesie di Alcuni Apatisti*, Biblioteca Nazionale Centrale, Florence

Rovai deprecated vices, particularly in those seven *Canzoni* against the seven deadly sins "depresse i vizi, e particolarmente in quelle sette fatte contro ai sette Capitali." This finds a parallel in the letter to Heinsius[91] and to a lesser extent in the letter to Vossius,[92] where however the allusion to the seven deadly sins is omitted. Common to the letters to Milton and Heinsius (but absent from that to Vossius) is a reference to the fact that Rovai knew Greek, French, Latin and Italian. Thus in the Heinsius letter *Graecas, Latinas, Gallicas litteras apprime calluit, <u>vernacula lingua ad stuporem</u> usque cultus et elegans*. The comparable section in the letter to Milton interestingly transfers that element of *stupor* from the vernacular to embrace *both* Latin and Italian: "intendeva benissimo la lingua Greca, parlava la Franzese, scriveva *stupendamente la Latina e la Toscana*,"[93] as though Rovai mirrored in a sense Milton's own skill — a skill which Dati has earlier acclaimed. In the letter to Milton, it is only at the end of the *vita*, as it were, that Dati refers to the sumptuous exsequies which are being prepared by Rovai's friends "Dagli Amici di esso a lui si preparano esequie sontuose," and, assuming the modesty *topos*, to those friends' inadequacy in asking him to pronounce the funeral oration "<u>solo in questo manchevoli</u> che dell' Orazione Funerale a me è stata imposta la Carica."[94] These features find a striking parallel in Dati's letter to Vossius: *Huic magnificas decrevit exequias amicorum erudita sodalitas, <u>hac re tantum imprudens</u> quod mihi funebris Orationis munus iniunxit)*[95] — a parallel so close as to suggest that in the letter to Milton Dati is actually *translating* his own Latin into Italian, but with a difference: now he has inverted their order in that they follow, rather than precede, the little *vita* of the poet. A brief character sketch of Rovai, describing him as polite, courteous, beloved of princes, of uncorrupted manners and most pious "Era manieroso, cortese, amato dai principi, di costumi incorrotti, e

---

MS. cl. II, IV 17, f. 216ᵛ: "Al signor Gabbriello Chiabrera in sua lode": "Tu di lei faune un bel pregio/al gran Pindaro Toscano." (7-8).

[91] Fontani, *Elogio di Carlo Roberto Dati*, 62: *alias quibus vitia huius aevi, et praecipue septem capitalia depressit.*

[92] Fontani, *Elogio di Carlo Roberto Dati*, 63-64: *vitiorum insectator acerrimus.*

[93] Italics are mine.

[94] *CM* 12, 298.

[95] Fontani, *Elogio di Carlo Roberto Dati*, 63.

religiosissimi,"[96] is followed by the statement that he died young without having published his works "morì giovane senza aver pubblicato l'opere sue."[97] But suddenly Dati introduces into his letter to Milton two additional points wholly absent from the corresponding letters to Heinsius and Vossius:

1) If Milton does compose the poem it will be a favor to the whole of Italy,[98] not just to Dati personally.[99] This is interesting not only in the given context of Milton's praise of Italy (expressed in his own Latin letter) and acknowledged by Dati, but also in view of Dati's earlier comment that his own *patria* counted it among its greatest treasures that it has in England one who magnifies their glories, loves their citizens, and celebrates their writers.[100] In other words, by composing this elegy Milton would indeed be contributing to that Italian treasure.

2) If Milton agrees, Dati states, when Rovai's poems are published, copies will be sent to him "e publicate che saranno le Poesie del Signor Francesco e le lodi del medesimo da me le ne saranno inviate le copie."[101] This final

---

[96] *CM* 12, 298. Cf. *pius in deum, dulcis amicis, principibus gratus* (to Heinsius [Fontani, *Elogio di Carlo Roberto Dati*, 62]); *pius in deum, principibus gratus, amicis morum integritate et ceteris animi dotibus pergratissimus* (to Vossius [Fontani, *Elogio di Carlo Roberto Dati*, 63]).

[97] *CM* 12, 298. Cf. *obiit cum nondum opera sua ad perfectissimam, quam sibi proposuerat ideam, adduxerit, et publici iuris fecerit* (to Heinsius [Fontani, *Elogio di Carlo Roberto Dati*, 62]); *carmina dum nimis accuratus ultra nonum annum premeret, morte oppressus inedita reliquit, quorum pars selectior brevi in lucem edetur* (to Vossius [Fontani, *Elogio di Carlo Roberto Dati*, 64]). Cf. Niccolo Rovai's dedicatory epistle to the reader, prefixed to his edition of *Poesie di Francesco Rovai Accademico Fiorentino* (Florence, 1652), f. 4ʳ: "Ebbe pensiero l'autore delle presenti poesie di mandarle alla stampa in vita sua, e però fece una scelta di quelle che furono stimate più riguardevoli, ed abbero maggior' applauso. Ma prevenuto in età di 42 anni dalla morte, gli fu negato il metterlo in esecuzione."

[98] Dati's statement to Vossius that Doni and Cavalcanti likewise make this request (Fontani, *Elogio di Carlo Roberto Dati*, 64), while lending further weight, is hardly comparable with "tutta la mia Patria."

[99] *CM* 12, 298: "se ella si compiacerà com'io spero di mandarmi in tal proposito qualche frutto del suo amenissimo ingegno si obbligherà non me solo, ma tutta la mia Patria."

[100] *CM* 12, 296: "che frà suoi pregi annovera d'aver nella grande Inghilterra ... chi le sue glorie magnifica, ama i suoi Cittadini, celebra i suoi Scrittori ..."

[101] *CM* 12, 298. Cf. his promise in his second letter to Milton to forward him (when published) a copy of his funeral oration on Prince Lorenzo of Tuscany (*CM* 12, 314).

attempt to persuade may also be intended as a respectful gesture, a return favor perhaps for Milton's own poems which he has promised to send to Dati.

But what of replies to Dati's request? Milton's letter of reply, if indeed he ever wrote one, does not survive, nor is there any evidence that he complied with Dati's request to write the poem on Rovai.[102] Given Milton's esteem for Dati and for things Italian, and his fond memories of Florentine academies and their members, it is tempting to suggest that he would not have refused a request like this — or rather that the Milton of the 1630s would not have refused. But this is the Milton of the turbulent 1640s embroiled in civic and domestic disturbances. It is difficult to disagree with Masson's comment that "Circumstanced as Milton was when he received this letter, he can hardly have been in a mood to respond sufficiently to its minute and overflowing *dilettantismo*."[103] But did he at least send Dati a letter of refusal? Or did he in fact compose and forward to Dati (with an accompanying letter) a now lost Latin elegy on Rovai? In view of the scrupulous way in which Milton seems to have gathered together every scrap of his verse (in particular his Latin verse) for publication,[104] the absence of a poem on Rovai from the 1673 edition of Milton's poetry (Rovai's death obviously post-dates the 1645 edition) seems to argue against its existence. Although the Columbia edition does not mention a poem on Rovai in its brief anthology of possible lost poetry by Milton,[105] it is not inconceivable that Milton did compose and send the poem, which may perhaps be lying somewhere in the archives of Florentine academies (perhaps with the text of Dati's funeral oration, if indeed such exists?) and will some day come to light. There are arguments for and against. In the only other extant letter from Dati to Milton dated 24 November/4 December 1648 (although written over a year after the one requesting the poem on Rovai) Dati refers to the fact that he had written to Milton at the end of the previous year. He does not however mention receiving the Rovai poem; instead, he seems to pick up points from Milton's own letter of the 21 April 1647, with the implication perhaps that

---

[102] As noted briefly by Masson, *Life*, III, 683.

[103] Masson, *Life*, III, 683.

[104] See 25 above, although a notable exception to this rule seems to be the *Carmina Elegiaca* discovered by Horwood with the Commonplace Book. See A.J. Horwood, ed., *A Common-place Book of John Milton, and a Latin Essay and Latin Verses Presumed to be by Milton* (Camden Society, London, n.s. 16, 1877).

[105] *CM*, 18, 266-271: "Fugitive, Lost, and Projected Works."

he has not received a personal communication since.[106] But where Milton had promised to send at least the Latin part of 1645 edition, now Dati replies by actually thanking him for not one, but two copies. So there has been some form of contact: Milton, by sending the volume[s] (perhaps one for Dati; another for the academy), has communicated at least in general terms since receiving the letter on Rovai. This may lend support to his possible compliance with the request. Did Milton include an accompanying letter with those volumes and/or did he also enclose on that occasion the Rovai poem? We may never know. There may be external evidence that Milton did indeed write more than the single extant letter to Dati. Salvini in the *Fasti Consolari* (Florence, 1717) states that Dati had planned to publish "letters" from Milton, and others.[107] The Columbia editors state: "This may imply more letters than the one known now."[108]

By contrast, there is in fact conclusive evidence that Heinsius complied with Dati's request. This is apparent from the existence of a long elegy entitled *De Pietate Academicorum Florentinorum, qui Francisco Rovaio praestantissimo Poetae parentarunt, eiusdemque Musas Posthumas typis divulgarunt*, which Heinsius sent with an accompanying letter to Dati from Venice on 17/27 September, 1647. It is obvious that this reply is an immediate one (*sine mora*).[109] He had intended to put the finishing touches to the poem, but was unable to do so because of travelling-companions who were "very foreign to the Muses," and thus denying him an opportunity for meditation.[110] He proceeds to praise Dati's *Vita di Pittori* and promises to write to Cavalcanti and Doni, to whom incidentally Heinsius's poem refers (along with Gaddi and Dati, [but not

---

[106] Masson, *Life*, III, 690, states that "Although the amiable young Italian had received no answer to his last, of Nov. 1647, there had meantime reached him, by some slow conveyance, those copies of the Latin portion of Milton's published volume of Poems which had been promised him as long ago as April of the same year."

[107] As noted in *CM* 18, 527. Cf. Masson, *Life*, III, 691. The others mentioned by Salvini are Isaac Vossius, Paganino Gaudenzio, Giovanni Rodio, Valerio Chimentelli, and Nicolas Heinsius.

[108] *CM* 18, 528.

[109] Fontani, *Elogio di Carlo Roberto Dati*, 64: *debebam profecto sine mora iis respondisse, si desiderio meo satisfactum vellem.*

[110] Fontani, *Elogio di Carlo Roberto Dati*, 65: *sed comites itineris habui a Musis maxime alienos, ut meditationi locus non esset.*

Milton])[111] as foremost among those academicians lamenting Rovai.[112] Heinsius would subsequently publish his *carmen* in his collected *Poemata*.[113] It is interesting to note however that it was not included in the posthumous edition of Rovai's own poetry *Poesie di Francesco Rovai Accademico Fiorentino* edited by Nicolo Rovai and published in Florence in 1652 (the volume which Dati promised to send Milton), and to which are prefixed laments by such fellow-academicians as Niccolo Strozzi, Alessandro Adimari, Cammillo Lenzoni, and Piero Salvetti. The explanation for this is probably quite simple. It seems likely that Dati's collection of *epicedia* on Rovai constituted a gesture that was quite independent from the forthcoming posthumous edition of Rovai's poetry, a gesture intended merely as a means of providing helpful material for Dati's own funeral oration and/or for recitation at those "private academies" and, perhaps ultimately, for preservation among their collections.[114]

    In his letter to Milton, Dati states that Vossius has complied with his request. Interestingly, however, the evidence would seem to suggest that at first he actually declined. Fontani includes a reply from Vossius to Dati dated Amsterdam 8/18 October, 1647,[115] which conveys in rather bland terms his regret at Rovai's death,[116] and continues by asking Dati why is he requesting that he should write:[117] surely his poem would seem inferior

---

[111] In a later letter to Vossius, dated 18/28 February 1653 (Petrus Burmannus, ed., *Sylloge Epistolarum a Viris Illustribus Scriptarum* [Leiden, 1727], III, 667-671) Heinsius would call Milton's Latin poems inelegant, and describe their prosody as frequently faulty. See French, *Life Records*, III, 320.

[112] *Fletibus Aoniis et Phoebeo ululatu/ad sibi constructos turba sonora rogos,/Praecipuum quos inter agunt ad sidera murmur/suada Cavalcanti, mellea suada Dati,/et cum Gaddiade, facundi Donius oris:/pectora Castalio bis duo sacra Deo* (7-12). I quote the text included by Jacopo Rilli at *Notizie*, 333. Heinsius may, of course, be speaking in general terms of the grief felt by fellow-academicians. It is quite possible moreover that he did not know that Dati had actually asked Milton to write such a poem.

[113] Cf. Rilli, *Notizie*, 333-334.

[114] Rilli, *Notizie*, 333, in referring to those who have written poems on Rovai's death singles out Heinsius ("ma più di tutti Niccolò Einsio nella seguente Elegia, che si trova a carte 23 e 24 delle sue poesie"), but mentions neither Milton nor Vossius.

[115] Fontani, *Elogio di Carlo Roberto Dati*, 66-68.

[116] Fontani, *Elogio di Carlo Roberto Dati*, 67: *Francisci Rovai Poetae insignis fatum ex animo doleo. Id si non facerem ei certe inviderem, cui tu oratione funebri parentares.*

[117] Fontani, *Elogio di Carlo Roberto Dati*, 67: *Verum ut quid meas lacrimas tuis interiungi postulas?*

by comparison with that of either Heinsius or Dati himself;[118] he wishes he could comply[119] but has himself seen nothing of Rovai's work.[120] He then concludes by looking forward to seeing such laments as that by Dati.[121] Fontani certainly assumes that Vossius did eventually give in to Dati's request, and indeed cites as evidence of this Dati's statement in the letter to Milton.[122]

Gabriello Chiabrera

Having made the request of Milton, Dati, despite his attempted transitional phrase "mà già che ho' cominciato a parlar della nostra lingua, e de' nostri Poeti,"[123] seems to branch off in a rather different direction. He does so by immersing himself in a literary discussion of a passage from Petrarch's *Trionfi*, remarking that Castelvetro has noted that passage's similarity to some Horatian lines imitated in one of the Italian sonnets of Gabriello Chiabrera.[124] Dati then zooms in upon this particular sonnet (which contains a reference to Venus's birth from the sea), and proceeds to illustrate Chiabrera by reference to the poetry of Horace, Tibullus and others. This lengthy exposition is wholly unparalleled in the corresponding epistles of Dati to Heinsius and Vossius. Moreover the entire passage, as argued below, seems to mirror on a methodological level the very forum of an academic debate to serve perhaps as a kind of *consolatio* for an English friend who has now lost that Italian paradise. Discourses on Petrarch

---

[118] Fontani, *Elogio di Carlo Roberto Dati*, 67: *Nempe ut tuae et Heinsii nostri quanto magis sint splendidae et ingeniosae, tanto meae ineptiores appareant?*

[119] Fontani, *Elogio di Carlo Roberto Dati*, 67: *vellem tamen libentissime postulato tuo satisfacere.*

[120] Fontani, *Elogio di Carlo Roberto Dati*, 68: *ego autem adeo infortunatus hactenus fui ut nihil quidquam tam egregii poetae viderim adeo ut mirari quidem eum liceat, amare non item.*

[121] Fontani, *Elogio di Carlo Roberto Dati*, 68: *spero me aliquando visurum doctas tuas lacrimas.*

[122] Fontani, *Elogio di Carlo Roberto Dati*, 68, states: "Dalle riferite espressioni del Vossio pare ch'e non volesse aderire alle persuasioni del Dati relativamente al cantar le glorie del Rovai, par eternarne la di lui memoria, ma da una lettera che Carlo medesimo scrisse al celebre Giovanni Milton Inglese affine di indurlo a volere anch' egli fare sullo stesso soggetto alcun poetico componimento, sembra ch'e si lasciasse vincere dalle attrattive dell' amicizia, e ner cantasse le lodi."

[123] *CM* 12, 298.

[124] On Chiabrera, see *DBI s.v.*; Alberto Viviani, *Gabriello Chiabrera* (Rome, 1938).

formed a regular part of meetings of such academies as the Apatisti. For example, on 16/26 May 1637 Antonio Malatesti had delivered a lecture to the Apatisti in exposition of some verses of Petrarch.[125] And Chiabrera, like Malatesti and Rovai, was an Italian academician.[126] In an exposition of Chiabrera (which in modern terms would amount to no more than a footnote), Dati pays an implicit compliment to Milton's erudition. The interesting point is that the inclusion of Chiabrera is done in so casual a way by Dati as to indicate not only his implicit acknowledgement of his addressee's familiarity with Chiabrera's poetry, but also the probability that they have indeed discussed this sonneteer's work on previous occasions.[127] It is very likely that even before his visit to Italy, Milton knew the works of this celebrated Italian poet, who had similarly turned to the worlds of pastoral and masque to produce *Gelopea* and *Il Rapimento di Cefalo* respectively.[128] It is almost certain that he would have discussed Chiabrera's work with fellow-academicians either in the more formal setting of the Svogliati or Apatisti, or else in informal scholarly conversation. In an excellent study of the possible influence of Chiabrera's pindaric poetry upon Milton's vernacular odes, Stella Revard has pointed out some affinities between the two poets, especially in their fusion of Christian and pagan themes within the given genre of the ode. She remarks that "Chiabrera was almost exactly the kind of poet the young Milton of the 1630s was aiming to be, Milton himself having composed in many of the modes in which Chiabrera excelled."[129] These affinities can only have been intensified by Milton's visit to Italy, by his participation in such academies as the Apatisti, whose meetings always ended with the

---

[125] Contained in Biblioteca Nazionale Centrale, Florence Cl. VII, 391. Among the ms letters in the Biblioteca Nazionale Centrale, Florence, is one by Dati (28 September/8 October 1658) on Petrarch's verse "Forse, o che spero, il mio tardar le duole." (Cl. VII, 583, f. 26ff.).

[126] Chiabrera was also a member of the Venetian Incogniti, and is included in *Le Glorie*, 64 with the following distich: *Maeonidem cantare novem docuere columbae,/mille cycni varium te docuere melos.*

[127] See Stella P. Revard, "Milton and Chiabrera," Di Cesare, 505-520 at 505. At 515 she states: "Given the concurrence of Milton's poetic interests during this period and Chiabrera's well-known accomplishments in the genre in which Milton was interested, we can hardly avoid speculating that Milton knew and had explored Chiabrera's Pindarics."

[128] Revard, "Milton and Chiabrera," 509, suggests indeed that these works should be added to the analogues or sources of Milton's masques.

[129] Revard, "Milton and Chiabrera," 505.

recitation of a new sonnet,[130] and by conversation with academicians, some of whom had known personally this Italian poet, who, after all, had just died (at Rome) in 1638 — the very year of Milton's visit to Italy.[131] And in many respects Chiabrera was very much a Florentine at heart.[132] In his epic poem *Firenze* he had depicted the banks of the Arno as a *locus amoenus*: "Già tutti i poggi, e del bell' Arno il piano/sotto tepido Sol rideva aprico,/ed oggimai facea poco lontano/Zeffiro udirsi de' fioretti amico" (I.4),[133] and had conveyed his love of the city itself, proclaiming: "Firenze nostra (è ben soverchio il dire/Di ciò che sempre ti favella il core,/Ma non debbo tacer)" (III.6).[134] Milton had voiced not very dissimilar sentiments in *Epitaphium Damonis*, 129-132 as he recalled with pleasure the attractions afforded by the banks of the river Arno: *O ego quantus eram, gelidi cum stratus ad Arni/murmura populeumque nemus, qua mollior herba,/ carpere nunc violas, nunc summas carpere myrtos,/et potui Lycidae certantem audire Menalcam.* In the course of his Florentine years (1585-1619) Chiabrera had moreover forged important links with many academies,[135] in particular the Accademia degli Alterati. It is certain for example that he was an acquaintance of Jacopo Gaddi, founder of the Svogliati, and, as noted above, a key member of the academic circle to which Milton belonged.[136] It was to Gaddi that Chiabrera had addressed one of his *sermoni*.[137] What is equally evident is that he was held in the highest regard by the young Dati himself. This esteem is strikingly apparent not only in the current letter, but also in Dati's subsequent works, not least in his preface to collected speeches from the Accademia della Crusca, where he cites Chiabrera's poetry on two occasions, admiring his beautiful verse, and singing the praises of one who can preserve in the

---

[130] Cochrane, *Tradition and Englightenment*, 19.

[131] See Revard, "Milton and Chiabrera," 505.

[132] See Laura da Riva, *Gabriello Chiabrera a Firenze* (a brief undated work, with no indication of its place of publication).

[133] Text is that of *La Firenze: Poema di Gabriello Chiabrera* (Ferrara, 1777), 8. Cf. Hannah Demaray, "Milton's Perfect Paradise and the Landscapes of Italy," *MQ* 8 (1974), 33-41.

[134] *La Firenze*, 40. Canto 3.6.

[135] Mag Cl VII, 356 of the Biblioteca Nazionale Centrale, Florence, entitled, *Poesie di Diversi non Ancora Stampate Raccolte da Più Manuscritti* 1650, includes Chiabrera, Malatesti, and Dati.

[136] See 8, 10-15 above.

[137] As noted by Revard, "Milton and Chiabrera," 506.

vernacular so much of ancient poetry.[138] Now in the letter to Milton Dati, through explicit and implicit praise of Chiabrera, reveals himself as a true academician, initiating a discussion by citing the work of an Italian poet (Petrarch), and illustrating his reference by highlighting parallels from both "ancient" and "modern" authors. In a sense then, Dati's methodology mirrors that academic tendency to be "in wandring mazes lost," to immerse oneself in the *eruditionis ambages.* But perhaps this is deliberately so. Revard appropriately asks: "Why should Chiabrera specially be cited in discussion that finally breaks down to a sequence of philological and mythological footnotes?"[139] She responds with the suggestion that perhaps Dati knew that Milton, like Chiabrera, was attempting to adapt classical material for vernacular performance.[140] Was he aware of the fact that Milton, like Chiabrera, had produced a vernacular rendition of Horace?[141] While such speculation is possible, there may be additional, though hitherto unnoticed, reasons which might help to explain why Dati should have focused on Chiabrera at this point. Perhaps Dati is recreating for his distant addressee the thought-world of such academies as the Apatisti, who from 1636 had indeed proposed that there should be alternate lectures on Petrarch's *Trionfi* and on the poetry of Horace respectively.[142] Also, as noted above, Dati's letter is a careful response to a Latin letter, in which Milton told him that only now has he discovered that his Italian friends (obviously Dati included) have received the separate copy of *Epitaphium Damonis,* which he had sent to them. He had then proceeded to highlight the emblematic references to Italian academicians in that poem.[143] Then, as we have seen, Dati, in response, picks up one by one a whole series of points made by Milton, with one notable exception: he does not make any reference whatsoever to Milton's stated comments about the *Epitaphium Damonis.* Instead, he proceeds to focus on a sonnet of Chiabrera. Perhaps this progression is no accident, given the fact that Chiabrera himself was the composer of a pastoral elegy entitled *Damone*

---

[138] *Prose Fiorentine Raccolte dallo Smarrito Accademico della Crusca* (Florence, 1661) I, 3-4. See Revard, "Milton and Chiabrera," 507.

[139] Revard, "Milton and Chiabrera," 508.

[140] Revard, "Milton and Chiabrera," 508.

[141] Milton rendered Horace, *Odes* 1.5 into English. See Revard, "Milton and Chiabrera," 508.

[142] Gori, f.15ᵛ; Lazzeri, *Intellettuali,* 60.

[143] *CM* 12, 48.

(Eclogue 4), an epitaph on the death of a certain Thyrsis![144] Has Dati perhaps in reading Milton's *Epitaphium Damonis* and in being reminded of that poem by Milton's explicit comments in the Latin letter, seen in his English friend's poem a possible echo and inversion of the pastoral roles in the Italian sonnet? In other words, has Chiabrera's deceased Thyrsis become to some degree the speaker of *Epitaphium Damonis*, with Damone, the speaker of the Italian poem as the lamented Damon (Charles Diodati)? While it is important not to overstate possible points of contact between the two poems, for example, the commonplace notion of a wolf ravaging the sheepfold ("Forse nel sangue dell' inferma greggia/l'insidioso lupo inaspra il dente?" [14-15]// *aut avidos terrere lupos praesepibus altis* [43]), perhaps Chiabrera has indeed contributed some minor details to Milton's far superior lament. For example Chiabrera's "itine pecorelle, ite caprette"(25), may recur in a transmuted form in the Miltonic refrain *ite domum impasti, domino iam non vacat, agni*.[145] Perhaps too the Italian poem's concluding image of the pastoral pipe consumed by grief and lamentation (40-43),[146] has become in Milton a confident announcement of a *fistula* undergoing another sort of transformation (155-160), a metamorphosis from pastoral to epic, which mirrors in a sense the apotheosis of Damon in a Christian heaven. Is it too fanciful to suggest that Dati's focus upon a poem of Chiabrera at this precise point in the letter might reflect his acknowledgement (albeit an unconscious or at least unstated one) of echoes of Chiabrera's work in Milton's own Latin poem? Whether or not this is the case, what follows is in many respects an attempt to re-enact on paper the acutely meticulous methodology of the Italian academies — academies in which both Chiabrera and Milton had once participated. All this perhaps by way of a *consolatio* for an English addressee so far removed both physically and emotionally from that Italian world.

Dati's *Consolatio* to Milton

The epistle's *consolatio* may not be limited to its methodology alone. Passages cited by Dati in the course of his erudite exegesis could be deemed to be particularly appropriate to Milton, who in that Latin letter

---

[144] See *Canzonette, Rime Varie, Dialoghi di Gabriello Chiabrera* ed. Luigi Negri (Torino, 1964), 425-426.

[145] Cf. Revard, "Milton and Chiabrera," 510.

[146] "Ed io cantando di soavi venti/la ben cerata mia sampogna empiea,/finchè in tiepidi pianti, ed in lamenti/m'ha posto, Tirsi, la tua morte rea." (40-43).

seemed to hint at his own marital difficulties. Thus he bewailed the presence of those whom perhaps proximity or some unprofitable tie had bound to him, whether by accident or by law (... *quos forte viciniae aut aliqua nullius usus necessitudo mecum sive casu sive lege conglutinavit*). These were the people who daily sat beside him, wearying and even exhausting him as often as they pleased (*illos nulla re alia commendabiles assidere quotidie, obtundere, etiam enecare mehercule quoties collibitum erit*).[147] At the time of writing the letter, his estranged wife Mary Powell had returned to his household, bringing with her the entire Powell family![148] Milton was undoubtedly caught up in the sorrows of domestic conflict. And these sorrows may even have found a public voice in the *Doctrine and Discipline of Divorce*, two editions of which had already appeared.[149] As noted above, Dati's wish for his friend's happiness is very probably a general indication of his acknowledgement of Milton's melancholy,[150] but did the shrewd Italian pick up Milton's possible hints in the letter at these marital problems, especially in the reference to an "unprofitable tie" of those bound to him by "law"? If so, then perhaps the passages from Petrarch, Horace, Chiabrera and Tibullus, which Dati quotes as if by accident, bear greater significance than has hitherto been noted. It is certainly possible that these extracts, conveying the cruelty of love and its associated torment, constitute Dati's discreet expression of his sympathy for Milton's implied marital difficulties, thereby contributing to the epistle's *consolatio*.[151] Milton had bemoaned an "unprofitable tie ... by law." It may be more than a coincidence that Dati's scholarly exposition begins with a quotation from Petrarch about the stern *laws* of love, which, despite their cruelty, must be obeyed. He introduces the stanza quite casually (deliberately so?), stating that the day before yesterday he has been reflecting on it ("L'altrieri mentre io faceva riflessione sopra quel ternario del Petrarca Trionf. d'Amor. c.3").[152] He proceeds to quote the relevant lines:

> Dura *legge* d'Amor, mà benchè obliqua
> servar conviensi pero ch'ella aggiunge

---

[147] *CM* 12, 46.

[148] See Nardo, "Academic Interludes," 209.

[149] In 1643 and 1644 respectively.

[150] Masson, *Life*, III, 683, even suggests that Dati "may have heard more particular rumours in Florence of Milton's marriage-mishap and its consequences."

[151] My point is anticipated, though not developed, by Masson, *Life*, III, 683.

[152] *CM* 12, 298.

di cielo in terra universale antiqua.[153]

[Cruel *laws* of Love, albeit difficult to be obeyed because they are stretched from the sky to the universal, ancient earth.]

Dati provides a gloss by Castelvetro, who had noted the similarity of these lines to Horace, *Odes* I. 33.10-12: *sic visum Veneri, cui placet impares/ formas, atque animos sub iuga ahenea/saevo mittere cum ioco,*[154] a passage likewise conveying the cruelty of love and, in particular, the incompatibility of certain couples. The context of the lines is not without relevance to the Dati/Milton context, for Horace's Ode is in itself an attempted *consolatio* for Albius,[155] who has been deserted by his mistress. The speaker begins by advising Albius not to grieve more than is tolerable: *Albi, ne doleas plus nimio memor/immitis Gycerae* (I.33.1-2). The implication is that instead of bewailing her desertion, he should try to forget his cruel sweetheart.[156] There follows a series of *exempla* of love-triangles: couples whose relationships did not last, in that one party fell in love with someone else. This particular *consolatio* is thus permeated by typically Horatian irony — no two people really remain in love — an irony surely not lost on Dati or indeed Milton. There follow lines 10-12, quoted above and noted by Castelvetro, describing the laws of Venus in the mock-solemn assertion of her decree (*sic visum Veneri*) and in the inclusion of wholly incompatible couples under a brazen yoke. That yoke (*iugum*), with its etymological link with *coniugium*, is a symbol of marriage. Significantly, however, it can also denote enslavement to a god or mistress.[157] And Milton himself (not unlike Albius) had in a sense been deserted by a female, whose return he had previously sought in vain. Now some years later, perhaps that eventual homecoming (along with her entire family) has come to epitomise a yoke of marriage that is simultaneously a yoke of enslavement — "an unprofitable tie ... by law."

Dati proceeds to cite an imitation of Horace's lines by Chiabrera in his fifth canzonetta. The speaker laments the arrival of the ashes which torture a lover, but this is the will of Venus, a cruel divinity born of the

---

[153] *CM* 12, 298. Italics are mine.

[154] *CM* 12, 300. Cited in error by Dati as I, 23.

[155] Quite probably Albius Tibullus. Cf. *Horace: The Odes*, ed. Kenneth Quinn (Macmillan 1980; rpt. Nelson 1992), 184.

[156] Quinn, ed., *Horace: The Odes*, 184: "The appropriate course to take, H. would have us believe, when a mistress walks out on you, is to do all you can to put her out of your thoughts."

[157] *OLD s.v.*2a.

ocean ("Ah che vien cenere/penando un amator benche fedele/cosi vuol Venere/nata nell' Ocean nume crudele"). Dati sees in these lines an echo of the Horatian ode discussed above, and also of Tibullus 1.2.39-40: *nam fuerit quicumque loquax is sanguine natam/is Venerem e rapido sentiet esse mari*, lines which amount to a threat against the betrayers of amorous secrets. The hissing sibilants, the depiction of Venus's birth from violence and more specifically from the sea, represent in forceful terms the cruelty of this deity. Dati continues by discussing in some detail the reading *rapidus* in Tibullus, recommending *rabidus* as more indicative of the goddess' cruelty.[158] The sheer weight of argument here is convincing. Dati begins by quoting with scholarly precision passages describing the sea (*mare*) (or its equivalent) as rapid (*rapidus*) from Catullus, Seneca, Valerius Flaccus, and Claudian. However, he observes that in these instances the context is that of a tempest or the fury of the sea, hence the appropriateness of the application *rapidus*. In Tibullus, however, the adjective "rapid" has little or no force, hence Dati suggests *rabidus*,[159] and cites in support of his reading such poets who have called the sea wild, savage, mad or angry as Virgil (*rabiem ... maris*),[160] Valerius Flaccus, Silius Italicus, and such others, who have applied the same adjective to lions and tigers, as Cornelius Gallus, Virgil *inter alia*.[161] In essence, this is an academic debate. Realising indeed that he has strayed from his purpose (which was to emend Tibullus and illustrate Chiabrera),[162] he focuses on references to Venus's birth from the sea in such "modern" writers as Natales Comes, Giglio Gregorio Giraldo, Martin del Rio, and highlights the association of the sea with cruelty in such authors as Aulus Gellius,

---

[158] Cf. P. Murgatroyd, *Tibullus* I (Bristol Classical Press, 1980), 303: "*rabidus* is a stronger word, and so has more point here, as it brings out better the goddess' cruelty. *Rapidus* appears in 44, and there seems little point in repeating the adjective within so few lines. The two words are often confused in the mss ... and the scribe's eye may well have wandered to line 44."

[159] *CM* 12, 304: "Mà a Tibullo leva tutta la bizzaria il dire "sentiranno i loquaci essere dal sangue/e dal rapido mar venere nata' piuttosto che "e dal rabbioso Mar Venere nata."

[160] Virgil, *Aeneid* 5.800-802: *fas omne est Cytherea meis te fidere regnis/unde genus ducis: merui quoque saepe, furores/compressi, et rabiem tantam coelique marisque* (*CM* 12, 304). Dati also cites Virgil's *rabies Scyllaea*.

[161] *Georgics* 2.151: *at rabidae tigres absunt ...* (*CM* 12, 306).

[162] *CM* 12, 306: "Mà troppo per avventura mi sono avanzato, e col discorso e con l'ardire; tornando adunque al mio primo scopo che fù di emendare Tibullo, e illustrare Chiabrera ..."

Tibullus, Catullus, Ovid, Homer, and Tasso.[163] He concludes by citing Horace and Seneca in support of Chiabrera's depiction of Venus as a "nume crudele."[164]

From a discussion that began with the cruelty of Love (Petrarch's depiction of Love's stern laws, and [by way of Castelvetro] Horace's ironic *consolatio* which in effect conveyed the incompatibility of certain partners), Dati has focused on Chiabrera's fusion of both Horace and Tibullus to present the torments inflicted by a cruel Venus born from the sea (a sea that is *rabidus* rather than *rapidus*, says Dati, in a lengthy footnote to Tibullus). *Venus* and *mare* become virtually identical in what is essentially an anti-feminist exegesis. If, as is possible, Dati did indeed know more about Milton's problematic marriage to Mary Powell, his *consolatio* seems to couch that knowledge with the utmost tact.

Final evidence of the Milton/Dati friendship is provided by another extant letter, dated Florence, 24 November/4 December, 1647.[165] Dati has once more chosen to write in Italian as a tribute to his addressee's ability to make that language appear not foreign, but familiar upon his lips ("sapendo che la mia lingua è a lei si cara, e familiare che nella sua bocca non apparisce straniera").[166] Here, as noted above, Dati thanks Milton for two copies of his poetry ("hò di poi ricevuto due copie delle sue eruditissime Poesie").[167] He praises the volume which, although small, is of value as it constitutes "a jewel from the treasure of Milton" ("quantunque piccolo racchiude in se valore infinito per esser una Gemma del Tesoro del Sig. Gio. Miltoni").[168] Dati then proceeds to inform him of his elevation to the Chair of Classics by the Grand Duke, vacant since the death of Giovanni Battista Doni of Florence.[169] It is noteworthy that Dati takes pains to spell out to his English addressee the precise honor associated with this appointment. This Chair, he says, was once held by the great

---

[163] *Gerusalemme Liberata* 16 "Ne te Sofia produsse, e non sei nato/dell'Azio sangue tu; te l'Onda insana/del mar produsse, e il Caucaso gelato/e le mamme allattar di Tigre Ircana" (*CM* 12, 310).

[164] *CM* 12, 310.

[165] *CM* 12, 312-314. The original letter is preserved in the British Museum. Ms. Add. 5016x.

[166] *CM* 12, 312.

[167] *CM* 12, 312.

[168] *CM* 12, 312.

[169] For a reference to Doni in Milton's Latin letter to Holstenius (*CM* 12, 42), see 21 above.

Angelo Poliziano and others.[170] Dati continues by announcing that he has had the honor of pronouncing the funeral oration for Prince Lorenzo of Tuscany, and concludes by telling Milton that fellow-academician Valerio Chimentelli has been appointed to a professorship of Greek literature at the university of Pisa: "Il Sr Valerio Chimentelli è stato eletto da S. Altezza per Professore delle Lettere Greche in Pisa con grande espettazione del suo valore"[171] — an item of news described in similar terms in Dati's Latin letter to Heinsius dated 25 November/5 December 1648: *clarissimus Valerius Chimentellus noster litterarum Graecarum professor electus in Academia Pisana maximam excitavit expectationem*.[172] Dati concludes his letter to Milton by conveying greetings from Frescobaldi, Coltellini, Francini, Galileo jr and others.[173] Although written some ten years subsequent to Milton's departure from the shores of Italy, Dati's letter, like that of 22 October/1 November 1648, would seem to reflect Milton's place within an important Italian academic network. But that network was not confined to Florence. In Rome and Naples Milton would once again take his place among Italian *litterati*. If in 1638 and 1639 the "love of the sweet muse" (*dulcis amor Musae* [*Ep. Dam.* 13]) detained him in Florence (*Tusca ... in urbe* [*Ep. Dam.* 13]), so the magnetism of "voice and verse" would likewise attract him to the academic world of Rome.

---

[170] *CM* 12, 314: "Il serenissimo Granduca mio Signor s'è compiaciuto di conferermi la cattedra, e lettura delle lettere umane dell' Accademia Fiorentina vacata per la morte dell' eruditissimo signor Giovanni Doni gentiluomo firoentino. Questa è carica onorevolissima, e sempre esercitata da gentiluomini, e litterati di questa patria, come già dal Poliziano, dà due Vettori, e due Adriani lumi delle lettere."

[171] *CM* 12, 314.

[172] Fontani, *Elogio di Carlo Roberto Dati*, 84-85.

[173] *CM* 12, 314: "I Signori Frescobaldi, Coltellini, Francini, Galilei et altri infiniti unitamente se inviano affetuosi saluti ... "

CHAPTER 5

Milton and the Accademia dei Fantastici

From Florence, Milton proceeded to Siena and then to Rome (*Florentia Senas, inde Romam profectus*), where he stayed for about two months (*ad bimestre fere spatium*).[1] This was to be the first of two visits to the eternal city — a city in which the institution of the *accademia* was fully established and flourishing. For the academies of Rome, like their Florentine counterparts, possessed the customary seicento accoutrements and associated formalities: they sported *imprese* and mottoes, offered sumptuous banquets, encouraged the performance of original compositions, and devoted much of their energies to enhancing the Tuscan tongue. Something of the nature of such can be gleaned from a reading of the *Diary* of John Evelyn, in which he recounts *inter alia* the reception he received in 1645 by the then leading academy of Rome: the Accademia degli Umoristi, which, like the Florentine Svogliati and Apatisti, took pains to entertain foreign *litterati*. Evelyn proceeds to refer to "several other Academies ... of this nature, bearing the like fantastical titles."[2] Indeed the phrase "fantastical titles" is particularly pertinent to the present purposes. For although, in contrast to the Florentine Svogliati, the minutes and archives of the academies that existed in seventeenth-century Rome[3] have hitherto failed to provide evidence of Milton's attendance at, or participation in, any of their meetings, there does exist rather different but no less interesting evidence that he did in fact establish links with at least one: the Accademia dei Fantastici.

Not much is known about the Fantastici Academy, whose laws and minutes do not survive. It seems to have originated in c. 1625 in the Convent of the Apostles through the agency and initiative of a certain

---

[1] *CM* 8, 122.

[2] For the whole passage, see *The Diary of John Evelyn*, ed. E.S. de Beer (Oxford 1955) II, 364-365, and 102-103 below.

[3] Cf. Johann Albert Fabricius, *Index Duplex Academiarum Italiae et Siciliae* appended to his *Conspectus Thesauri Literariae Italiae* (Hamburg, 1749), 251-252.

Alberto Fabri.[4] Its *impresa* consisted of a loom ("tela"), while its motto *quidlibet audendi*, borrowed from Horace,[5] was intended no doubt to reflect its members' undaunted willingness to undertake any type of composition. And such versatility is exemplified by a volume of poetry entitled *Poesie de' Signori Accademici Fantastici di Roma* printed at Rome in 1637 and undoubtedly accessible to Milton during his sojourn in that city. One of the contributors to that volume, Giovanni Martino Longo, was described as the "acerrimo propagatore de' Fantastici" by a certain Giuseppe Malatesta Garuffi, who cites an allusion to the academy and its *impresa* in one of Longo's madrigals.[6] The other contributors were: Andrea Barbazzi, Antonio Bruni, Anton Francesco Tempestino, Bernardo Evangelista, Benedetto Benetti, Benedetto Rigogli, Carlo Spada, Francesco Carducci, Fulvio Testi, Gabriel Marino, Martino Longo, Giovanni Salzilli, Niccolo Strozzi and Vittorino Venturelli. And, as noted below, there is conclusive evidence that at least one of these academicians was well known to Milton. As for the Fantastici academy itself: although it published a further volume in 1655 entitled *Poesie in Lode d'Alessandro VII*,[7] its life was to be short-lived, for by 1688 it had in fact become extinct.[8]

(i)   Giovanni Salzilli's "Written Encomium"

Milton's links with the Fantastici are suggested by a four-line Latin encomium which one of its members, Giovanni Salzilli, composed in his honor, and by Milton's own Latin poem entitled *Ad Salsillum Poetam Romanum Aegrotantem*,[9] in which he addresses the sick academician, wishes him a speedy recovery and praises his skill as a poet. Virtually

---

[4] See Giuseppe Malatesta Garuffi, *Italia Accademica* (Rimini, 1689), 11; Bartolomeo Piazza, *Eusevologio Romano* (Rome, 1690), Tractate XII; Maylender, *Storia*, II, 347.

[5] *pictoribus atque poetis/quidlibet audendi semper fuit aequa potestas.* (Horace, *Ars Poetica*, 9-10). Cf. Maylender, *Storia*, II, 347.

[6] Maylender, *Storia*, II, 347: "Osate o Cigni alteri, alme Febee/pinger su questa *Tela* eterni esempii/di *Fantastiche Idee*;/Sianvi o canori Apelli,/chiari carmi i color, penne i pennelli./Ma se Fulmini mai mortali, ed empii/d'obblio, d'invidia rintuzzar bramate,/fortunati vogliate/fabbri d'alti stupori,/pingervi lo splendor de' vostri allori." Italics are mine.

[7] See Maylender, *Storia*, II, 347.

[8] See Maylender, *Storia*, II, 347.

[9] For a text and translation of this and other Latin poems by Milton which are directly associated with the Italian trip, see the Appendix to the present study.

nothing is known of Salzilli, apart from the fact that he contributed fifteen Italian poems (11 sonnets, 3 canzoni, 1 ottava) to the 1637 Fantastici collection.[10]   Freeman is probably correct in his assumption that since Salzilli's contribution amounts to some eleven per cent of the entire volume, he was in fact a highly regarded poet.[11] Not included in this collection, but lying among the archives of the Biblioteca Nazionale Centrale of Florence is a hitherto unnoticed ms. sonnet by Salzilli in praise of a certain Giulio da Montevecchio for his *Scorneide*, a satire on G.B. Scornio of Pisa.[12]

It was probably during Milton's first, rather than second, visit to Rome that he met this Italian poet and academician, since in both the 1645 and 1673 editions of Milton's works *Ad Salsillum* precedes *Mansus*,[13] which has a Neapolitan context. That Salzilli survived the illness alluded to in the headnote to *Ad Salsillum* and described in the poem proper is evident from the existence of a letter addressed to him by Tommaso Stigliani, (dated Matera, 25 March/4 April 1644).[14] Unfortunately this does not reveal very much in biographical terms. Stigliani apologises for not writing to his friend, excusing his *otium* by stating that *he* is an old man. This may imply that in 1644 his addressee was comparatively young.[15] The letter employs a mythological subtext: Apollo is depicted as abandoning his followers when Venus abandons her worshippers: "Suole questo benedetto Apollo abbandonare i suoi seguaci, quando Venere abbandona i suoi cultori."[16] Is this perhaps an implicit acknowledgement of Salzilli's sound knowledge of classical mythology? Italian moreover was not the only language in which Salzilli composed. He is the author

---

[10] *Poesie de' Signori Accademici Fantastici di Roma* (Rome, 1637), 148-169.

[11] James A. Freeman, "Milton's Roman Connection: Giovanni Salzilli," *MS* 19 (1984), 87-104, at 97.

[12] See G. Mazzatinti, *Inventari dei Manoscritti delle Biblioteche d'Italia* (Florence, 1890), 96: II, IV, 22 (Magl. Cl XXIV num 41; Cl VII, num 518, 481, 462, 591, 308, 595, 459; Cl XXV, 524; Cl XXIV, 57): *Relaz. di Costantinopoli di Cristoforo Valiero* 1615 f.1ff; Salsilli Giovanni, sonetto in lode di Giulio da Montevecchio per la sua Scorneide e la "Scorneide del Signor Conte Giulio di Monte Vecchio" in beffe del canonico G.B. Scornio pisano (f. 80ff); "Altra copia della Scorneide" (f. 88ff) "Altra copia della medesima" (f. 104ff).

[13] See Douglas Bush, *A Variorum Commentary on the Poems of John Milton: Vol I: The Latin and Greek Poems* (New York, 1970), 263.

[14] Tomaso Stigliani, *Lettere* (Rome, 1664), 248-250.

[15] Stigliani, *Lettere*, 250.

[16] Stigliani, *Lettere*, 250.

also of the following four-line *Latin* poem in praise of Milton, to which *Ad Salsillum* cleverly replies:

> Ad Ioannem Miltonem Anglum triplici
>   poeseos laurea coronandum Graeca nimirum,
>   Latina, atque Hetrusca, Epigramma
>   Ioannis Salsilli Romani.
>
> Cede Meles, cedat depressa Mincius urna;
>   Sebetus Tassum desinat usque loqui;
> At Thamesis victor cunctis ferat altior undas,
>   Nam per te, Milto, par tribus unus erit.

[An Epigram by Giovanni Salzilli, of Rome, to John Milton, an Englishman, who deserves to be crowned with a threefold laurel-wreath of poetry: Greek certainly, Latin and Tuscan.

Yield Meles; let Mincius yield with lowered urn; let Sebetus cease to speak constantly of Tasso. But let the victorious Thames carry his waves higher than all the rest, for through you, Milton, he alone will be equal to all three.]

Here, as in other such encomia, *Ioannes Milto Anglus* is presented as a polyglot.[17] In the prose title Salzilli states that Milton deserves to be crowned with a threefold laurel-wreath — one of Greek, one of Latin and one of Tuscan. In addition to his compositions in Greek and Latin already noted, Milton, as stated above,[18] had by the time of the Italian journey composed his Italian sonnets, hence validating the inclusion of the *laurea Hetrusca*.

The chief feature of Salzilli's tribute is the use of a river to represent a famous poet of that region: Meles (Homer), Mincius (Virgil), Sebetus (Tasso). These three rivers are to yield to the Thames, representative of the London-born Milton, which victoriously carries its waves higher than all the rest since through Milton it alone is equal to the other three taken together (*par tribus unus erit*).[19] The tribute is a great compliment, ranking Milton above three famous epic poets. Salzilli is thereby going one stage further than he had in one of his own Italian sonnets entitled "Che l'età nostra ha scrittori sì di verso, come di prosa eguali a gli Antichi," which had stated that Tasso surpassed Virgil himself:

---

[17] Cf. the tributes of Francini and Dati at 40 and 47 above.

[18] See 23 above.

[19] For the phraseology of *par ... unus*, cf. Michael Marullus, *Ep.* 2.9.5-6 (*Ad Antonium Principem Salernitanum*): *sic modo par unus cunctis, ex omnibus unum/non potes, ut cupias, deligere ipse parem.* Text: Marullus, *Carmina*, ed. A. Perosa (Zurich, 1951).

> E pur' io veggio al gran Maron simile
>   De la tromba di Manto il Tasso herede,
>   Che'l suono accresce, e'l suo retaggio eccede,
>   E la pietà d'Enea si prende a vile.(5-8)[20]

[And I also see Tasso, like the great Virgil, heir to the trumpet of Manto, who augments the sound and exceeds his heritage, while the piety of Aeneas is regarded as worthless.]

Now Milton outshines not only Virgil, but also Homer, and even Tasso.

(ii)   Milton's *Ad Salsillum*

That *Ad Salsillum* is a reply to the Latin tribute is suggested by the fact that it echoes some of these features.[21] Milton actually mentions the extent to which his poetry has been admired by Salzilli and alludes to his judgement (*camoena nostra cui tantum est cordi,/quamque ille magnis praetulit immerito divis*. [7-8]).[22] The perfect tense *praetulit* seems indeed to point to one occasion in particular — the writing of the encomium — , while the *magni ... divi* are Homer, Virgil and Tasso, said to be surpassed by Milton in the encomium itself.[23] In qualifying his statement by saying that this preference was undeserved (*immerito*), he expresses in a miniature or condensed form that element of modesty which is evident on a much grander scale in the Latin prose preface to the tributes as a whole, where he states that the ensuing encomia go far beyond what he actually deserves.[24]

---

[20] *Fantastici*, 150.

[21] As briefly noted by Parker, *Biography* I, 173, and by Anthony Low, "*Mansus*: In Its Context," *MS* 19 (1984), 105-126, at 105.

[22] ["to whose heart my poetry is so dear and which he preferred, quite undeservedly, to the mighty gods."]

[23] Cf. Revard, *Milton and the Tangles of Neaera's Hair*, 225.

[24] *Haec quae sequuntur de auctore testimonia, tametsi ipse intelligebat non tam de se quam supra se esse dicta, eo quod praeclaro ingenio viri nec non amici ita fere solent laudare ut omnia suis potius virtutibus quam veritati congruentia nimis cupide affingant, noluit tamen horum egregiam in se voluntatem non esse notam; cum alii praeserim ut id faceret magnopere suaderent. dum enim nimiae laudis invidiam totis ab se viribus amolitur sibique quod plus aequo est non attributum esse mavult, iudicium interim hominum cordatorum atque illustrium quin summo sibi honori ducat negare non potest.* Hale, *Milton's Languages,* 92-93, briefly analyses this prose preface, in which he sees Milton performing a syntactical balancing act.

In *Ad Salsillum* Milton uses the Latinised form *Milto* to refer to himself. It may be significant that he should choose this, rather than, say, *Miltonius*[25] or *Miltonus*,[26] since this is precisely the form which had been used by Salzilli both in the prose heading (*Ad Ioannem Miltonem*) and in the distich proper (*nam per te, Milto, par tribus unus erit*).[27] Moreover Milton introduces himself as *alumnus ille Londini Milto* (9), the emphatic *ille* perhaps suggesting "that same *Milto* mentioned by you in the encomium." Similarly, in line 17 it is "this same" Milton who wishes Salzilli every good fortune (*Tibi optat idem hic fausta multa Salsille.*)

Implicit in Salzilli's tribute is the contrast between the *Ioannes* who is an Englishman (*Ad Ioannem Miltonem Anglum*) and the *Ioannes* who is an Italian and native of Rome (*Epigramma/Ioannis Salsilli Romani*). This heading may be echoed in the title of Milton's poem (*Ad Salsillum poetam Romanum ...*). Milton develops this contrast on a climatic level in lines 9-16, which are marked by a gradual progression from the inclement weather of England with its fierce winds and panting gusts to the essential order of Italy, its peoples and the intellectual prowess of its youth. The description of Milton leaving England, his arrival in Italy and the many learned friends whom he met in the course of his trip also occurs in the Italian encomium by Francini,[28] who, as noted above, praises Milton's virtue and outlines the reasons which led him to travel to Italy.[29]

Perhaps the closest parallel between Salzilli's encomium and Milton's poem is the motif of a river associated with, and even representative of, the poet of its region. In the concluding lines of the poem Milton describes in detail the effect which Salzilli's *cantus* will have upon his native river, the Tiber:

> Tumidusque et ipse Tibris hinc delinitus
> spei favebit annuae colonorum;
> nec in sepulchris ibit obsessum reges
> nimium sinistro laxus irruens loro;
> sed frena melius temperabit undarum
> adusque curvi salsa regna Portumni. (36-41)

---

[25] *Miltonius* occurs in the heading to Manso's tribute: ... *ad Ioannem Miltonium Anglum.* See 130 below.

[26] *Miltonus* occurs in Selvaggi's tribute: *Graecia Maeonidem, iactet sibi Roma Maronem,/Anglia Miltonum iactat utrique parem.*

[27] As noted by Bush, *Variorum*, 264.

[28] See 39-41 above.

[29] For a discussion of this tribute, see 38-43 above.

[And the swollen Tiber himself, charmed by the strains, will favour the yearly hope of the farmers and will not seek to besiege kings in their tombs by rushing along with the left rein too slack, but he will keep the reins of his waves under better control all the way to the salty kingdom of curved Portumnus.]

As a result of Salzilli's poetry, the swollen Tiber will curb its waves. This passage is a development of, and elaboration upon, the river motif which was the characteristic feature of Salzilli's compliment.[30] Now Milton subtly inverts the whole, for whereas Salzilli had described the Thames, representative of Milton, carrying its waves higher than all the other rivers (*At Thamesis victor cunctis ferat altior undas*), Milton depicts Salzilli's river, the Tiber, as curbing its waves (*sed frena melius temperabit undarum* [40]) and hints at a parallel between the envisaged healing of Salzilli, who had required *levamen* (30), and the calming of the Tiber which had been *tumidus* — an adjective which can also denote illhealth.[31] Neither will have any connections with death. Salzilli, it is hoped, will recover his strength; the Tiber will not invade the tombs of kings. Line 41 in its reference to the *curvi salsa regna Portumni*[32] may even play on Salzilli's name (*Salsillus* is the Latinised form). Milton may also be drawing a parallel between Salzilli and Portumnus, the god of harbors and gates, and perhaps reacting once again to the river motif as expressed in the tribute. The imperious tone of Salzilli's encomium as a whole is indeed compatible with such an authoritative figure as Portumnus himself.

A further parallel is the notion of Milton's versatility in a wide range of languages, both ancient and modern. Salzilli had deemed him worthy of a threefold laurel: of Greek, Latin and Italian. These languages are represented in the distich proper by Homer, Virgil and Tasso. It could be argued that *Ad Salsillum* illustrates this versatility in practice through

---

[30] For the occurrence of the river motif in Salzilli's first Italian sonnet, see 94 below.

[31] E.g. Cicero, *Tusc.* 3.9: *membrum tumidum ac turgidum*. Cf. Hugo Grotius, *Anapaesti in Morbum Fratris*, who uses the adjective to describe mental illhealth: *pellat tumidos/pectoris aestus, et vesanos/animi fluctus, sopor ut reddat/mite serenum*. (*Poemata Collecta* [Leiden, 1617], 262, lines 7-10).

[32] Milton's phrase *salsa ... regna* finds a parallel in an Italian poem addressed to Jacopo Gaddi by the Florentine academician Francesco Rovai. At *Poesie di Francesco Rovai*, 293, stanza 5, Rovai states: "Potea su'l dorso all' Ocean profondo/Alzar vele novelle e nuovi legni,/potea ne salsi regni/porto trovar dov'è più cupo il fondo./In piane ime campage/Erger motagne e i più superbi calli/sforzar dell' Alpi ad abbassarsi in valli." Included in Fabricius, *Conspectus*, 291-295. On Rovai and his possible links with Milton, see 61-71 above.

its echoing of phrases and passages from Greek, Latin and possibly Italian literature.[33]

The *laurea Graeca* can be seen at certain stages in the poem, perhaps most obviously, in the specific use of Greek names, such as the allusion to lyric poetry in the tradition of Alcaeus and Sappho (*Lesbium ... melos* [22]), and the reference to Hebe (23) and Paean (25). More implicitly, the description of the violent wind (11-13) may, as Freeman suggests,[34] echo Hesiod's account of the violently panting Typhoeus in *Theogony* 826ff., and Pindar's elaboration of the same in *Pythian* 1. While links are of a rather tenuous nature, the possibility does exist that the contrast between a bellowing obstructing wind (the act of Typhoeus) and the love of poetry (the hymn which Phoebus inspires in Aetna) underlies Milton's poem, in which a strong wind almost impeded his journey to Italy in his lofty aim of enhancing his love of poetry and Italian culture. Moreover the wind finds a parallel in the *profunda bilis* (19) which breathes through (*spirat* [20]) the sick Salzilli and has no respect for the fact that he is a skilful poet (17-22). Less obvious is the possible Greek background to the *decentes ... suras* attributed to Deiopea (4). This may recall the comely ankles (καλλίσφυρον ... Ἥβην) of Hebe in *Odyssey* 11. 603. Furthermore in depicting Deiopea dancing before Juno's couch, Milton may have invented a function which parallels Hebe as cup-bearer to Jupiter.[35]

The *laurea Latina* of Salzilli's encomium is also evident in Milton's poem, which contains many allusions to themes and *topoi* from classical Latin literature. The opening line, describing the scazontic meter — particularly apt for the subject since the lameness of the Muse[36] parallels the sickness of the poet, Salzilli (*O Musa gressum quae volens trahis claudum* [1]) — may recall Ovid's description in *Remedia Amoris* 377-378: *liber in adversos hostes stringatur iambus,/seu celer, extremum seu trahat ille pedem*. But, in contrast to the ill addressee, the Vulcan-like Muse of the poem rejoices in her limping gait (*Vulcanioque tarda gaudes*

---

[33] Freeman, "Milton's Roman Connection," 96, states: "By alluding to so many Greek, Latin, and modern Italian practices, Milton thus politely justifies Salzilli's epigram as well as his own accomplishment."

[34] Freeman, "Milton's Roman Connection," 94.

[35] As suggested by Bush, *Variorum*, 264.

[36] For a discussion of the metrics of the poem, see S.M. Oberhelman and J. Mulryan, "Milton's use of classical meters in the *Sylvarum Liber*," *MP* 81 (1983), 131-145, at 137-138.

incessu [2]).[37] The fusion of the female *Musa* with the limping male deity
Vulcan may owe something to *Aeneid* 8, where as Vulcan rouses himself
from sleep to approach his forge Virgil, in a very homely simile, compares
him to a woman (*femina*) tending to her household chores.[38] And Milton
seems to pick up other themes and ideas from Virgil's *Aeneid*. Thus the
reference to Deiopea dancing before Juno's couch (*cum decentes flava
Deiope suras/alternat aureum ante Iunonis lectum* [4-5]) may recall a
scene from *Aeneid* 1, where Juno bribes Aeolus to raise a storm by
offering Deiopea as a reward.[39] The Virgilian context is appropriate since
Milton seems to envisage himself as another Aeneas, leaving his own
"nest" (*suum linquens nidum* [10]), and although differing from Virgil's
hero in that he has evaded stormy weather (*pessimus ... ventorum* [11]),
resembling him in that he too has reached Italy (*venit feraces Itali soli ad
glebas* [14]). Possible echoes of the *Aeneid* continue in the course of the
poem. Milton mentions Faunus (27) and Evander (28).[40] Faunus is alluded
to several times in *Aeneid* 7,[41] while Evander plays an important role in
book 8.[42] Finally, the description of the calming of the Tiber in lines 36-41
may echo in a general sense Virgil's account in *Aeneid* 8.[43] Milton's lines
however are much more closely related to Horace, *Odes* 1.2. 13-20,
describing the swelling of the Tiber:

> vidimus flavum Tiberim retortis
> litore Etrusco violenter undis
> ire deiectum monumenta regis
>   templaque Vestae;
> Iliae dum se nimium querenti
> iactat ultorem, vagus et sinistra
> labitur ripa Iove non probante u-
>   xorius amnis.[44]

---

[37] Cf. *Elegia Septima* 81-82; *Naturam non Pati Senium*, 23-24; *Paradise Lost* 1. 740-
746.

[38] Virgil, *Aeneid* 8. 408-415.

[39] Virgil, *Aeneid* 1. 71-73.

[40] *Ad Sals.* 27-28: *Querceta Fauni vosque rore vinoso/colles benigni, mitis Evandri
sedes...*

[41] Virgil, *Aeneid* 7. 47-49; 7. 81-82 etc.

[42] Virgil, *Aeneid* 8. 152ff. See also 7.43, 11.139.

[43] Virgil, *Aeneid* 8. 86-89: *Thybris ea fluvium, quam longa est, nocte tumentem/
leniit, et tacita refluens ita substitit unda,/mitis ut in morem stagni placidaeque
paludis/sterneret aequor aquis, remo ut luctamen abesset.*

[44] For an interesting adaptation of these lines in a Cambridge context, cf. Andrew
Marvell, *Ad Regem Carolum Parodia*, 12-16: *vidimus Chamum fluvium retortis/litore*

[We have seen the yellow Tiber, his waves hurled violently back from his Tuscan bank, advance to lay low the king's monument and Vesta's shrine, while he boasts that he is the avenger of Ilia's importunate complaints, and over his left bank glides far and wide, without the approval of Jupiter — a river too devoted to his wife.]

Milton inverts Horace, where the Tiber had turned against his own city, invading the *monumenta regis*. Such will not be the case in Salzilli's Rome (*nec in sepulchris ibit obsessum reges* [38]). Where Horace had described the Tiber flooding on the left bank (*vagus et sinistra/labitur ripa*), Milton states that this will not occur (*nec ... ibit .../ nimium sinistro laxus irruens loro* [38-39]). An Horatian ill-omen of a river turning against its own city, a gross perversion of the natural order of events, hinting, as Quinn suggests, "at the misguided division of Roman against Roman,"[45] has now been transformed into a Miltonic symbol of harmony, reconciliation and calm. And this is appropriate in that it thereby parallels the hoped-for physical calming of Salzilli's ailments so graphically described in lines 19-20. Milton also seems to invert the structural progression of Horace's ode from the flooding river (one of many ill-omens) to a prayer addressed to a series of deities that they come to the help of Rome. The speaker of Horace's poem asks: *quem vocet divum populus ruentis/imperi rebus?* (25-26), a question which he tries to answer by invoking Apollo (32), Venus (*Erycina ridens* [33]) or Mars (*almae/filius Maiae* [42-43]). He then considers the possibility that perhaps the god is already here, having assumed the human form of Augustus (*sive mutata iuvenem figura* [41]), who should thus delay his return to the world of the divine and by his presence assist the people of Rome (*serus in caelum redeas diuque/laetus intersis populo Quirini* [45-46]). Milton *precedes* his description of the calming of the Tiber with an invocation to a series of deities to come to the assistance of a private rather than a public need; a physical rather than a moral illness: Salus (23),[46] Phoebus, and then, as in Horace, an alternative form of a god: *sive tu magis Paean/libenter audis* (25-26).

The echo of Horace at this point is particularly appropriate given Milton's description of Salzilli at lines 21-22: his illness is all the more outrageous in that it has failed to show any respect for the fact that he is

---

a dextro violenter undis/ire plorantem monumenta pestis,/templaque clausa. Text: *Andrew Marvell: The Complete Poems*, ed. Elizabeth Story Donno (Penguin, 1996), 199.

[45] Quinn, ed., *Horace: The Odes*, 122.

[46] On Milton's poem vis-à-vis the genre of the hymn to Health (Hygeia/Salus), see Revard, *Milton and the Tangles of Neaera's Hair*, 224-226.

cultus and that upon his Roman lips he founds *Lesbium melos*: *Nec id pepercit impia quod tu Romano/tam cultus ore Lesbium condis melos* (21-22). Salzilli is presented here in terms which clearly recall Horace. This seems to work on two levels: 1) in the use of the adjective *Lesbium* to refer to Greek lyric poetry in the tradition of Alcaeus and Sappho of Lesbos; 2) in the idea of "nationalising" that poetry to make it sound upon Roman lips. In *Odes* 1.1.34 Horace had used the phrase *Lesboum ... barbiton* (the lyre of Lesbos) to describe the instrument of his own lyric poetry, and in so doing had presented himself as following Sappho and Alcaeus of Lesbos. Similarly in *Odes* 1.32.4-5, in stating that he was planning Latin verse in the manner of Alcaeus, Horace used the phrase *Lesbio ... civi* to describe the latter.[47] That contrast between the Greek lyric poet (*Lesbio ... civi*) and the Latin song (*Latinum carmen*) occurs elsewhere in Horace. For example, in *Epistles* 1 he had issued the great boast that he was the first to show the iambic rhythms of Paros to Latium,[48] using the meter and spirit of Archilochus: although he is a *Latinus*, he has made Alcaeus known — Alcaeus who was spoken before on "no other lips" (*hunc ego, non alio dictum prius ore, Latinus/vulgavi fidicen* [*Ep.* 1.19.32-33]). Horace's *non alio ore* becomes in *Ad Salsillum* the *Romano ... ore* (21-22) of Salzilli, a phrase which, Masson suggests, signifies Italian rather than Latin verse, since it was as an Italian poet that Salzilli had achieved fame in Rome.[49] In the absence of any Latin poems by Salzilli (with the exception of the distich in Milton's honor) it is difficult to argue the case, but perhaps the important point is that irrespective of the language (whether Latin or Italian), Salzilli, like Horace before him, has in a sense "nationalised" Greek lyric poetry upon "Roman" lips. Milton, whose own interest in Horace is attested by his translation of *Odes* 1.5,[50] sees Salzilli as following in the footsteps of the great lyric poet. It is interesting in this regard that Tomaso Stigliani in that letter to Salzilli noted above, when referring to his own apparent *otium* and failure to write to his friend, cites with colloquial ease a line of

---

[47] Horace, *Odes* 1.32.3-5: *age dic Latinum,/barbite, carmen,/Lesbio primum modulate civi*. Cf. Ovid, *Tr.* 3.7.20.

[48] Horace, *Epistles* 1. 19.23-24: *Parios ego primus iambos/ostendi Latio.*

[49] David Masson ed., *The Poetical Works of John Milton*, (London, 1874), III, 346.

[50] Carey, ed., *Milton: Complete Shorter Poems*, 99, suggests a date of c. 1629. However, other dates proposed range from 1626 to 1655.

Horace.[51] This casual inclusion of an Horatian motto in a letter to Salzilli conveys perhaps its author's expectation that his addressee would pick it up quite easily. It is indeed very probable that Salzilli knew his Horace exceptionally well. This is evident from a reading of his Italian sonnets included in the *Fantastici* volume, some of which are Horatian not only in spirit, but also in language, thus validating the Miltonic viewpoint of his Italian friend and poet as in effect a second Horace, one who *Romano/tam cultus ore Lesbium condis melos* (21-22). On a general level, *Ad Salsillum* seems to invoke an important Horatian dictum, namely, poetry as a monument impervious to the destructive powers of wind and rain. Freeman is probably correct[52] in reading into Milton's choice of the adjective *impotens* (to describe the north wind, the *pessimus ... ventorum*), an echo (although I would term it an inversion) of the famous *Ode* 3.30 of Horace: *exegi monumentum ...*[53] And in support of this possible Horatian subtext is perhaps the fact that, as noted above, the closing lines of Milton's poem actually invert *Odes* 1.2.13-20, lines which had described the ravaging forces of the Tiber upon "monuments" (*ire deiectum monumenta regis* [15]), albeit literal rather than figurative.[54]

Milton's obvious Horatian echoes in *Ad Salsillum* can be seen as a sincere compliment to his addressee. The implication of this is that if Milton, in Salzilli's tribute, can surpass Homer, Virgil and Tasso, then perhaps Salzilli in Milton's poem can surpass Horace. It seems likely moreover that Milton is acknowledging the Horatian tone and spirit of some of Salzilli's own Italian compositions. One example will serve as an illustration. Salzilli's first sonnet in the *Fantastici* volume[55] establishes what is in essence an Horatian contrast between poetry and other obsessive occupations. Entitled "S'antepone la dignità della Poesia all' utile de gli altri studi," the sonnet censures the "alma vil" ("vile soul") which follows gold, and pursues the misleading tracks of Aeculapius and of Paean ("Calchi pur' alma vil, serva de l'oro,/D' Esculapio, e Peon l'orme fallaci" [1-2]). Salzilli sets up a contrast between the vocations of

---

[51] Tomaso Stigliani, *Lettere*, 249: "le quali quando non son di negozio, son sempre oziose e superflue, così faccio io coi miei, e così ho caro che quegli facciano con me, dicendo con Orazio *Hanc veniam petimusque damusque vicissim.*"

[52] Freeman, "Milton's Roman Connection," 96.

[53] Horace, *Odes* 3.30. 1-5: *Exegi monumentum aere perennius/regalique situ pyramidum altius,/quod non imber edax, non Aquilo impotens/possit diruere aut innumerabilis/ annorum series et fuga temporum ...*

[54] Surprisingly, Freeman does not adduce Milton's *monumenta* (15) in support of his argument that *impotens* recalls Horace's famous *exegi monumentum* ode (3.30).

[55] *Fantastici*, 148.

medicine and poetry, betraying an Horatian detachment from materialistic pursuits and a sense of pride in the poet who is elevated from the masses. Medicine is no more than legacy-hunting. Whereas the mad populace causes the forum to resound with tumultuous noise, the poet in virtue of his noble desire is raised to the heights of mount Pindus where he can reap the laurel of glory and escape the ravaging forces of Time, that tributary to Lethe which sweeps away other men's spoils.[56] The progression of the sonnet, from a description of an obsessive occupation (medicine), to the speaker's rejection of such, and by contrast, his elevation to a place where he can reap metaphorical rewards (especially the laurel), seems to recall Horace, *Odes* 1.1 (like Salzilli's sonnet, the first poem in a series). Horace's poem begins by outlining the vain obsessions of other men (chariot-racing, politics, business, farming, overseas trade, leisure, war, hunting), and proceeds to highlight the speaker's desire to achieve the heights of fame, with a statement of metaphorical rewards, including ivy-garlands, symbolising his recognition as bard. If he can be ranked among the great lyric poets, then he will strike the very stars with his head.[57] As Quinn comments on the decisive line 23 of Horace's poem, "Horace likes introducing himself at a key point in the rhetorical structure of an Ode."[58] Similarly, it is not until the sestet of his sonnet that Salzilli introduces himself.

Finally, it may also be possible to observe the *laurea Hetrusca* in Milton's poem. Freeman outlines some possible points of contact between *Ad Salsillum* and Salzilli's own Italian poems in the *Fantastici* volume.[59] Some of these are tenuous, as, for example, the fact that "both men speak to Phoebus Apollo" and the statement that Milton's poem "politely incorporates certain ideas that Milton knew were very important to his Roman friend."[60] But there are some more striking parallels: for example,

---

[56] *Fantastici*, 148, lines 9-14: "Ch'io d' altre nerci avaro, ergo sublimo/Nobil desire a le più eccelse mete,/Per poggiarne di Pindo a l'erte cime./Qui fecondo di gloria Allor si miete,/E qui de' nomi altrui le spoglie opime/Non porta il Tempo tributario a Lete."

[57] Horace, *Odes* 1.1. 29-36: *Me doctarum hederae praemia frontium/dis miscent superis; me gelidum nemus/Nympharumque leves cum Satyris chori/secernunt populo, si neque tibias/Euterpe cohibet nec Polyhymnia/Lesboum refugit tendere barbiton;/quodsi me lyricis vatibus inseres,/sublimi feriam sidera vertice.* The theme recurs at *Odes* 4.3, although the tone is very different. Horace emphasises that since the poet is chosen at birth by the Muse, no other career (boxing, charioteering, soldiering) is open to him.

[58] Quinn, ed., *Horace: The Odes*, 120.

[59] Freeman, "Milton's Roman Connection," 97-100.

[60] Freeman, "Milton's Roman Connection," 99.

Freeman's suggestion that perhaps the reference to Paean in *Ad Sal.* 24-26,[61] the sole occurrence of this proper noun in Milton, may show the influence of the opening lines of that first sonnet discussed above: "Calchi ... D'Esculapio, e Peon l'orme fallaci" (1-2).[62] Also the river-motif of *Ad Salsillum* (and indeed of Salzilli's Italian tribute) may assume additional significance in view of its occurrence in Salzilli's first Italian sonnet, whereby the poet in acquiring the laurel of immortality escapes Tempo, the tributary to Lethe ("qui fecondo di gloria allor si miete,/e qui de' nomi altrui le spoglie opime/non porta il Tempo tributario a Lete").[63] Two further links between Salzilli's Italian poems and *Ad Salsillum* may be added: 1) Milton's self-description as an *alumnus ille Londini Milto* in line 1 (with the etymological link between *alumnus* and *alo-alere*, and the juxtaposition with a capital city [London] as agent of the nurturing) may draw upon the opening of Salzilli's sonnet *Al Signor Giacomon* ("Già veggio, *altrice* gloriosa, in seno/*nutrir Roma* a l'insubria un germe altero").[64] 2) Milton's description of, and implied escape from, a virtual English tempest (an exaggerated description of the cold northern climate), and subsequent arrival in a calm haven (*Ad Sals.* 10-16) finds a general parallel in Salzilli's *La Poesia Trionfante*: addressing Poetry, Salzilli praises her as a safe haven in the storms of human life ("Per le naufraghe vie/de l'humane procelle/Tu sarai calma a le tempeste mie"),[65] and proceeds to state that he longs not for Castor or Pollux as guides, but only for the light of poetry ("Di Castore, e Polluce/non vagheggio le stelle,/se scorta m'è la tua gradita luce").[66] And perhaps this is the subtext of *Ad Salsillum*. For Milton has escaped the inclement weather of England, and has followed his own guiding light, travelling to the fertile climes of Italy (*animi causa*). In Italy and perhaps even in Salzilli himself is epitomised that *Poesia Trionfante*, which by the end of *Ad Salsillum* celebrates a triumph of her own by validating that *monumentum*, that edifice of eternity, through subtle echo and inversion of Horace.

The most striking parallel between *Ad Salsillum* and Salzilli's Italian poetry, although not developed by Freeman, is provided by a sonnet entitled "Ricco Mercante ucciso in duello, per volersi vendicar

[61] *Ad Sals.*, 24-26: *Tuque Phoebe morborum terror/Pythone caeso, sive tu magis Paean/Libenter audis ...*

[62] Freeman, "Milton's Roman Connection," 99.

[63] *Fantastici*, 148.

[64] *Fantastici*, 154.

[65] *Fantastici* 157.

[66] *Fantastici*, 157.

d'una parola ingiuriosa."[67] The *argumentum* of the poem is rather odd: the speaker, a merchant, recalls the sea voyages which he had to endure as a beggar until a calm wind brought him to his native land as a rich man. Some insult which he received led him to participate in a duel, which in turn brought about his death:

> D'Humano fasto a le grandezze intento,
>> Lunga stagion per l'Oceano infido
>> Mendico errai, fin ch'al bramato lido
>> Ricco m'addusse poi tranquillo vento.
> Hor mentre qui nel cumulato Argento
>> D'un' eterno gioir la speme affido,
>> Ecco, ò folle pensier, nel patrio nido,
>> Di propria voglia al mio morir consento.
> D'acerbo detto un momentaneo scorno
>> Vendicar volli, e la nemica sorte
>> Spese del viver mio l'ultimo giorno.
> Flutti, e scogli nel Mar con petto forte
>> Sostengo, e poscia di lontan ritorno,
>> Da un falso accento a mendicar la Morte.

> [Intent on the grandeur of human pomp, I wandered as a beggar for a long time across the treacherous ocean until a tranquil wind brought me as a rich man to the shore for which I had yearned. Now while I was trusting in the hope of eternal joy in the money I had made, behold, o foolish thought, in my native nest, I of my own free will agreed to my death. I wanted to avenge the temporary shame of a harsh word, but hostile Fate extinguished the last day of my life:
>> With a strong breast I endured waves and rocks in the sea, and then I returned from far away to beg for Death in a false tone of voice.]

The merchant, "intent on the grandeur of human pomp," was assisted by a tranquil wind ("tranquillo vento") which brought him ashore. He describes the land as his "native nest" ("nel patrio nido"). Milton's situation is exactly the reverse.[68] He too has travelled, but he has *left* his native land — his "nest" (*qui suum linquens nidum* [10]) in order to see the cities and learned youth of Italy. He describes moreover a wind which, far from being "tranquil" and of assistance to the traveller, is in fact a *pessimus ... ventorum* (11), which almost proved an obstruction to his journey:

---

[67] *Fantastici*, 155.

[68] Freeman, "Milton's Roman Connection," 100, who does not quote the poem, briefly notes some parallels: "The word 'nest' ('nido') unites this odd poem to *Ad Salsillum*: Milton speaks of leaving his *nidum*, enduring fierce (not 'quiet') winds and imploring Paean, enemy of Death, to heal his friend."

diebus hisce qui suum linquens nidum
polique tractum, (pessimus ubi ventorum,
insanientis impotensque pulmonis
pernix anhela sub Iove exercet flabra) (10-13)

[[Milton], who recently left his own nest and region of the heavens
(where the worst of winds, powerless to control its madly heaving
lungs, swiftly puffs its panting blasts beneath the sky.]

But the riches that Milton can receive upon arrival at *his*, as it were,
"bramato lido," — the *feraces Itali soli ... glebas* (14) — are spiritual and
intellectual rather than the material wealth enjoyed by Salzilli's rich man
("ricco" [4]). In Salzilli, the "nido" is closely associated with death, as the
speaker asserts "nel patrio nido,/Di propria voglia al mio morir consento"
(7-8) and reiterates the theme in the last line " ... a mendicar la Morte."
Milton inverts this. The fact that he is leaving his "nest" is balanced by the
dismissal of death as he invokes *Salus* (23) and Phoebus/Paean (24-25),
restorers of life and opponents of death. Thus instead of a merchant
begging for death, Milton is virtually "begging" for a life as he prays for
the speedy recovery of Salzilli:

> ... o Salus, Hebes
> germana, tuque Phoebe morborum terror
> Pythone caeso, sive tu magis Paean
> libenter audis, hic tuus sacerdos est![69]
> Querceta Fauni, vosque rore vinoso
> colles benigni, mitis Evandri sedes,
> siquid salubre vallibus frondet vestris,
> levamen aegro ferte certatim vati. (23-30)

[O sweet gift of the gods, o Health, sister of Hebe, and you, Phoebus
— or whether you more willingly attend under the name of Paean —,
terror of diseases ever since your slaughter of Python, this man is your
priest! Oak-groves of Faunus, and you, hills abundant in the dew of
grapes, abode of the gentle Evander, if any health-giving plant blooms
in your valleys, bring it eagerly to your sick bard.]

Indeed the situation is quite the reverse of Salzilli's poem. Unlike the
merchant who has received an insult and is seeking vengeance ("per
volersi vendicar d'una parola ingiuriosa"), Milton has received words of
praise — the encomium itself (described in lines 7-8) — and wishes to

---

[69] Cf. Hugo Grotius, *Poemata Collecta* (Leiden, 1617), 261, *Anapaesti in Morbum
Fratris*, lines 23-26: ... *si forte tamen,/si respiciat nos alma Salus,/et placato numine
Paean/aegrum melius servet alumnum.*

return a compliment. Instead of bringing death upon himself by avenging "un momentaneo scorno," Milton praises Salzilli and wishes him every good fortune (*tibi optat idem hic fausta multa Salsille* [17]).

Milton in replying to Salzilli's Latin distich inverts features of the tribute itself and, moreover, through subtle echoes of Greek, Latin and Italian literature, seems to justify the claim that he is worthy of the *triplex ... laurea*. In short, *Ad Salsillum* moves beyond its ostensible purpose as a get-well wish for an Italian friend and academician to constitute a highly skilful reply to a commendatory poem.

On a more general level, it is tempting to consider Milton's poem in relation to seicento academic practices. One of the characteristic features of Italian academies was the emphasis on wordplay. This manifests itself on a variety of levels. As noted in chapter 2, members of the Florentine Apatisti even invented anagrams of their own names, anagrams by which they were known in the academy and under which their works were frequently published. Is it possible that the element of wordplay in *Ad Salsillum* (and indeed in *Mansus*) owes something to this tendency and perhaps to other more specific etymological practices of Italian academies? One such practice worth mentioning is an exercise entitled "lingua ionadattica" or "lingua fagiana." As Nardo notes, this was a game, probably invented by a castrato (valet to a prominent cardinal), in which words with similar first syllables were exchanged."[70] Could this help to explain the predominance in this 41-line poem of words beginning with *sal-*? It might of course be argued that this is inevitable in view of the name of the poem's addressee (hence *Salsillo* [6], *Salsille* [17]), but it is tempting to wonder if there is not some reflection of such academic wordplay in the occurrence of **salus** (23), **salubre** (29) and **salsa** (41).[71] Is there also a possible word wrap in lines 4-5: suras/ **alt**ernat, thereby resulting in an ingeniously concealed English translation of the first syllable of the addressee's name? Through emphasis upon *sal-* words and also through the phrase *salsa regna* (41), the poem could indeed be seen to contain an implicit cooking metaphor, amplified perhaps in the use of the culinary verb *condere* to describe Salzilli's own poetic practices (*tam*

---

[70] Nardo, "Academic Interludes," 213.

[71] The same practice may even underlie the predominance of "dis"- words in *Paradise Lost* 9. 6-9: " ... foul *dis*trust, and breach/*dis*loyal on the part of Man, revolt,/and *dis*obedience: On the part of Heaven/now alienated, *dis*tance and *dis*taste." See Christopher Ricks, *Milton's Grand Style* (Oxford, 1963), 69-72; Neil Forsyth, "Of Man's First Dis," Di Cesare, 345-369, neither of whom however relates the passage to Italian academic practice.

cultus ore Lesbium condis melos [22]).[72] And if Milton seems to play on the first syllable of his addressee's name, it is possible that he plays also on its final two syllables in such phrases as *sentis illud* (3), *ille* (8), *alumnus ille* (9) and *sic ille* (31). Perhaps then Milton's poem demonstrates a wit (*sal*) of its own through employing the sort of etymological play so beloved of that academic world in which he participated.

---

[72] If so, then Milton's possible pun finds a parallel in a later work: the volume celebrating members of the Venetian academy of the Incogniti: *Le Glorie*, 66, *s.v.* Anton Giulio Brignole Sale Genovese: <u>*SAL*</u> *erit insulsum, salibus nisi* <u>*condiat*</u> *illud/hic Ligur, ex ipso qui SALE nomen habet.* Cf. in a general sense Milton's letter to Charles Diodati (*CM* 12, 22): *Nae ipsum te nuper Salutis condum promum esse factum oportet, ita totum Salubritatis penum dilapidas*; cf. also *Prolusion* VI. See in general, Roslyn Richek, "Thomas Randolph's Salting (1627): its text, and John Milton's Sixth *Prolusion* as Another Salting," *ELR* 12 (1982), 102-131.

CHAPTER 6

"Voice and Verse"
Leonora Baroni, Milton, and Italian *Accademici*

Just as *Ad Salsillum* suggests Milton's links with an academy of Rome, his friendship with one of its members, and his knowledge of that member's Italian poetry, so his epigrams in praise of the soprano Leonora Baroni can be seen to mirror in a variety of ways the much wider context of the seicento Italian academy and, more precisely, an encomiastic trend in vogue in Rome in the late 1630s.

Milton's three Latin epigrams in praise of Leonora differ from *Ad Salsillum* (and indeed *Mansus*) in that they were not composed as a tribute which he had received. On the contrary, Milton, in acknowledgement of the outstanding quality of Leonora's singing, takes the initiative and conveys his admiration by composing poems in her honor. In so doing, he seems to take his place among many academicians of Italian and other nationalities who proclaimed this diva in an anthology entitled *Applausi Poetici Alle Glorie della Signora Leonora Baroni* compiled by Vincenzo Costazuti and published at Rome in 1639. Milton's poems are not included in the volume, and it is probably unwise to assume, with Byard, that they were actually intended to be included.[1] It is highly probable nonetheless that the composition of such reflects his reaction to, if not his participation in, an essentially academic literary trend current at the time.

What is indisputable is that this Leonora, daughter of the famed Adriana Baroni,[2] possessed an outstanding vocal talent. She was also an extremely polished instrumentalist. She would sing to the accompaniment of her mother (on *lira*) and sister (on harp), but frequently she accompanied herself on theorbo, harp or viol. She was also gifted

---

[1] Thus Margaret Byard in an otherwise excellent discussion in "Adventurous Song: Milton and the Music of Rome," Di Cesare, 305-328 at 322-323, refers to "the three Latin epigrams he wrote and intended for a volume of poetry dedicated to her."

[2] See Alessandro Ademollo, *La Bell' Adriana ed Altre Virtuose del Suo Tempo alla Corte de Mantova* (Citta di Castello: Lapi, 1888).

intellectually as she was the composer of over thirty arias.[3] It is not certain on which of his two visits to Rome Milton actually heard Leonora sing. The reference to Tasso's madness in his second epigram may favor the second visit. After his first visit to Rome Milton travelled to Naples, where he met Manso, the patron of Tasso.[4] And Manso's *Vita* of Tasso (1621) had indeed promulgated the story of Tasso's madness as a consequence of his love for a certain Leonora. It was after his sojourn in Naples that Milton made his return visit to Rome. Could the Tasso reference thus reflect conversations which he had held with Manso on the subject, or even suggest his reading of Manso's *Vita*?[5] What music Leonora performed is also unknown.[6] As women were not permitted to participate in religious celebrations,[7] Milton must have heard her at a private concert in Rome, perhaps in the Baroni house itself, perhaps at one of the many sumptuous musical entertainments overseen by Cardinal Francesco Barberini. It is surely not without significance that the Cardinal would own a personal copy of the Leonora *Applausi*.[8] And such private musical gatherings, irrespective of their location, did in fact constitute an academy in microcosm. As Hammond states:

> Cardinal Francesco Barberini's private musical establishment was most conspicuously employed for a number of entertainments in the 1630s described in his financial records as accademie, a term applied in seventeenth century Rome to almost any organised gathering, as Doni referred to his viol consort as "l'académie de mes violes." Musical academies, often involving the finest musicians in Rome, were presented in private houses such as those of the Baroni family and Luigi Rossi.[9]

---

[3] See Frederick Hammond, *Music and Spectacle in Baroque Rome: Barberini Patronage Under Urban VIII* (London, 1994), 86.

[4] See 118 below.

[5] Cf. 179-184 below.

[6] For a useful study of the musical context of Milton's visit to Rome, see Byard, "Adventurous Song," *passim*.

[7] See Alessandro Ademollo, *I Teatri di Roma nel Secolo Decimo-settimo* (Rome, 1888), 25; J. S. Smart, "Milton in Rome," *MLR* 8 (1913), 91-92; G.L. Finney, "Chorus in Samson Agonistes," *PMLA* 58 (1943), 649-664 at 658.

[8] Cardinal Barberini's copy is Biblioteca Apostolica Vaticana Stamp. Barb. JJJ. VI. 67. See Hammond, *Music and Spectacle*, 86, 302.

[9] Hammond, *Music and Spectacle*, 103.

It is known moreover that the Baroni household received foreigners hospitably. It was there, for instance, that his Roman debut was made by the French viola da gambist André Maugars,[10] who by a felicitous coincidence heard Leonora sing during the precise years of Milton's sojourn (1638-1639). His extravagant testimony to her abilities is as follows:

> elle l'entend parfaitement bien, voire mesme qu'elle y compose: ce qui fait qu'elle possède absolument ce quelle chante, et qu'elle prononce et exprime parfaitement bien le sens des paroles ... Elle chante ... avec une douce gravité. Sa voix est d'une haute estendüe, juste, sonore, harmonieuse ... [11]

> [She understands [music] perfectly well, and even composes. All of this means that she has absolute control over what she sings, and that she pronounces and expresses the sense of the words perfectly ... She sings with ... gentle seriousness. Her voice is of high range, accurate, sonorous, harmonious ...][12]

Maugars proceeds to convey her ability to transport the listener to the realms of the divine. Thus her music

> me surprit si fort les sens et me porta dans un tel ravissement, que j'oubliay ma condition mortelle, et creuz estre desia parmy les anges, jouyssant des contentemens des bienheureux. [13]

> [had such an overwhelming effect on me and transported me into such ecstasy that I forgot my mortal condition and thought that I was already among the angels, enjoying the pleasures of the blessed.][14]

The words might just as easily have been Milton's. Byard's analysis of the musical context of Rome in the late 1630s suggests among other things that Leonora's performance would have given Milton "probably for the first time, an opportunity to hear a talented woman singing with

---

[10] Hammond, *Music and Spectacle*, 86, 302.

[11] André Maugars, *Response Faite à un Curieux sur le Sentiment de la Musique d'Italie, Escrite à Rome le Premier Octobre 1639*, ed. Ernest Thoinan (Paris, 1865), 37.

[12] tr. Walter H. Bishop, "Maugars' Response Faite a un Curieux sur le Sentiment de la Musique d'Italie," *Journal of the Viola da Gamba Society of America* 8 (1971), 5-17 at 13.

[13] Maugars, *Response*, 37-38.

[14] Bishop, "Maugars' Response," 13.

professional skill and technique."[15] That may indeed be a further contributory factor to the elaborately encomiastic nature of his epigrams.

But there is another hitherto unnoticed possible venue where Milton may have heard Leonora sing: that of the highly reputable Accademia degli Umoristi, of which Leonora was actually a member: more accurately, she was its only female member.[16] The Umoristi met in the house of Paolo Mancini on the Corso. There no doubt Leonora enthralled her fellow-academicians with her music and intelligence. Among the elite membership of this academy were numbered no fewer than four cardinals: Francesco Barberini himself, his brother Antonio Barberini, together with Cardinals Montalto and Mazari. It also included the celebrated musicologist Giovanni Battista Doni. Among the contributors to the Leonora *Applausi* is a further Umoristi member: Lelio Guidiccioni.[17] This combination of factors surely raises the tantalising possibility that Milton during either or both of his sojourns in Rome participated in the life of its foremost academy. What is particularly striking is the fact that the Umoristi hospitably entertained foreign visitors to Rome.[18] We can catch a telling glimpse of its character and setting from the description of his reception there by John Evelyn in 1645, only six years after Milton's visit:

17 Feb 1645

> The 17, I was invited (after dinner) to the Academie of the Humorists, kept in a spacious Hall, belonging to Signor Mancini, where the Witts of the Towne meete on certaine daies, to recite poems, & prevaricate on severall Subjects &c: The first that Speakes is cal'd the Lord, & stands in an eminent place, & then the rest of the virtuosi recite in order: by these ingenious Exercises besides the learn'd discourses, is the purity of the Italian Tongue daily improv'd: This roome is hung round, with enumerable devises or Emblems all relating to something of *humidum* with Motos under them: Several other Academies there are of this nature, bearing the like fantastical titles. It is in this Accademie of the Humorists where they have the Picture of Guarini the famous Author of Pastor fido, once of this Society:
>
> Over against this lives Hippolito Vitelesco the greate Statue Colector, and he has a vast store of them & of the most esteem'd in

[15] Byard, "Adventurous song," 322.

[16] Hammond, *Music and Spectacle*, 86.

[17] Guidiccioni's Latin encomium of Leonora occurs at *Applausi*, 196: *Parcite Romulei LEONORAM extollere Cygni/Ipsa suis Siren laudibus una satis./Nam Siren voce haec, labiis Pitho, Aonis arte,/Fronte Charis, Hebe est ambrosia, igne Venus.*)

[18] Arthos, *Italian Cities*, 90.

Rome to an incredible value [and his action, as a Comedy:] but the best
part of the day we spent in hearing the Academic exercises.[19]

Again, the description might perhaps just as easily have been Milton's.
Indeed, as has been noted elsewhere, Milton's first-hand observation of,
and participation in, certain Italian practices (academic and otherwise)
may have been just as influential as literary analogues. It seems difficult to
believe, for example, that he was actually unaware of the academic vogue
of Leonora encomia and that he did not see in manuscript or hear in
recitation some of the tributes which were to be included in the 1639
volume of *Applausi*. These tributes may have been circulating in Rome
during either or both of his sojourns in that city, and some of them may
even have made their debut in an academic context. It is evident moreover
that Milton had already made the acquaintance of at least one such
encomiast. Among the tributes included in the Leonora volume is a Latin
poem by the academician Lucas Holstenius, the Vatican Librarian,[20] who
actually conducted Milton around the Library, showed him manuscripts,
and presented him with a copy of one of his own works: the *Demophili
Democratis et Secundi Veterum Philosophorum Sententiae Morales*
(Rome, 1638).[21] This present, a bilingual edition of the axioms of the later
Pythagoreans, is important evidence of Holstenius actually familiarising
Milton with his own work. They surely shared and discussed many more
of his compositions, whether in manuscript or in printed form. The learned
librarian even asked Milton to undertake a scholarly errand on his behalf:
to transcribe parts of a Medicean codex for him at the Laurentian Library
in Florence[22] — an implicit tribute perhaps to his English guest's erudition.

---

[19] *The Diary of John Evelyn*, Vol. II, 364-365. Cf. the account of Richard Symond,
which states that the Umoristi met late every Sunday afternoon, (British Museum
Egerton MS 1635, ff. 47v-49) and describes the rooms and the order of the
proceedings (sometimes in Latin, sometimes in Italian).

[20] Holstenius's Latin tribute occurs at *Applausi*, 201-203.

[21] In his letter to Holstenius of 20/30 March 1639 (*CM* 12, 38-44, at 40), Milton
states: *mox in Musaeum comiter admisso, et conquisitissimam Librorum
supellectilem, et permultos insuper Manuscriptos auctores Graecos, tuis
Lucubrationibus exornatos, adspicere licuit quorum ... partim tua opera etiamnum
editi, passim ab eruditis avide accipiuntur; quorum et unius etiam duplici dono abs te
auctus dimittor*. For the identification, cf. Leo Miller, "Milton and Holstenius
Reconsidered," Di Cesare, 573-587, at 574.

[22] See Milton's letter to Holstenius (*CM* 12, 38-44, at 42), in which he states that he
has asked his Florentine friends about the possibility of examining the manuscript, the
transcription of which Holstenius had commissioned to him (*Iam illud vero quod mihi
negotium dedisse videbare de inspiciendo codice Mediceo sedulo ad amicos retuli ...*)
He has however been informed that in that particular library nothing may be copied

But perhaps just as importantly, it was Holstenius who introduced Milton to leading musical circles in Rome.[23] Furthermore, the broad network of acquaintances actively forged by Milton in the course of his Italian sojourn would lend support to the suggestion that he had read (or heard) some of the poems in Leonora's honor.[24]

---

except by prior permission. They have suggested that perhaps Holstenius may accomplish this task through commissioning Giovanni Battista Doni (who is now in Rome) but is daily expected in Florence.

[23] In the same letter Milton views the cordial reception he received from Cardinal Barberini at a musical entertainment as the consequence of Holstenius' recommendation. (*CM* 12, 40). J.S. Smart, "Milton in Rome," 91-92, points out that this musical entertainment was Rospigliosi's opera *Che Sofre, Speri* presented on 27 February 1639; G.L. Finney, "Chorus," 658, states that it could not have been here that Milton heard Leonora sing since women were not allowed to sing at the Palazzo Barberini. Hammond, *Music and Spectacle*, 236, describes the *Che soffre, speri* as the "most fully documented of Cardinal Barberini's operas," of which *argomenti* survive for both the 1637 and 1639 versions. This comedy was based on a story by Boccaccio. Its synopsis stated: "The principal intent of the comedy must be instruction together with delight" (Hammond, *Music and Spectacle*, 199). At 276 Hammond usefully summarizes its main contents as follows: "Carnival 1639; commedia in musica; Palazzo Barberini, inauguration of Barberini theatre; Francesco Barberini; text and addition of Fiera di Farfa by Rospigliosi; music by Virgilio Mazzocchi, additional music by Marco Marazzo." He proceeds (235-236) to quote the description of the seating accommodation on that occasion as recounted by the new Modenese resident Massimiliano Montecucceoli: "While I and many others were walking in a little cortile where Cardinal Antonio had told me to wait until he had seated the people of lesser importance in order to give me and those who were with me a better place, we saw him then enter the salone and almost immediately come out with someone whom he was pushing forward and bitterly threatening, and I heard him say in particular 'I'll teach you to be insolent' and then with his hand he hit him very hard with a stick that he held, five or six strokes. The one he hit was a young man of c. 25, of excellent manners and with a long habit of silk (i.e. an ecclesiastic). When I had entered, I saw Cardinal Barberini arrive in the salone; he went around from row to row with most civil manners, and with the greatest courtesy made everyone squeeze in as much as possible with the result that there was room for six hundred people more." (Cf. Ademollo, *I Teatri*, 30-31). In Milton's account in *DS* it is Francesco (the brother of Antonio) who greeted him. Cf. Campbell, *A Milton Chronology*, 65. Thus, according to Milton, it was Francesco Barberini who sought him out at the door, took him by the hand and escorted him inside to the performance: *Tum nec aliter crediderim quam quae tu de me verba feceris ad praestantissimum Cardin. Franc. Barberinum, iis factum esse, ut cum ille paucis post diebus ἀκρόαμα illud musicum magnificentia vere Romana publice exhiberet, ipse me tanta in turba quaesitum ad fores expectans, et pene manu prehensum persane honorifice intro admiserit.* (*CM* 12, 40).

[24] Campbell, *A Milton Chronology*, 64-65 perceptively notes: "there was a vogue for poems *ad Leonoram*, and JM's contribution to this genre was a gesture directed to his Italian acquaintances rather than the singer."

The *Applausi*, some 267 pages in length, contains poems in five languages. The majority are in Italian, others in Latin, Greek, Spanish and French — languages in which the polyglot Milton was undoubtedly fluent.[25] The volume as a whole is marked by the highly extravagant nature of the pieces, which praise not only Leonora's voice, but also her beauty, chastity and moral character.[26] Leonora is seen as a key force motivating and unifying the cosmos itself,[27] as a tenth muse and as an ideal image of beauty. The emphasis upon her beauty may be connected with the fact that some of the poems are in praise of a portrait of Leonora painted by a certain Don Fabio della Cornia.[28]

On a reading of Milton's epigrams, it might be remarked that differences are more noteworthy than similarities.[29] His poems are on the whole less extravagant, they do not mention her beauty or chastity and even when they do praise her singing, the emphasis is more on the effect of her song upon the listener than on the quality of her voice *per se*. There are nevertheless several parallels which, while not necessarily indicating *imitatio* on the part of Milton, do serve to create an interesting perspective from which to view his poems, illustrate some common reactions to the beauty of her voice, and highlight an important academic context.

One aspect of Milton's treatment which merits comparison with the poems of the *Applausi* is the association of Leonora's song with a divine presence. This is the major theme of his first epigram:

---

[25] In *Ad Patrem* (79-85) Milton mentions Latin, Greek, French, Italian and Hebrew among the languages which his father enabled him to acquire. Francini's encomium attributes to him knowledge of English, Spanish, French, Italian, Greek and Latin. See 40 above.

[26] See, for example, Berlingiero Gessi, who praises Leonora under the three titles: La Bellezza (*Applausi*, 31-38); L'Honesta (*Applausi*, 39-46); La Musica (*Applausi*, 47-54). On Leonora in general, see A. Ademollo, *La Leonora di Milton e di Clemente IX* (Milan, 1885); Eugene Schuyler, "Milton's Leonora," *Nation* 47 (18 October, 1888), 310-312; M. Allessandrini, "Una celebre cantatrice alla corte di Urbano VIII," *Scenario* 11 (April, 1942). 152ff; *The New Grove's Dictionary of Music and Musicians* (London, 1980), II, 171-172; *DBI* VI, 456-458, which contains a full bibliography.

[27] See, for example, *Applausi*, 3 (by an anonymous author).

[28] Some of the poems are entitled "Per lo Ritratto della Signora Leonora Baroni fatto dal Sig. D. Fabio della Cornia."

[29] See Ademollo, *La Leonora*, 10. Bush, *Variorum*, 148, states: "If he saw any of the poems that went into the *Applausi*, they do not seem to have left clear marks on his own."

Ad Leonoram Romae canentem
Angelus unicuique suus (sic credite gentes) [30]
  obtigit aethereis ales ab ordinibus.
Quid mirum, Leonora, tibi si gloria maior,[31]
  nam tua praesentem vox sonat ipsa Deum!
Aut Deus, aut vacui certe mens tertia caeli   5
  per tua secreto guttura serpit agens;
serpit agens, facilisque docet mortalia corda
  sensim immortali assuescere posse sono.
Quod si cuncta quidem Deus est, per cunctaque fusus,
  in te una loquitur, cetera mutus habet.   10

[To Leonora singing at Rome
Each person (believe this o peoples) has been allotted a winged angel
from the celestial ranks. What wonder then if, Leonora, you have a
greater glory, for your very voice proclaims the presence of God.
Either God or certainly the third mind has left an empty place in the sky
and secretly progresses, coiling its way through your throat. Coiling its
way, it progresses, and easily teaches hearts that are mortal gradually
how to grow accustomed to a sound that is immortal. For if God is
indeed all things and is diffused through all things, it is in you alone that
he speaks, while holding everything else in silence.]

Contrary to William Cowper's opinion of this poem's inferiority to
Milton's other Leonora pieces,[32] the first epigram is in fact a masterful
study of the power of inspiration and of the enchanting effect of music
upon the listener. Diane McColley, in an excellent analysis of the piece,
illustrates the variety of ways in which Milton through a "condensation of

---

[30] For a study of this epigram in the context of contemporary angel lore, see Diane K.
McColley, "Tongues of Men and Angels: *Ad Leonoram Romae Canentem*," *MS* 19
(1984), 127-147; see also Robert H. West, *Milton and the Angels* (Athens, 1955). For
an example of a Renaissance Latin poem on the subject of a guardian angel, see M.
Antonio Bonciario, *Angelus Custos*, in *Carmina Illustrium Poetarum Italorum*, ed.
G.G. Bottari (Florence, 1719-1726), II, 404-405 (abbreviated hereafter to *CIPI*).
Some of the poets of the *Applausi* associate Leonora herself with angels, e.g. Claudio
Marazzani, who speaks of her angelic appearance ("Resta in mirare angelici sembianti"
[71]). Fulvio Testi calls her "l'Angioletta mia" (156); Ludovico d' Agliè praises her
"angelici accenti" (211).

[31] Cf. *Applausi*, 72: *quidni igitur mirum potui qui audire canentem/si moveor, si te,
vel lapis, ipse cano?* (3-4).

[32] "I have translated only two of the three poetical compliments addressed to Leonora,
as they appear to me far superior to what I have omitted." (William Cowper, *Latin
and Italian Poems of Milton Translated Into English Verse* [London, 1808], 42.)

opposites"[33] proclaims a self-conscious ability to reconcile voice and verse. Leonora's voice moreover is depicted as proclaiming the very presence of God. Thus she surpasses the common fortune of mortals, who possess not God but a guardian angel. When she sings, God himself speaks.

The progression of the epigram from the *angelus unicuique suus*, to *credite*, to *aut deus* creeping *secreto per guttura* bears an interesting similarity to *Comus* 212ff. There the Lady had asserted her belief that God would send her a guardian angel to protect her life and honor.

> "O welcom pure-eyed Faith, white-handed Hope,
> Thou hovering Angel girt with golden wings,
> And thou unblemished form of Chastity,
> I see ye visibly, and now *believe*
> That he, the Supreme Good, t'whom all things ill
> Are but as slavish officers of vengeance,
> Would send a *glistring Guardian* if need were
> To keep my life and honour unassailed."
>   (*Comus*, 212-219)[34]

Then as the Lady proceeds to sing her song she is praised by Comus, whose subsequent "encomium," as it were, acknowledges, like Milton's epigram, a secret presence in the singer:

> Can any mortal mixture of Earths mould
> Breathe such Divine inchanting ravishment?
> Sure *something holy* lodges in that brest,
> And with these raptures moves the vocal air
> To testifie *his hidd'n residence*."
>   (*Comus*, 243-247).

But if Milton is echoing himself, he also seems to turn to academic tributes in Leonora's honor. The *Applausi* likewise emphasises the otherworldly and indeed divine nature of Leonora's singing. Carlo Eustachio, for example, states that the harmony of her voice and her words do not seem to be of an earthly quality ("L'armonia di tua bocca, e le parole/Non son cosa terrena à chi l'ascolta").[35] Similarly, Ferdinando Barbazzi states that her singing and beauty are out of this world ("Non è terreno il canto,/E non è già la tua beltà terrena." Indeed she can unite heavenly song and

---

[33] McColley, "Tongues," 129.

[34] Italics are mine.

[35] *Applausi*, 61: "The harmony and the words of your mouth are not an earthly thing to him who hears them."

heavenly beauty beneath a human veil ("Accoppi insieme sotto humana veste/Con celeste beltà, canto celeste").[36] The theme recurs in a poem by Francesco Caetani.[37]

Closely related to this is the notion that the harmony of the spheres[38] can be transported to an earthly and human level, thereby enabling mortal hearts to grow accustomed to an immortal sound. This may be implicit in Milton's puzzling reference to a *mens tertia* (5), which has left the heavens, enters Leonora's throat and makes its presence felt among mortals. There has been widespread disagreement among scholars as regards the exact meaning of *mens tertia*, which has been interpreted as the sphere of Venus,[39] the Holy Spirit (as described by Saint Paul)[40] and even one of the angelic ranks.[41] There are two further possibilities: firstly, it may be an allusion to the last of the three categories (*musica mundana*, *musica humana*, and *musica instrumentalis*) into which Boethius had divided music;[42] secondly, it could be a subtle reference to the harmony of the spheres, which has deserted the heavens (hence *vacui ... coeli*), enters Leonora and enables a mortal to grow accustomed to an immortal sound.[43] It is as if the heavens themselves have been bereft of their harmony and are thus silent. This interpretation of the passage may be strengthened by the fact that the theme occurs in the *Applausi*. Leonora's song is depicted as transporting the harmony of the spheres to the earth. Thus Andrea

---

[36] *Applausi*, 121.

[37] *Applausi*, 142: "Io con stupor de la Natura accolto/Scorgo quanto hà di bel mole Celeste/Se ti miro LEONORA, ò se t'ascolto." (9-11) ["Whether I gaze at you, Leonora, or whether I listen to you, seized with amazement at Nature, I perceive the extent of its beauteous heavenly mass."]

[38] For Milton's *Prolusion* on this theme, and for its possible academic recasting, see 50-51 above.

[39] See Thomas Keightley, *The Poems of John Milton* (London, 1859) *ad loc.*

[40] See Bush, *Variorum*, 149, who cites "the third heaven" of 2 *Cor.* 12.2.4.

[41] See McColley, "Tongues," 139-142.

[42] *De Musica* I.II: *Tertia est musica, quae in quibusdam consistere dicitur instrumentis. Haec vero administratur aut intentione, ut nervis, aut spiritu ... aut percussione.* For a discussion of Boethius' classification, see S.K. Heninger, *Touches of Sweet Harmony: Pythagorean Cosmology and Renaissance Poetics* (California, 1974) 101-104.

[43] It is important to observe the musical connotations of the noun *sonus* (8). Cf. Cicero, *De Or.* 1.59: *ab acutissimo sono usque ad gravissimum sonum*; Cicero, *N.D.* 2.58: *in tibiarum cantibus varietas sonorum*. Cf. in a general sense Milton, *At A Solemn Musick*, 17-18: "That we on Earth with undiscording voice/May rightly answer that melodious noise."

Barbazzi states that her enticing music transports the heavenly spheres to
the earth ("... le tue vaghe note, e lusinghiere/Portano in Terra le celesti
Sfere").[44] Giovanni Bentivoglio says that when Leonora sings, the
harmony of the spheres, which is unfamiliar to mortal men, comes and
actually dwells in their midst:

> Se canti, ò LEONORA, ecco ci sueli
> Il concerto de' Cieli, à noi mal noto.
> Co'l tuo canto gentil, tù sol far puoi
> De l'armonia del Ciel fede trà noi. (29-32)[45]

> [If you sing, o Leonora, lo here on earth is the harmony of the heavens
> which is unfamiliar to us. With your noble singing you alone can make
> us believe that the harmony of the heavens is in our midst.]

Milton's concluding lines convey the idea that God speaks in
Leonora alone but holds all other thing in silence (*Quod si cuncta quidem
Deus est, per cunctaque fusus,/in te una loquitur, cetera mutus habet.*
[10]). MacKellar thinks that Milton is expressing here "a pantheism which
was current at the time and with which he must have become acquainted
in the Italian academies, if he had not met it earlier."[46] This is however
highly speculative. A more appropriate context in which to read these lines
(especially vis-à-vis the contrast between a *mutus deus* who nevertheless
loquitur in Leonora alone) is that of a poem in the *Applausi* by Francesco
Ronconi, which states that on account of Leonora's singing the spheres
are rendered motionless, the birds lose their flight, the winds lose their
course and the result is amazement and *silence* in the listener:

> COSMO, cui diede il Cielo
>   Di LEONOR sì spesso udir le note,
>   Dì, con qual' arte à sì soavi accenti
> Stanno le sfere immote,
> Perdon gli Augelli il volo, il corso i venti?
> Tacito ti confundi?
> Col silentio rispondi;
> Perche tanti stupori altrui distingua,
> Non hà voci la lingua.[47]

---

[44] *Applausi*, 19, lines 5-6.

[45] *Applausi*, 174.

[46] Walter MacKellar, ed., *The Latin Poems of John Milton* (*Cornell Studies in
English*, vol. 15 [New Haven, 1930]), 246.

[47] *Applausi*, 151.

[Cosmo, whom Heaven has so frequently granted to listen to the notes of Leonora, tell me in response to what skill do the spheres stand motionless at such sweet tones, the birds lose their flight, the winds lose their course? Are you confused and silent? You respond with silence. Your tongue has not the voice with which to distinguish such great marvels of another.]

Giovanni Bentivoglio tells the heavens themselves to be quiet and to pay attention to Leonora's sweet singing:

> Se canti, e spieghi al Ciel note amorose,
> > Degni sono del Cielo i dolci accenti;
> Tacete, ò Cieli, ad ascoltarla intenti;
> Aure vinte tacete, e vergognose.[48]

[If you sing and display your amorous notes to Heaven, your dulcet tones are worthy of Heaven; Be quiet, o ye heavens, be intent on listening to her, be quiet, o breezes, conquered and ashamed.]

Another theme which is common to Milton's epigrams and the poems of the *Applausi* is that of the soothing power of Leonora's song. This is a major theme of the second epigram.

> Ad eandem
> Altera Torquatum cepit Leonora poetam,
> > cuius ab insano cessit amore furens.
> Ah miser ille tuo quanto felicius aevo
> > perditus, et propter te, Leonora, foret!
> Et te Pieria sensisset voce canentem   5
> > aurea maternae fila movere lyrae,
> quamvis Dircaeo torsisset lumina Pentheo[49]
> > saevior, aut totus desipuisset iners,
> tu tamen errantes caeca vertigine sensus
> > voce eadem poteras composuisse tua;   10
> et poteras aegro spirans sub corde quietem
> > flexanimo cantu restituisse sibi.[50]

> [To the same
> Another Leonora captivated the poet Torquato, who became mad on account of his insane love for her. Ah how much more happily would that poor man have been ruined in your life-time and on your account,

---

[48] *Applausi*, 178.

[49] Cf. *Applausi*, 62: *Dircaeo ... cantu* (7)

[50] Cf. *Applausi*, 202 (Lucas Holstenius): *carmen flexanimum, diserta verba,/dulces blanditias, iocosque doctos.* (21-22)

Leonora! And had he heard you singing with your Pierian voice and heard the strumming of the golden strings of your mother's lyre, even though he had rolled his eyes more savagely than Dircaean Pentheus or had been utterly dull and senseless, still, through your voice you could have calmed those senses reeling in their blind wanderings, and breathing repose into the depths of his troubled heart, through your soul-moving song, you could have restored him to himself.]

Milton speaks of Tasso's love for another lady named Leonora — a love which drove him insane. If Tasso had heard Leonora Baroni singing, his madness could have been assuaged. Even if he had rolled his eyes more fiercely than Pentheus, Leonora's song would have soothed his aching heart and restored him to his senses. The connection between Tasso's madness and Leonora had been popularised even in England from an early date, as is testified by John Eliot's reference to it in 1593: "This youth fell mad for the love of an Italian lass, descended of a great house, when I was in Italy."[51] Similarly Scipio Gentili seems to accept it in the prefatory stanzas to his Latin translation of the *Gerusalemme Liberata*, published in London in 1584.[52] But perhaps it was in Italy and more precisely through Milton's Neapolitan friend and host Giovanni Battista Manso, whose *Vita* of Tasso had appeared in 1621, that the story was most widely known.[53] Indeed Manso's erroneous and frequently false account was believed, since he had known Tasso personally. In the *Vita* Manso states that while Tasso was staying with him at Naples he had the opportunity to examine his melancholy.[54] He describes Tasso's obsessive delusions, and links his name with Leonora d'Este. He was seized, Manso says, with an "alto e nobilissimo amore."[55] Milton's *altera ... Leonora* is interesting in that Manso had in fact referred to three Leonoras, of one of whom Tasso was enamoured: "Tre Leonore una delle quali fù l'amata di Tor":[56] 1) Leonora

---

[51] John Eliot, *Ortho-epia Gallica* (London, 1593).

[52] *S. Gentilis Solymeidos libri duo priores de T. Tassi Italicis expressi* (London, 1584).

[53] See C.P. Brand, *Torquato Tasso: A Study of the Poet and of his Contribution to English Literature* (Cambridge, 1965), 207-209.

[54] Manso, *Vita di Torquato Tasso*, 72-76 proffers a somewhat extravagant explanation of Tasso's madness: a close friend Maddalo gave the poet's love away at court; there followed a duel in which Tasso wounded his opponent and was then wounded himself by one of his opponent's friends. Tasso was then put into custody to protect him from further attacks; but he regarded this as imprisonment, and this marked the onset of his madness.

[55] Manso, *Vita di Torquato Tasso*, 48.

[56] Manso, *Vita di Torquato Tasso*, 50.

d'Este;[57] 2) Contessa San Vitale;[58] 3) a damigella of Leonora d'Este.[59] If the reference does reflect Milton's conversations with Manso, the Leonora epigrams would, of course, have to be dated to his second visit to Rome.

While the *Applausi* does not compare Leonora with any of those women supposedly beloved of Tasso, nor does it refer to Tasso's madness specifically, it does nevertheless emphasise on several occasions the soothing power of Leonora's *cantus*. Fabio Leonida, for example, states that her song has the power to calm the Furies themselves ("Ma di questa Sirena è vero vanto/Placar la furia de le Furie stesse").[60] This is extended to embrace the fury of war. Gasparo de Simeonibus asserts that as a result of her singing, both swords and hearts are placated "Fatti molli in un punto i ferri, e i cori."[61] It is with a "Pierian voice" (*te Pieria ... voce canentem* [5]) that Leonora sings, in accompaniment to the strings of her mother's lyre (*aurea maternae fila movere lyrae* [6]).[62] As is inevitable, the poets of the *Applausi* likewise associate Leonora with the Muses.[63] At times she is a tenth Muse;[64] at others the Muses serve her.[65] The Pierides taught her how to play the lyre.[66]

---

[57] Manso, *Vita di Torquato Tasso*, 51.

[58] Manso, *Vita di Torquato Tasso*, 57.

[59] Manso, *Vita di Torquato Tasso*, 59.

[60] *Applausi*, 118. ["But this Siren possesses the true boast that she placates the fury of the Furies themselves."]

[61] *Applausi*, 167.

[62] The reference to *maternae ... lyrae* would seem to indicate Milton's acknowledgement of the fact that Leonora's mother, Adriana Baroni, was also a musician.

[63] Vincenzo Marescotti, *Applausi*, 258, alludes to her in the phrase "Questa canora Musa" ["This tuneful Muse."]

[64] Thus Alfonso Pallavicini, *Applausi*, 12, states "Ma, perche chiare prove/Sian di ciò frà i Mortali,/Una Musa frà lor prende i natali/Aggiunta à l'altre nove,/Che le vince, E LE ONORA/Non men casta, e più bella e più canora." ["But so that there may be clear proofs of this among mortals, a Muse is born in their midst, is added to the other nine, who conquers and honors them and is no less chaste, but more beautiful and more musical."] Cf. Michael Marullus, who envisages Alessandra Scala as a tenth Muse, as, for example, in *Ep.* 3.15, addressed to her father: *plus multo tamen, o beate amice, est,/quod Scalam Latio pater dedisti/aucturam numerum novem sororum/casto carmine, castiore vita* (9-12). Cf. *Ep.* 3.4. *De Alexandra Scala Bartholomaei Scalae Filia: Auxerat Aonias Sappho, dea facta, sorores,/et poteras numero cedere, Roma, novo,/dulcia cum Scalae miratus carmina Apollo,/dixit: "Habes numerum tu quoque, Roma, tuum."*

[65] Thus Domenico Benigni, *Applausi*, 108, states: "Gran vanto è sì; ma che le Muse ancelle/Portino sù'l tuo crin toscano alloro,/Pregio è più bello ..." ["This is a great

On a very general level the hypothetical element which is the characteristic feature of Milton's second epigram, as he envisages the consequences had Tasso heard Leonora's beautiful singing,[67] is also to be found in the *Applausi*. Fabio Leonida imagines what would have happened if those tormenting furies of the underworld had heard her pleasing song:

> S'udisse i vaghi suoi soavi accenti
>   l'augel di Titio, e d'Ission la rota,
>   l'un resterebbe satio, e l'altra immota,
>   e fine hauria'l martir di que' dolenti.[68]

> [If the bird of Tityos and the wheel of Ixion had heard her graceful, sweet tones, the one would have remained satisfied and the other motionless, and the torture of those sufferers would have ended.]

The final point of similarity between Milton's Latin epigrams and the poems of the *Applausi* is the depiction of Leonora as a Siren,[69] and, more specifically, as Parthenope, daughter of Achelous, reputed to have been washed ashore near Naples, where a tomb was erected in her honor.[70] This equation is particularly apt and perhaps inevitable,[71] since, like Parthenope, Leonora herself was a Neapolitan noted for her singing. Milton's third epigram is devoted entirely to this theme. Lines 1-4

---

boast, yes; but it is a finer merit that the Muses, your handmaids, are placing Tuscan laurel on your hair."]

[66] Thus Gregorio Porcio, *Applausi*, 188: *Illic te Virtus artes, te turba Sororum/ Pieridum docuit fila canora Lyrae,/cui Phoebea manus, triplex et Gratia chordas/pollice praetentans sollicitabat ebur.*

[67] This hypothetical element is conventional in itself. Cf. Castiglione, *De Elisabella Gonzaga Canente: Audiat Aeneas hanc si tam dulce querentem,/flens ultro ad litus vela dabit Lybicum./Quod si dura nimis, blandisque immota querelis/mens fera propositum non remoretur iter,/invitam ad litus portabunt aequora classem,/ flaminaque ad fletus officiosa pios,/excidet atque animo regnum dotale, nec unquam/ Dardanius Latium navita classe petet.* Text is that of *CIPI*, III, 304.

[68] *Applausi*, 119.

[69] Cf. the description of the Sirens in *Comus* 251-256: "I have oft heard/My mother Circe with the Sirens three,/Amidst the flowry-kirtl'd Naiades/Culling their potent hearbs, and balefull drugs,/Who as they sung, would take the prison'd soul,/And lap it in Elysium ..."

[70] For an interesting survey of Parthenope vis-à-vis Leonora and Sabrina, cf. Revard, *Milton and the Tangles of Neaera's Hair*, 147-151.

[71] Bush, *Variorum*, 148, states: "... the volume has many allusions to the Sirens and some to Parthenope ... but these were almost inevitable."

constitute a question addressed to Naples: why does she boast of the Siren
and of the famous shrine of Parthenope and of the "Chalcidian pyre" on
which she was placed:

> Ad eandem
> Credula quid liquidam Sirena Neapoli iactas,
>   claraque Parthenopes fana Acheloiados,
> litoreamque tua defunctam naiada ripa
>   corpora Chalcidico sacra dedisse rogo?

> [To the same
> Why, credulous Naples, do you boast of your clear-voiced Siren and of
> the famous shrine of Achelous's daughter, Parthenope, and that when
> she, a naiad of the shore, died on your coasts, you placed her sacred
> body upon a Chalcidian pyre?]

In actual fact this Siren is alive, has exchanged the noisy Posillipo
for the lovely Tiber and holds her audiences spellbound:

> Illa quidem vivitque et amoena Tibridis unda
>   mutavit rauci murmura Pausilipi.
> Illic Romulidum studiis ornata secundis,[72]
>   atque homines cantu detinet atque deos.

> [Indeed, she is alive and has changed the murmurs of the hoarse
> Posillipo for the pleasant waters of the Tiber. There, honored by the
> favorable enthusiasm of the sons of Romulus, she captivates both men
> and gods with her song.]

The contrast between noisy Naples[73] and the peaceful setting of Rome is
highlighted by the echo in *amoena Tibridis unda* of Virgil's idyllic
description of the Tiber in *Aeneid* 7,[74] scene of the "promised land," as it
were, of Aeneas and his men.

Leonora as a Siren is a recurring theme in the *Applausi*: "ò bella
Sirena,"[75] "questa Sirena,"[76] "vaga Sirena,"[77] "la dolce Sirena,"[78] *ut notis*

---

[72] For the use of the genitive plural *Romulidum*, cf. Gasparo de Simeonibus, *Applausi*,
170: *Haud falsa Harmoniae ludit imagine,/quae dignos LEONORA fert/plausus
Romulidum.*

[73] Carey, ed., *Milton: Complete Shorter Poems*, 259, suggests that *murmura* refers to
the rumble of traffic in the tunnel which pierces Mount Posillipo.

[74] Virgil, *Aeneid* 7. 30-32: *hunc inter fluvio Tiberinus amoeno/verticibus rapidis et
multa flavus harena/in mare prorumpit.*

[75] *Applausi*, 19.

[76] *Applausi*, 118.

Siren caneres superbis,[79] "La Sirena immortale,"[80] "Fastosetta Sirena,"[81] "Syrene de la mer d'amour,"[82] *pudica Siren,*[83] "altra Sirena."[84] Fabio Leonida states:

> Da le rive del Mincio alma, e canora
> Sirena uscì, cui de l'aurata cetra
> Febo arricchisce: Amor de la faretra,
> E de la face, e del suo straLE ONORA.[85]

[From the banks of the river Mincius has emerged a divine, harmonious Siren, whom Phoebus enriches with his golden lyre, and whom Cupid honors with his quiver, torch and dart.]

— a theme treated in an even more elaborate fashion by Lelio Guidiccioni.[86]

That notion of emulation, implicit in Milton's question as to why Naples boasts of the Siren and of the honors paid to Parthenope when in fact she is very much alive in the person of Leonora, underlies Vincenzo Costazuti's injunction that Fama should cease to speak of Parthenope since the latter has a rival in Leonora.[87]

Milton's emphasis upon the fact that the Siren is not dead but actually lives in Leonora (*illa quidem vivitque* [5]) finds a general parallel in Giulio Rospigliosi's poem on a portrait of Leonora, in which he praises the artist's skill, saying that through him the Siren is no mere myth but a living being:

---

[77] *Applausi*, 121.

[78] *Applausi*, 129.

[79] *Applausi*, 146.

[80] *Applausi*, 155.

[81] *Applausi*, 157.

[82] *Applausi*, 180.

[83] *Applausi*, 201.

[84] *Applausi*, 250.

[85] *Applausi*, 117.

[86] *Applausi*, 196: *Parcite Romulei LEONORAM extollere Cygni/Ipsa suis Siren laudibus una satis./Nam Siren voce haec, labiis Pitho, Aonis arte,/Fronte Charis, Hebe est ambrosia, igne Venus.*

[87] *Applausi*, 252: *Syrenum variis mulcens concentibus auras/lusit in aequoreis turba canora vadis./Parthenopen nunc Fama sile: nam marmoris undis/ aemula iam Minci tollitur ora lacus./Immo ELEONORAE resonat dum gloria cantus/maiori patrius laude resultat honos./Illa viris pariunt mortem modulamina vocis,/istud viva melos reddere saxa potest.*

Per te questa de' cor dolce Sirena
Non è finta, *ma vive*; e i lumi ardenti
Scoccan dal vago ciglio amabil pena.[88]

[On account of you this Siren with her sweet heart is not feigned, *but lives*, and her blazing eyes dart from their graceful lids a lovely pain.]

Indeed one of the Italian tributes resembles Milton's poem in that it depicts the Siren exchanging one dwelling-place for another and in fact coming to the city of Rome. Thus just as Milton describes Leonora/Siren abandoning the *rauci murmura Pausilipi* (6) for the *amoena Tibridis unda* (5) and captivating her audience by the power of her song, so Fulvio Testi envisages her as a Siren who has left the shore of Parthenope, has arrived at Rome and moves her audience with her singing:

Fastosetta Sirena,
    Che da Partenopei liti odiosi
Sù la Romana arena
Se' venuta à turbar gli altrui riposi;
E con la dolce pena
Del divin canto, e de' begli occhi ardenti
Con flagello di gioia il cor tormenti.[89]

[O magnificent Siren, you who have come from the tedious shores of Parthenope to Roman sand to disturb the repose of others, and with the sweet pain of your divine song and of your beautiful burning eyes torment the heart with a whip of joy.]

Parthenope is mentioned in two further poems in the *Applausi*. Gregorio Porcio states that Leonora was reared by Parthenope (*Mox te Parthenope blandas Sirenas, et inter/Sebethi Nymphas fovit amica sinu.*[7-8]),[90] while Lucas Holstenius addresses her as the *pulchrae Parthenopes canora proles.*[91]

Perhaps that well-known phrase "When in Rome, do as the Romans do" is an apt description of Milton's essentially reactionary experiences in the eternal city — experiences exemplified by his Latin scazontes to

---

[88] *Applausi*, 185. Italics are mine.

[89] *Applausi*, 157.

[90] *Applausi*, 188.

[91] *Applausi*, 201: *Phoebi delicium, pudica Siren,/Pulchrae Parthenopes canora proles/Inter purpureos adulta Cygnos,/Qui Mantus liquidas natant per undas;/Quo te carmine praedicam, tuasque/Quo tentem numero explicare laudes?* (1-6)

Salzilli and by his Latin epigrams to Leonora. Thus he assumed a not insignificant place among Seicento Italian academicians by replying to an encomium in his honor, but also by composing his own encomia in praise of a Neapolitan soprano. But Milton's links with Naples were to extend far beyond the present context. Whereas Leonora, as Parthenope, had left Naples to be reborn in Rome, Milton himself by contrast would leave the eternal city for Naples. There he too would experience a very meaningful process of reinvention and self-discovery.

CHAPTER 7

Milton and the Accademia degli Oziosi

In December 1638, or possibly early January 1639, Milton proceeded from Rome to Naples (*Neapolim perrexi*),[1] a city which could in itself boast of no fewer than thirty academies.[2] It was to the founder of the Accademia degli Oziosi,[3] namely, Giovanni Battista Manso, Marquis of Villa,[4] that Milton was introduced through the agency of a still unidentified "certain hermit," with whom he had travelled from Rome. In *Defensio Secunda* Milton writes:

> Illic per Eremitam quendam quicum Roma iter feceram ad Ioannem Baptistam Mansum, Marchionem Villensem, virum nobilissimum atque gravissimum (ad quem Torquatus Tassus insignis poeta Italus de amicitia scripsit) sum introductus.[5]

> [There I was introduced by a certain hermit, with whom I had journeyed from Rome, to Giovanni Battista Manso, Marquis of Villa, a very noble and authoritative man (to whom the illustrious Italian poet Torquato Tasso wrote concerning friendship).]

But it was not only as a founder of an academy that Manso was acclaimed. Milton acknowledges the fact that it was to Manso that Tasso had addressed his *Dialogue on Friendship*. Here was a poet and biographer, himself a befriender of Tasso and Marino, and above all a true Neapolitan

---

[1] *DS, CM* 8, 122.

[2] Fabricius, *Conspectus*, 250, lists under Naples the following academies: "Addormentati, Ardenti, Arditi, Armeristi, Assettati, del Cimento, Camilli Columnae, Erranti, Incogniti, Incolti, Infuriati, Intronati, Investiganti, Laurentiana, Lunatici, Oscuri, Oziosi, Partenii, Pigri, del Pontano, Rauvivati, Rinnomati (Rinnovati potius), Rozzi, Scatenati, Segreti, Sicuri, Sireni, Svegliati, Uniti, Volanti."

[3] On the Oziosi, see Maylender, *Storia*, IV, 183-190. Cedric Brown, *John Milton: A Literary Life*, 62, incorrectly states that Manso was founder of the Umoristi.

[4] On Manso, see Angelo Borzelli, *Giovan Battista Manso* (Naples, 1916).

[5] *CM* 8, 122-124.

Maecenas.[6] And Milton himself, like those Italian poets before him, was to have the good fortune of being on the receiving end of Manso's hospitality. During his sojourn in Naples, Manso conducted him through the city and Vice-regent's palace (*qui et ipse me per urbis loca et Proregis aulam circumduxit*)[7] and visited him more than once at his own lodgings for the purpose of seeing him (*et visendi gratia haud semel ipse ad hospitium venit*).[8] It is as though Manso were almost an Evander figure, leading his newly arrived guest on a guided tour of a city. And that this was a friendship, an *amicitia*, is indicated by the terms (*amicissimo; amicus*) enshrouding Milton's references to Manso not only in the *Defensio Secunda*, but also in the prose *argumentum* to *Mansus* and in that poem as a whole. Manso even seems to have presented Milton with gifts while he was in Naples — gifts described in the *Epitaphium Damonis* in pastoral terms as two wonderfully engraved cups (*bina ... pocula* [*Ep. Dam.*, 181-183]),[9] but as De Filippis and others have convincingly argued,[10] probably two books of Manso's own compositions: the *Erocallia* (1628) and the *Poesie Nomiche* (1635). This argument is supported by hitherto unnoticed evidence elsewhere of Manso's apparent custom of presenting copies of his own compositions as farewell gifts to guests leaving Naples. Thus Jacopo Gaddi, friend and fellow-academician of Milton during his Florentine sojourn, states that when he was leaving Naples he received from Manso a present of one of his *Dialogues*.[11] Milton's esteem for Manso's *pocula* is highlighted by his comment that he had been keeping them for his close friend Charles Diodati (*Ep. Dam.*,180-181), himself of an Italian family. Hence the appropriateness that these presents should be <u>Italian</u> works. This would indeed seem to lend support

---

[6] Jacopo Gaddi in his *De Scriptoribus*, 121, praises Manso as one *qui Tassi, Marini, aliorumque huius aevi praestantium ingeniorum Maecenas fuit, aut amicus et laudator omnis expers livoris ac malignitatis.*

[7] *DS, CM* 8, 124.

[8] *CM* 8, 124.

[9] For a full description in ekphrastic terms of these *pocula*, cf. *Ep Dam*, 181-197.

[10] Michele De Filippis, "Milton and Manso: Cups or Books?" *PMLA* 51 (1936), 745-756; Donald C. Dorian, "Milton's *Epitaphium Damonis*, lines 181-197," *PMLA* 54 (1939), 612-613. Cf. John Black, *Life of Torquato Tasso* (Edinburgh, 1810), II, 467.

[11] Jacopo Gaddi, *De Scriptoribus*, 121: *In exordio primi Dialogi quem inscribit Gesualdum ab Alph. Gesualdo Archiep. Neapolis, et Card. Decano eloquenter describit atque concelebrat litoralem oram urbemque Neapolis quam ego celebraveram allocutione non incuriosa multos menses anteaquam viderem aut scirem nobilissimum <u>hoc opus a Marchione mihi donatum ea ipsa qua Neapoli profectus sum hora.</u>*

to De Filippis' thesis.[12] Milton had thus treasured presents of Italian prose and verse from an Italian *amicus*, to be given in turn to his own Anglo-Italian friend. But the untimely death of that friend in London while Milton was in Italy would prevent this ever happening.[13]

Interesting however is the fact that appended to one of these *pocula*, one of these Italian works by Manso, namely the *Poesie Nomiche*, was a whole series of Italian encomia of Manso. Whether it was through reading these or through other possible sources, Milton, both in the prose preface to *Mansus* and in the poem proper, betrays his awareness of the high reputation which Manso has achieved among Italians. This, he states, is on account of his "intellectual ability, his devotion to literature and also his bravery in war" (*vir ingenii laude, tum literarum studio, nec non et bellica virtute apud Italos clarus in primis est.*) And not only was Manso the addressee of Tasso's *De Amicitia*, his name was also included in the *Gerusalemme Conquistata*:

> Ad quem Torquati Tassi dialogus extat de amicitia scriptus;[14] erat enim Tassi amicissimus; ab quo etiam inter Campaniae principes celebratur, in illo poemate cui titulus *Gerusalemme conquistata*, lib 20.

---

[12] Cf. Milton's *Elegia Sexta* 89-90, in which the poems *patriis meditata cicutis* promised to Diodati by Milton (along with the *Nativity Ode*) are most likely Milton's own Italian sonnets. See John Carey, "The Date of Milton's Italian Poems." For an argument against (based on similar wording in a Latin poem by May), see Leo Miller, "Milton's *Patriis Cicutis*," *N & Q*, n.s. 28 (1981), 41-42.

[13] Diodati died in London and was buried on 27 August 1638. For arguments as to when and where in Italy Milton received the news of his death, see John T. Shawcross, "*Epitaphium Damonis*: lines 9-13 and the Date of Composition," *MLN* 71 (1956), 322-324, who argues that it was in April in 1639 while Milton was in Florence (since lines 9-13 refer to Italian crops [there being two wheat harvests (March/August) annually in the Arno valley], and thus two had elapsed since Diodati's death). This argument is countered by W.R. Parker, "Milton and the News of Charles Diodati's death," *MLN* 72 (1957), 486-488, who argues that Milton heard the news when he was in Naples (i.e. December 1638 or January 1639) and that it was this that led him to cancel his journey to Sicily and Greece. Shawcross responds in Rose Clavering and John T. Shawcross, "Milton's European Itinerary and his Return Home," *SEL* 5 (1965), 49-59. For the evidence pointing to the fact that Milton sent a separate copy of the *Epitaphium Damonis* to Italian academicians, see 55-56 above. For the apparently unique copy of an anonymous edition of the poem discovered in the British Museum (C. 57.d.48) by Leicester Bradner and dated by him to c. 1640, cf. *TLS* 18 August (1932), 581, and 55 above.

[14] The full title of Tasso's Dialogue is *Il Manso, overe Dell' Amicitia Dialogo del Sig. Torquato Tasso al Molte Illustre Sig. Giovanni Battista Manso* (Naples, 1596). Prefixed to the work are a dedication and five sonnets from Tasso to Manso.

> Fra cavalier magnanimi, e cortesi
> Risplende il Manso — [15]

[Addressed to whom there exists a dialogue of Torquato Tasso on friendship; for he was a great friend of Tasso; by whom he is also celebrated among the princes of Campania in that poem which is entitled Gerusalemme Conquistata, bk. 20.
Among great-hearted and magnanimous courtiers
Manso is resplendent]

Milton can hardly have failed to notice Manso's intellectual standing. By the time of their meeting, the Neapolitan Marquis, already a septuagenarian, had acquired national fame, having seen through press a virtual life-time's work, embracing religious, philosophical, biographical and secular topics. Among such were a biography of St Patricia (*Vita, virtù, e miracoli principali di S. Patricia Vergine* [Naples, 1611]), platonic dialogues on love and beauty (*Erocallia* [Venice, 1628]),[16] miscellaneous minor poems (*Poesie Nomiche* [Venice, 1635]),[17] and a biography of Tasso (*Vita di Torquato Tasso* [Venice, 1621]).

A celebrated Neapolitan and befriender of poets, Manso was also a promoter of learning and of scholarship. Although De Filippis has convincingly shown that in some of his works, most noticeably in his *Vita* of Tasso, he plagiarised a whole series of anecdotes pertaining to other writers,[18] it is likely that his seventeenth- as opposed to his twentieth-century reputation was not blemished in this way. On the contrary, evidence would seem to point to the high regard in which he was held, not only as poet and biographer, but also as the very nucleus of the Accademia degli Oziosi.

If Milton did actually participate in the life of one or more of the Neapolitan academies, it is the Oziosi that must rank at the top of the list

---

[15] Milton cites only the relevant lines. The entire canto is as follows: "e di Circello e d' Ansa altri marchesi,/e'l figlio, indegno di fortuna avversa,/gli animi avranno al vero onore accesi,/ e'l conte di Loreto, e quel d'Anversa./Fra' cavalier magnanimi e cortesi/risplende il Manso, e doni e raggi ei versa./Ma cieco oblio giá non asconde e copre/del buon duca di Sora il nome e l'opre."

[16] *Erocallia ovvero dell' Amore e della Bellezza* (Venice, 1628). For the possibility that this was one of the *pocula* given by Manso to Milton, see De Filippis, "Milton and Manso," *passim*, and 134-135 below.

[17] *Poesie Nomiche, ... Divise in Rime Amorose, Sacre, e Morali*, ed. A. Berardelli (Venice, 1635).

[18] Michele De Filippis in his *Anecdotes in Manso's Life of Tasso and their Sources* (Berkeley, 1936), illustrates that at least 91 of the 100 anecdotes Manso relates of Tasso have in fact literary sources.

of possibilities. This was one of the more highly esteemed, not only in the city of Naples itself, but also by comparison with other Italian academies of its day.[19] Founded by Manso, it met in its initial years in the convent of San Maria delle Grazie.[20] In 1615 as a consequence of the transfer of the University of Naples from the monastery of St Dominic to the palace outside the Gate of Constantinople in Naples (today the National Museum), the Oziosi took over the abandoned monastery.[21] Among Manso's predecessors as principle of the Academy were Annibale Brancaccio (1621), Francesco de Pietri (1622), and then, at Manso's own instigation, the famous "poet of the marvellous"[22] Giambattista Marino (1624), an appointment not without some controversy.[23] It was upon the death of Marino in 1625 that Manso himself became head of the Oziosi, a position which he was to hold until his own death on 28 December 1645. Manso held meetings of the academy in his villas at Puteoli and Bisaccio, where he also received foreign visitors. Since by the time of Milton's visit Manso was no longer in possession of the Bisaccio villa, it is probable that it was at the Puteoli villa, with its beautiful coastal setting, that he played host to Milton.[24] And Manso's abode was celebrated in contemporary verse and prose in terms reminiscent of a *locus amoenus*. Indeed Manso himself in his *Vita di Torquato Tasso* had offered his own enticing description:

> Dimorava all' hora il Manso nella dilettevolissima piaggia del mare, in un bel casamento alquanto sopra gli altri elevato, ed attorno attorno di bellissimi giardini circuito.[25]
>
> [Manso lived on a most delightful sea-shore, in a beautiful house somewhat elevated above the others and encompassed all around by very beautiful gardens.]

---

[19] Cf. Maylender, *Storia*, IV, 183.

[20] Maylender, *Storia*, IV, 183.

[21] Maylender, *Storia*, IV, 186.

[22] The phrase is that of J.V. Mirollo, *The Poet of the Marvelous: Giambattista Marino* (New York, 1963).

[23] Maylender IV, *Storia*, 187.

[24] For an attempt to ascertain the location of Manso's villa, see Joseph C. Walker, *Historical Memoir on Italian Tragedy* (London, 1799), Appendix V: *An Attempt to Ascertain the Site of the Villa near Naples, in Which the Marquis Manso Received Tasso and Milton. With Notices of the Manso Family.*

[25] Manso, *Vita di Torquato Tasso*, 208.

According to the *Vita* it was the beauty of such surroundings (the foliage, verdure, aroma and purity of the air) that had enabled Tasso to recover from his melancholy.[26] Obviously conducive to *otium*, this was an ideal setting for meetings of an academy entitled "Oziosi." This name had been chosen by Francesco de Pietri, who in so doing was careful to point out that the *otium* signified thereby was not "idle or negligent, but pertaining to literature and virtue."[27] In order to signify the importance of what was essentially an active *otium*, de Pietri invokes Cicero's reference to Scipio's statement: *numquam ... minus otiosum esse quam cum otiosus ... esset*[28] — that he was "never less 'at leisure' than when he was 'at leisure.'" Would this contrast between intellectual activity and slothful inertia be remembered much later by the poet of *Paradise Lost*?[29] Apparently, it was also de Pietri who invented the *impresa* and motto of the Oziosi: an eagle sitting upon a hill with his gaze fixed upon the sun, with the motto *Non Pigra Quies*.[30] That the aim of the academy was to live up to its *impresa* and motto is evident from a reading of its scrupulous statutes — an important document (in a seventeenth-century hand) discovered and published by Carlo Padiglione in 1878.[31] Strikingly noticeable is the hierarchical, exceedingly prescriptive and formal nature of these statutes. This manifests itself in a variety of ways, not least of which is the stated requirement that the academy should possess a whole series of administrators with specifically designated tasks: a Leader (*Principe*) and two assistants (*Assistenti*),[32] three advisers (*Consiglieri*),[33] a Secretary

---

[26] Manso, *Vita di Torquato Tasso*, 208: "i quali dalla vegnente primavera, di nuove frondi, e di variati fiori tutti rivestiti, con la verdura, e col soave odore di quelli, e molto più con la purità dell' aria per sì fatto modo Torquato dalla sua invecchiata malinconia ricrearono."

[27] Francesco de Pietri, *I Problemi Accademici overe le Più Famose Questioni Proposte nell' Illustrissima Accademia degli Oziosi di Napoli* (Naples, 1642), Proemio: "non già dell' ozio scioperato, o neghittosa, ma del letterario e virtuoso."

[28] Cicero, *De Officiis*, 3.1.

[29] See Nardo, "Academic Interludes," 218.

[30] See Maylender, *Storia*, IV, 183.

[31] Carlo Padiglione, *Le Leggi dell' Accademia degli Oziosi in Napoli Ritrovate nella Biblioteca Brancacciana* (Naples, 1878).

[32] Padiglione, *Le Leggi*, 10: "Dovrà dunque essere il capo di tutta l'Academia et del governo etiamdio il nostro Principe, a cui si daranno due Assistenti: Si perche l'accompagnino et aggiutiuno nel governo, come perche in assenza di lui possano successivamente tenere le sue veci."

(*Secretario*), whose responsibility it is to look after the Academy's library, compositions by its members, and letters for foreigners,[34] a treasurer,[35] and a *Recivitore* in charge of such practical details as choice of location of the academy, care of its members, and accommodation and treatment of foreigners: "Il Recivitore, al cui peso sarà il luogo dell' Academia il ricevere de gli Academici, e'l accomodare, e'l honorare degli Forestieri."[36] All of these positions were to be decided on the basis of annual elections, with the exception of the *Secretario*, who was permanent.[37] The actual meetings of the academy are equally prescriptive, consisting of readings (*lettioni*), compositions (*compositioni*) and ensuing questions.[38] *Lettioni*

---

[33] Padiglione, *Le Leggi*, 10: "Se gli eleggeranno oltr' a gl' assistenti tre altri Consiglieri, co' quali doverà l'istesso e suoi Assistenti, partecipare, et ricevere parere nelle cose più gravi dell' Accademia."

[34] Padiglione, *Le Leggi*, 10: "A questi tre officiali si deono aggiungere tre altri ministri, et cio sono il Segretario che dovra haver' cura de libri dell' Academia, delle Compositioni degli Academici, è delle lettere per gli Forestieri."

[35] Padiglione, *Le Leggi*, 10: "Il Tesoriere, che dovrà riscuotere, conservare, et spendere tutto quello, che sarà mestiere per l'Academia."

[36] Padiglione, *Le Leggi*, 10.

[37] Freeman, "Milton's Roman Connection," 90, suggests that the martial sound of such offices as principe, assistenti, consiglieri, recivitore, censori, bidello, protettore, luogotenenti may echo in Milton's hell. This is developed by Nardo, "Academic Interludes," 218-219. I would add to these the possible significance of the fact that the demons in hell are known (on earth) by a variety of names: "Then were they known to men by various names" (*PL* 1.374). Is this a reflection on a demonic level of that custom whereby Italian academicians were known by a variety of names (sometimes, though not always, by anagrams of their own names)? That Milton was familiar with this custom is surely undeniable, given that he corresponded with such academicians as Carlo Dati who was variously known as Timauro Antiate and Currado Bartoletti (only the latter is an anagram of Carlo Roberto Dati). Similarly his prose correspondence mentions Piero Frescobaldi, who was known by the anagram of Bali Scoprifode. Compare Agostino Coltellini, again mentioned by Milton. His anagram was Ostilio Contalgeni. Benedetto Buommmattei was Boemonte Battidente. (Benedetto Fioretti published under the name of Udeno Nisieli). Milton emphasises on more than one occasion the precise practice of one demon assuming a variety of names, or, more accurately, being known by various names. He presents the demons in hell, i.e. an existence prior to that in which they had acquired on earth different names: "Nor had they yet among the sons of Eve/Got them *new names*" (*PL* 1. 364-365). Later he states: "Then were they known to men by *various names*,/And various idols through the heathen world./Say, Muse, *their names then known*, who first, who last,/Roused from the slumber, on that fiery couch" (1. 374-377). Italics are mine.

[38] Padiglione, *Le Leggi*, 18: "Gli esercitii da farsi nell' Academia perciochè sono lo strumento principale a conseguire il fine da noi desiderato, dovranno essere con molta

moreover should pertain to poetry, rhetoric, mathematics, and all aspects of philosophy, and to the exposition of authors who have written on these subjects.[39] But the reading of any material related to theology or the Scriptures was forbidden: "vietando che non si debba leggere alcuna materia di Teologia, ò della Sacra Scrittura, delle quali per riverenza dobbiano astenerci,"[40] and the latter point was true of the majority of Italian academies as a rule.[41] The prescriptive nature and high expectations of the Oziosi are epitomised in those statements in the statutes about "obedience." It is this which is recommended as one of the principal virtues of its participants. Such obedience should be shown above all in the observation of the academy's rules and in the ability to endure criticism in cases of transgression: "L'obbedienza dovrà essere una delle principali virtù da essercitarsi da ciascun Accademico perciocchè senz' ella non può alcuna virtuosa unione alcun tempo durare in istato .... Quest' obbedienza dovrà primieramente mostrarsi nell' osservanza di queste regole, ed in suffrire con animo ben composto, le reprensioni che saranno date à trasgressori d'esse, et appresso in ricevere prontamente gli esercitii che saranno à ciascheduno imposti."[42]

The academy's statutes thus betray a strict hierarchical format with conformity as the rule and aberration readily censured. And such characteristics would hardly have escaped the notice of the youthful Milton. It is tempting to speculate that if the Accademia degli Oziosi was attended by the future defender of liberty, the poet who seems indeed to parody such hierarchy in his depiction of hell in *Paradise Lost*,[43] for him at least it surely must have presented some negative, as well as positive, aspects. What is undeniable is that there existed some form of religious tension between Manso and Milton. *In Defensio Secunda* Milton says that on his departure from Naples, Manso apologised that although he had wanted to, he had been unable to show him greater hospitality in that city.

---

sollecitudine posti in opera dagli Academici, saranno principalmente trè, et cio sono le lettioni, le Compositioni, e le questioni ad esseguire;" cf. Maylender, *Storia*, IV, 184.

[39] Padiglioni, *Le Leggi*, 19: "La materie delle lettioni dovrà essere intorno all Poetica, alla Ritorica, alle discipline Matematiche, et à tutte le parti della filosofia, et intorno alla Spianatione delli Autori ch' hanno delle sopradette materie scritto;" cf. Maylender, *Storia*, IV, 184.

[40] Padiglione, *Le Leggi*, 19.

[41] Nardo, "Academic Interludes," 222.

[42] Padiglione, *Le Leggi*, 24. Cf. 25: "Ma sopra tutti gli atti di ubbedienza è richiesto principalmente a tutti gli Academici l'osservanza di queste presenti regole."

[43] See Nardo, "Academic Interludes," 219.

This was because Milton had been unwilling to be more guarded on the
subject of religion:

> discedenti serio excusavit se, tametsi multo plura detulisse mihi officia
> maxime cupiebat, non potuisse illa in urbe, propterea quod nolebam in
> religione esse tectior.[44]

> [As I was departing, he seriously apologised that even though he greatly
> desired to pay me much greater services, he had been unable to do so in
> that city, on account of the fact that I was unwilling to be more discreet
> about the subject of religion.]

Milton proceeds to admit that while he had decided not to introduce
the subject, when asked about his religious convictions he did not
dissemble in spite of the consequences:

> sic enim mecum statueram de religione quidem iis in locis sermones
> ultro non inferre; interrogatus de fide, quicquid essem passurus, nihil
> dissimulare.[45]

> [for I had formed the resolution not to initiate discussions voluntarily
> about religion in those regions; but that when interrogated about my
> faith, I would dissimulate nothing no matter what I was destined to
> suffer.]

It is necessary to weigh up Milton's self-presentation here, in particular his
stated caution about not introducing the topic of religion, within the
context of the *Defensio Secunda* as precisely that — a defence in which
the more mature Milton is aiming to appear not as a provocative youth, but
as a defender of the Protestant faith in Catholic Italy. It is noteworthy that
Milton's is an unwillingness (*nolebam*)[46] to be *in religione tectior*. It is
probable that the uneasiness or cause of offence, if such there was,
occurred in informal conversation between Manso and Milton. That Milton
did in fact broach religious topics, at least in private conversation with
Italian academicians, is evident from his comment in his letter to Carlo
Dati, who, Milton states, was inclined to excuse his former freedom of
speech on the topic of Catholicism (*quoties de vestris ritibus nostro more*

---

[44] *CM* 8, 124.

[45] *CM* 8, 124.

[46] The *CM* translation "because *I had not thought proper* to be more guarded on the
point of religion" (8, 125) is inaccurate here as it fails to convey the force behind
nolebam.

loquendum erit).[47] Milton had hoped that Dati would secure similar indulgence from his fellow-academicians upon receipt of the Latin part of the 1645 volume (in a few pages of which there were some anti-papal sayings).[48] Was the Catholic Manso simply too sensitive? He was, after all, considered a man of such piety that on the feast of San Gennaro, when the saint's blood miraculously became liquid, it was he who was given the honor of carrying the blood in procession.[49] Another possibility however cannot be ruled out. Perhaps Milton's *nolebam in religione esse tectior* refers to a more formal incident, even in the Oziosi Academy itself. It is tempting to wonder if the youthful Protestant found himself unable to maintain that "obedience" prescribed by the statutes. Did he transgress the Oziosi's ban on theological subjects?[50] Suffice it to say at this point that, irrespective of the cause, there existed between the elderly Catholic Neapolitan and the youthful Protestant Londoner an unease on religious grounds which seems eventually to have restricted at least to some degree the social circles into which Manso felt himself able to introduce Milton.[51] That said, it is equally important also not to exaggerate the issue. If it was a tension, the evidence seems to suggest that it was a good-humored one — a tension that seems to underlie Manso's two-line Latin "written encomium" which he composed in Milton's honor, and which, as noted above, Milton was subsequently to prefix along with other such tributes to the 1645 volume of his poetry. The light-hearted tone of this distich, discussed below, as indeed of *Mansus* as a whole (in particular, in terms of

---

[47] *CM* 12, 50. See 59-60 above.

[48] *CM* 12, 50.

[49] Cf. Arthos, *Italian Cities*, 102.

[50] Or had Manso in particular, or the Oziosi in general, in some way or other come to learn of, say, Milton's anti-papal gunpowder epic *In Quintum Novembris*, in which the Eucharist is described in the pagan phrase *panificos ... deos* (56), while the triple-crowned pope (*tricoronifer* [55]), a secret adulterer, is the recipient of a dream vision inspired by none other than Satan himself, disguised as a Franciscan (90-132), and is himself a key instigator of a conspiracy involving death and destruction? Such of course is mere speculation.

[51] For the possibility of such religious tension at its worst, cf. Milton's probably exaggerated comments in *DS* about rumors of threats to his life from Jesuits in Rome: *Romam autem reversurum monebant mercatores se didicisse per literas parari mihi ab Iesuitis Anglis insidias si Romam reverterem; eo quod de religione nimis libere locutus essem* (*CM* 8, 124). Contrast Stoye, *English Travellers Abroad*, 180, who regards the fact that Milton was not molested, together with the appearance of so many Englishmen in central Italy, indicative that "The sad fate of John Mole, arrested for heresy at Rome in 1609 and imprisoned there for over twenty years because he refused to abjure, belonged to a phase that was now past."

the treatment of religion in both [!]), suggests that the friendship between the two men was neither marred nor even threatened in any serious way. Instead of either party taking offence, this tension seems to have been relaxed through learned repartee whereby a jocular Latin distich was answered by a good-humored Latin poem, in which Milton actually seems to poke fun at Manso's gentle criticism,[52] while also praising his addressee and invoking contemporary Italian encomia to do so.[53] The success of Milton's poem lies precisely in this fusion of humor[54] and panegyric.[55] Humor seems to underlie many of the stances assumed by both speaker and addressee in *Mansus*. At times Manso is a centaur figure, the hospitable Chiron welcoming guests into his *nobile antrum*; on a more elevated note, Milton is a swan ranking among fellow-swans, taking his own place in an important literary tradition in England, and thereby revealing pride in his heritage, but also flying to the shores of Italy[56] and finding a ready home in its fertile climes.[57] Immortality is a key theme in the poem. It is rendered possible through the power of the written word, through Manso's composition of biography, through Manso's own name inscribed in the pages of Tasso, through Milton's poetic biography, as it were, of Manso, through Milton's projected *Arthuriad*,[58] through being remembered after death by a close friend and by posterity as a whole, through virtue elevating the self into the celestial ranks. *Mansus* is thus a verse epistle that moves beyond its ostensible purpose of a token of gratitude to a Neapolitan host. A celebration of, as well as a longing for, *amicitia*, it is a poem of contrasts: a piece that is both personal and formal, both serious and good-humored, both conventional and innovative. Moreover through an intricate labyrinth of textual allusion, analogy and verbal reminiscence Milton reveals himself as a classicist, steeped in Greek and Latin literature, but also, and no less interestingly, as a man of his time, a Renaissance Englishman, echoing neo-Latin and vernacular poetry composed in both England and Italy. But if the poem sets up a series of parallels and contrasts between England and Italy — their

---

[52] See Low, "*Mansus*," at 107.

[53] See 137-148 below.

[54] Low, "*Mansus*," 119, states: "There is a subtle undercurrent of amusing grotesquerie, a shared joke."

[55] See Ralph W. Condee, "*Mansus* and the Panegyric tradition," *SR* 15 (1968), 174-192, reprinted in his *Structure in Milton's Poetry*, 85-103.

[56] For the flight motif in Milton's descriptions of his travels to Italy, see 2 above.

[57] For Oziosi academicians as swans, see 144 below.

[58] *Mansus* 78-84.

climates, their poets, their ancient traditions, their national identities —
then Manso himself can perhaps serve as a bridge between these different
worlds. As for Milton: by answering a two-line Latin distich by a one
hundred-line verse epistle, he too, like many Neapolitan academicians, has
composed his own "written encomium" of Manso.

CHAPTER 8

From "Angel" to "Angle": Manso and Milton

Like *Ad Salsillum, Mansus* is a poem of gratitude in a very specific sense in that it seems to reply to a Latin distich composed in Milton's honor by an Italian academician. Manso's "written encomium" is as follows:

> Ioannes Baptista Mansus, Marchio
> Villensis Neapolitanus ad Ioannem
> Miltonium Anglum.
>
> Ut mens, forma, decor, facies, mos, si pietas sic,
> non Anglus verum hercle Angelus ipse fores.
>
> [Giovanni Battista Manso of Naples, Marquis of Villa
> to John Milton Englishman
>
> If your religion were as your mind, beauty, charm, appearance,
> character, you would be not an Angle, but by Hercules a very
> angel.]

Read on a superficial level, Manso's two-line distich seems to amount to no more than a tribute to the physical and moral qualities which Milton possesses, praising his *mens, forma, decor, facies* and *mos*.[1] But with the phrase *si pietas sic* a different note is struck and the reader is even surprised. Manso is emphasising what he sees to be the one possible shortcoming: Milton's religious convictions. If his *pietas* were as outstanding as his physical appearance, he would be an "Angel" rather than an "Angle." The pun is not original with Manso.[2] Rather, it recalls an incident narrated by Bede in his *Ecclesiastical History* and by Milton's

---

[1] For similar praise of Milton's intellectual and physical prowess, cf. Carlo Dati's tribute discussed at 46-52 above.

[2] As noted by Parker, *Biography*, II, 827 and by Low, "*Mansus*," 106.

day virtually proverbial:[3] Gregory the Great, on seeing strange youths who had been brought to Rome for sale, made enquiries regarding their nationality and punned that because of their fair appearance they were not *Angli* but *Angeli*. Bede's version merits full quotation since it is possible that Milton recalled the entire incident as he replied to Manso's distich:

> Nec silentio praetereunda opinio quae de beato Gregorio traditione maiorum ad nos usque perlata est, qua videlicet ex causa admonitus tam sedulam erga salutem nostrae gentis curam gesserit. dicunt quia die quadam cum advenientibus nuper mercatoribus multa venalia in forum fuissent conlata, multi ad emendum confluxissent et ipsum Gregorium inter alios advenisse ac vidisse inter alia pueros venales positos candidi corporis ac venusti vultus, capillorum quoque forma egregia. quos cum aspiceret interrogavit, ut aiunt, de qua regione vel terra essent adlati dictumque est quia de Britannia insula cuius incolae talis essent aspectus. rursus interrogavit utrum idem insulani Christiani an paganis adhuc erroribus essent implicati. dictum est quod essent pagani. at ille intimo ex corde longa trahens suspiria, "Heu, pro dolor!" inquit "quod tam lucidi vultus homines tenebrarum auctor possidet, tantaque gratia frontispicii mentem ab interna gratia vacuam gestat!" rursus ergo interrogavit quod esset vocabulum gentis illius. responsum est quod Angli vocarentur. at ille: "Bene" inquit, "nam et angelicam habent faciem et tales angelorum in caelis decet esse coheredes. quod habet nomen ipsa provincia de qua isti sunt adlati?" responsum est quia Deiri vocarentur idem provinciales. at ille: "Bene" inquit, "Deiri, de ira eruti et ad misericordiam Christi vocati. rex provinciae illius quomodo appellatur?" responsum est quod Aelle diceretur. at ille adludens ad nomen ait: "Alleluia, laudem Dei Creatoris illis in partibus oportet cantari."[4]

Milton, citing Bede, was later to summarize the whole in his *History of Britain*:

> Howbeit not long after, they had the Christian Faith preached to them by a nation more remote, and (as a report went, accounted old in Bedas time) upon this occasion.
> The Northumbrians had a custom at that time, and many hundred yeares after not abolished, to sell their children for a small value into any foreign land. Of which number two comely youths were brought to Rome, whose fair and honest countenances invited Gregory Archdeacon of that city among others that beheld them, pitying their

---

[3] An earlier version of the story occurs in Paulus Diaconus, *S. Gregorii Magni Vita, Patrologia Latina*, ed. Jean-Paul Migne, LXXV, 50 (see Low, "*Mansus*," 125, n. 7).

[4] Text is that of B. Colgrave & R.A.B. Mynors, eds., *Bede's Ecclesiastical History* (Oxford, 1969), 132-134.

condition, to demand whence they were; it was answered by some who
stood by that they were Angli of the province Deira, subjects to Alla,
king of Northumberland, and by religion pagans. Which last Gregory
deploring, framed on a sudden this allusion to the three names he heard:
that the Angli so like to Angels should be snatched *de ira*, that is, from
the wrath of God, to sing Halleluia.[5]

As Low has rightly observed,[6] Manso's use of the pun has a wide
range of semi-humorous connotations and implications. He is assuming the
stance of the Christian Gregory, pitying the handsome yet pagan
newcomer, Milton, and thereby perhaps highlighting that religious tension
noted above. Milton, it might be thought, recognises the subtle
implications of the distich and adapts and inverts some of the features in
Bede's account of the incident. Thus it is possible to go further than Low's
suggestions[7] by arguing that Milton is echoing *specific details* of the
incident (in Bede) and turning the whole upon its head, alluding to such
themes as physical beauty, the contrast between the civilised Italian and
the barbarous foreigner, the notion of an angel and even including an
element of wordplay, which was the chief characteristic of the original.
Thus he cleverly acknowledges the sting implicit in Manso's distich and
sets out to counter those implications by inverting particular details of the
story, applying them in a totally different context and, in short, making
Manso himself the butt of the joke.

One important theme underlying Bede's version and implicit in
Manso's tribute is that of a foreigner coming to a new land. Both allude to
the handsome appearance of the newcomer. In Bede, Gregory had noticed
boys who were fair-skinned (*candidi corporis*), had charming faces
(*venusti vultus*) and beautiful hair (*capillorum quoque forma egregia*)[8] —
features which led Gregory to remark that they resembled angels. Manso's
distich likewise emphasises beauty. Assuming the stance of Gregory, he
praises the newcomer's *forma* and *facies*, but goes one stage further as he
admires his intellectual and moral qualities: his *mens*, *decor* and *mos*. The
theme recurs in an inverted form in *Mansus* as Milton applies it to Manso
himself and, subtly replying to the distich, he too praises both physical

---

[5] *CM* 10, 142.

[6] Low, "*Mansus*," 107.

[7] Low, "*Mansus*," 107, states that Manso "no doubt ... expected [Milton] to recognize
the famous pun on which his distich is based, and also to grasp some of the
implications of the allusion, implied by the context in which it was originally spoken."

[8] Cf. Paulus Diaconus, *S. Gregorii Magni Vita*, 50: ... *pueros venales positos lactei
corporis ac venusti vultus, capillos quoque praecipui candoris habentes.*

beauty and intellectual prowess. Manso, he says, possesses an old age which is spring-like (*Hinc longaeva tibi lento sub flore senectus/vernat* [*Mans.* 74-75]), his handsome features are still intact, enjoying the youthfulness of Aeson (*et Aesonios lucratur vivida fusos,/nondum deciduos servans tibi frontis honores* [*Mans.* 75-76]),[9] while his intellect and wit are very alert indeed (*ingeniumque vigens et adultum mentis acumen.* [*Mans.* 77]). But there is a stark contrast between the essential youthfulness of the *pueri* and Manso's *longaeva ... senectus* which can only attempt to preserve its youthful looks. This contrast is all the more emphatic if, as scholars have suggested, line 76 (*nondum deciduos servans tibi frontis honores*) is a hint at the fact that Manso wore a wig,[10] since this would be a skilful and ironic inversion of the boys' *capillorum ... forma egregia* admired by Gregory. The theme of physical beauty is later associated with Milton himself. Just as Bede had described the *venusti vultus* and, as noted above, the beautiful hair of the boys, so Milton alludes to his own *vultus* (91) which, he hopes, will be carved in marble, and to his hair (*comae*) which will be crowned with laurels (92-93).[11]

The influence of Manso's tribute upon Milton's poem works on another equally important level, namely, the contrast between the civilised Italian and the uncivilised foreigner. Gregory's pun was the consequence of questions concerning the particular region of the earth from which the *pueri* had come. On asking whether the inhabitants of their island are

---

[9] Cf. Milton, *El.* 2. 7-8: *O dignus tamen Haemonio iuvenescere succo,/dignus in Aesonios vivere posse dies.*

[10] Masson, *Poetical Works*, III, 535, cites evidence from the *Pinacotheca* of a certain Janus Nicius Erythraeus that Manso wore a wig:

" ... and, as is the fashion in the club-meetings of the Blessed Virgin, in which he was ranked as one of the members (*ut mos est in sodalitiis B. Virginis, in quibus ille numerabatur*), he would good-humoredly bear to have his defects publicly exposed. If bid lick the ground with his mouth, or kiss the feet of his club-fellows, he would not refuse, or escape the authority of the master of the revels; nor was he less obedient if he were ordered to snatch from his head the periwig with which he concealed his baldness (*caliendrum e capite quo calvitiem occultabat*), but immediately did as he was ordered, and made no scruple about exhibiting, amid the great laughter of the beholders, his perfectly bald head (*neque dubitabat, magno intuentium cum risu, caput pilis nudum ostendere*)."

Low, "*Mansus*," 119, states " ... one may hardly doubt that the old man did a double-take when he read these words" (i.e. lines 74-77). Contrast Revard, *Milton and the Tangles of Neaera's Hair*, 216, who somewhat oddly regards Milton's line as a reference to "the many laurels of honor that the old man had bestowed upon him."

[11] *Mans.* 91-93: *Forsitan et nostros ducat de marmore vultus,/nectens aut Paphia myrti aut Parnasside lauri/fronde comas. At ego secura pace quiescam.*

Christian or Pagan,[12] he is told that they are pagans who have come from Britain.[13] Gregory has initiated the discussion.[14] Milton describes himself in *Mansus* as a *iuvenis* — like the *pueri* in Bede and thereby contrasting with Manso, the *fortunate senex* (49), *diis dilecte senex* (70) and father figure *Manse pater* (25). More specifically, he is a "young foreigner" (*iuvenis peregrinus* [26]) and describes Britain from the perspective of the Italian — cold and northern (*Mans.* 24-29).[15] However, he proceeds to defend his native land, stating that it possesses eloquent and cultured poets. As opposed to the implications of Manso's tribute, the British race is not a *genus incultum* (35).

Another feature of Manso's tribute which may be echoed in *Mansus* is the element of wordplay, which occurs no fewer than three times in Bede's account: *Angli/Angeli*; *Deiri/de ira*; *Aelle/Alleluia*. The last of these is a pun on a name (*adludens ad nomen*). Milton in depicting the withdrawal of Apollo to Chiron's cave seems to play on Manso's name in the line *nobile man̲s̲ueti cessit Chironis in antrum* (60).[16]

The final point of Manso's distich in relation to *Mansus* is the reference to an angel (*Angelus*). Gregory had likened the *pueri* to angels because of their physical appearance. Manso certainly praises among other things Milton's *forma* and *facies*, but hints that an equation with an angel is impossible because of Milton's protestantism (*si pietas sic,/non Anglus, verum hercle Angelus ipse fores*). It is noteworthy that the theme of angels, and, in particular, the nature of an angelic *facies*, had occurred in Manso's *Erocallia* (1628) which, according to De Filippis and others,[17]

---

[12] *interrogavit utrum idem insulani Christiani an paganis adhuc erroribus essent implicati.*

[13] *de Britania insula, cuius incolae talis essent aspectus.* Cf. Paulus Diaconus, 50: *dictumque est quia de Britania insula cuius incolae tali omnes decore niterent.*

[14] Contrast Milton's statement in *DS* that he had decided not to *introduce* the subject of religion: *sic enim mecum statueram de religione quidem iis in locis sermones ultro non inferre* (*CM* 12, 124).

[15] *Mans.* 24-29: *Ergo ego te Clius et magni nomine Phoebi/Manse pater, iubeo longum salvere per aevum/missus Hyperboreo iuvenis peregrinus ab axe./Nec tu longinquam bonus aspernabere musam,/quae nuper gelida vix enutrita sub Arcto/imprudens Italas ausa est volitare per urbes.* For a useful discussion of Milton's lines vis-à-vis their Hyperborean context, cf. Revard, *The Tangles of Neaera's Hair*, 217-218.

[16] Cf. the possible pun on Salzilli (*Salsillus*) in *salsa regna* (*Ad Salsillum* [41]) discussed at 87 above. For punning in *Mansus* in relation to Ovid, see 157-158 below. For verbal play in Italian academies, see 8, 31-32 above.

[17] See De Filippis, "Milton and Manso," *passim.*

may have been one of those two books (*bina ... pocula*) described in *Epitaphium Damonis* as gifts given by Manso to Milton. In *Dialogue* VII of the *Erocallia*, Manso discusses the appearance of angels, and in so doing cites examples from both the Old and New Testament of the equation of angels with light.[18] Thus "an angel is the image of God, the manifestation of a hidden light, a pure and most splendid mirror" (*Angelus est imago Dei, manifestatio occulti luminis, speculum purum splendidissimum*).[19] He invokes other examples of the association of angels with light,[20] in particular their possession of a natural radiance in accordance with their intellect: *Angeli perficiuntur duplici lumine, lumine scilicet naturali, prout sunt intellectus quidam, et lumine gratuito perficiente ad actus hierarchicos, et utrumque lumen est unum in omnibus.*[21] Is it possible then that at the end of a poem composed as a response to Manso's encomium, Milton, as well as inverting the implications of the distich itself, is also echoing Manso's own discussion of angels? In the closing lines of the poem he envisages himself transcending the boundaries of this earthly existence, and colors the whole with pervasive light imagery. Thus it is an *ignea virtus* (96) that leads to heaven. His own *vultus* is suffused with radiant light (*purpureo suffundar lumine vultus* [99]). Now admitted to the celestial or perhaps even angelic ranks he can look down, smile (*ridens* [99]) (in defiance?) upon Manso and his world, and applaud himself (*plaudam mihi* [100]).[22] Although there is no mention of an angel, the notion of applause in a celestial context may recall the heavenly hosts of Milton's *Elegia Tertia*, who applaud the Bishop of Winchester with their jewelled wings (*agmina gemmatis plaudunt caelestia pennis* [59]). The smiling countenance (*ridens purpureo suffundar lumine vultus*) anticipates perhaps the description of Raphael in *Paradise Lost* 8. 618-619 as an angel "with a smile that glowed/Celestial rosy-red." In any case, the speaker's self-association with *lumen* is

---

[18] *Erocallia* (Venice, 1628), 687-688: "... onde nelle sacre lettere dell' antico testamento si disse, *Qui facis Angelos tuos spiritus et ministros tuos ignem urentem* e parimente nel nuovo *Facies eius erat ut Sol, et pedes eius tanquam columna ignis,* e nell' uno e nell' altro gli Angioli dell' ordine superiore sono propriamente Serafini chiamati, percioch' essi, in cui primieramente l' Angelica Natura risplende, sono più di tutti gli altri luminosi e ardenti."

[19] *Erocallia*, 688.

[20] *Erocallia*, 688: *Cum lux illa prima facta est, Angeli creati intelliguntur.*

[21] *Erocallia*, 688.

[22] Revard, *The Tangles of Neaera's Hair*, 223 notes that Milton uses the phrase *plaudam mihi* in *Prolusion* 6, where he congratulates himself upon being more successful than Orpheus and Amphion.

striking, as though by the end of the poem his *facies* (in accordance with some of those sources cited by Manso in the *Erocallia*) does indeed possess the characteristics of an *Angelus*. There is a contrast moreover between Milton smiling from the heavens (99) and Marino, depicted earlier as smiling from a bronze monument (*vidimus arridentem operoso ex aere poetam* [16]), the erection of which was seen as an instance of Manso's *pietas* towards a dead friend (*nec manes pietas tua cara fefellit amici* [15]).[23] Milton, while certainly considering the possibility of a monument being built in his honor (91-93), goes one stage further by envisaging a heavenly, as opposed to an earthly, reward. In this respect he surpasses Marino. The phrase *plaudam mihi* (100)[24] contrasts sharply with the *plausumque virorum* (52) — the applause of mankind — which, he had stated, would be received by Manso himself. The implication of lines 94-100 is that even Milton, the supposed pagan — *ipse ego* (95) — can be an *angelus*, but since Manso is not willing to recognise the fact, Milton will have to applaud himself. The passage elaborates upon the Christian/pagan theme which was important in Bede and implicit in Manso's tribute. Milton has inverted the original, subverting the pagan world of the poem and ascending to a Christian Heaven.[25] Thus in replying to a "written encomium," Milton challenges its author's assumptions by depicting *inter alia* an *Anglus* who can perhaps also be an *angelus*!

[23] Cf. *pia* .../*officia* (17-18)

[24] Cf. Horace, *Satires* 1.1.66-67: *mihi plaudo/ipse domi*.

[25] Just as Chaucer's Troilus transcended the labyrinth of his pagan existence and, assuming a Christian stance, laughed at the world which he had left behind. (*Troilius and Cresside* V 1807-1827). Noteworthy in particular are lines 1821-1822: "And in hymself he lough right at the wo/Of hem that wepten for his deth so faste." (Text: *The Works of Geoffrey Chaucer*, ed. F.N. Robinson [London, 1957]).

CHAPTER 9

Mansus and Italian Encomia of Manso

As well as cleverly responding to a Latin distich, *Mansus* takes its place among the many Italian encomia *Poesie Diversi a Gio. Battista Manso, Marchese di Villa* which Manso had received from fellow-academicians and other contemporary *litterati*, and had appended to his own collection of Italian verse *Poesie Nomiche* (Venice, 1635).[1] While parallels are virtually inevitable in view of the laudatory nature of these pieces addressed to a great patron of the arts, there are nevertheless some similarities which may in themselves be sufficient to suggest that Milton was familiar with these tributes. This is all the more likely in view of the argument of Black and De Filippis, discussed above, that the *Poesie Nomiche* constituted one of the *bina pocula* presented by Manso to Milton.[2]

That Milton was very much aware of the great esteem in which Manso was held by his fellow Italians is indicated by the prose preface and the poem proper. In the preface, as noted above,[3] he states that Manso has achieved distinction *apud Italos*[4] for his intellectual abilities (*ingenii laude*), his devotion to literature (*literarum studio*) and his bravery in war (*bellica virtute*). Contemporary tributes, as might be expected, had likewise stressed Manso's versatility in the fields of literature and warfare. A certain Antonio

---

[1] The title *Poesie Nomiche* is derived from the Greek νόμος, used in the sense of "a type of early melody created by Tarpander for the lyre as an accompaniment to Epic texts" (H.H. Liddell & R. Scott, *A Greek-English Lexicon* [Oxford, 1968], 1180). This is extended to embrace the type of verse itself. (See under *Poesia Nomica* in the *Grande Dizionario della Lingua Italiana* [Turin, 1981], XI, 521).

[2] De Filippis, "Milton and Manso," *passim*.

[3] See 120 above.

[4] Milton is probably using *apud* in the sense of "among." It can however be translated in the more specific sense of "in the writings of ..." as designating the author of a work.

Biaguazzone, for instance, has two poems which make this point: "Loda la mano impiegata nell'armi e nello scriver d'Amore;"[5] "Loda l'imprese dell'armi e i dialoghi dell'Amore."[6] Here the poet marvels at the way in which Manso has achieved distinction in battle and in poetry with the "sword" and "golden plectrum" respectively: through these means Manso has opened up for himself the way to immortal life; Manso indeed is worthy of a double laurel-wreath in that he knows how to use the pen and brandish the sword:

> Qual può fregio adeguar tue glorie tante?
>   Tu col ferro, e col plettro aureo, e canoro,
>   MANSO, à vita immortal t'apri la strada.
> Ben si deve al tuo crin doppio l'alloro,
>   Che sai la penn' oprar, rotar la spada,
>   Di par saggio guerriero, e prode Amante (9-14)[7]

> [What adornment can equal such great glories of yours? You, Manso, with the sword and with the golden, tuneful plectrum have opened up for yourself the way to immortal life. Your hair is well-deserving of a double laurel-wreath in that you know how to use the pen and brandish the sword, you who are equally a wise warrior and a brave lover.]

The same point is made by Scipione Sambiasi: "Glorioso colla spada e colla penna."[8] Similarly Anello Sarriano praises Manso's "valor" and "canto": Manso deals death with the sword, and life with the pen, and knows how to use brave valor in war, and harmonious song in peace.[9] The theme recurs in Scipione Errico: "Loda l'attioni nella guerra e lo studio nelle scienze"[10] and in Gio. Battista Comentati: "Lodato nella guerra e nella pace,"[11] who praises intelligence and invincibility in arms as represented by Apollo and Mars respectively: it is with difficulty that the speaker can discern whether wise

---

[5] *Poesie Nomiche* (Venice, 1635), 266: ["He praises the hand which is employed in arms and in writing about love."]

[6] *Poesie Nomiche*, 266: ["He praises his exploits in arms and his dialogues on love."]

[7] *Poesie Nomiche*, 266.

[8] *Poesie Nomiche*, 280: ["Glorious with the sword and with the pen."]

[9] *Poesie Nomiche*, 301: *"Dà morte con la spada, e vita con la penna*: MANSO, che sai trattar forte, e canoro/Ne la guerra il valor, in pace il canto." (3-4)

[10] *Poesie Nomiche*, 302: ["He praises his exploits in war and his study in the sciences."]

[11] *Poesie Nomiche*, 304. ["He is praised in war and in peace."]

Apollo or fierce Mars shines ("risplende") more through Manso.[12] One poem, by Andrea Vittorelli, is entitled "Loda nella militia e nella dottrina";[13] another, by Vincenzo Petrone, entitled "Paragona le lodi nel guerreggiare e nello scrivere,"[14] achieves a parallel between Apollo and Mars, the palm and the laurel, Bellona and the Muses, the spear and the lyre, the sword and the pen, blood and ink:

> MANSO, se tu guerreggi, o se tu scrivi
>   Sii seguace d' Apollo, o sii di Marte,
>   L'hoste nel campo atterri, e i nomi avvivi
>   Ne l'immortali tue famose carte.
> O se la Palma, o se l'Allor coltivi,
>   Hor con Bellona, hor con le Muse à parte,
>   Per l'hasta per la lira eterno vivi,
>   Raro prodigio di Natura, e d'Arte.
> O se la spada, o se la penna adopri,
>   Col sangue, e con l'inchiostro i tuoi valori,
>   E ne i petti, e ne i fogli a noi discopri. (1-11)[15]

[Manso, whether you are engaged in battle or whether you are writing, whether you are a follower of Apollo or of Mars, you terrify the enemy in the battle-field and you bring names to life in your immortal, renowned pages. Or whether you cultivate the palm or the laurel — at one time associated with Bellona, at another with the Muses — , through the spear and the lyre you live eternally, a rare marvel of Nature and of Art. Or whether you employ the sword or the pen, with blood and with ink you reveal to us your courage both in your breast and in your pages.]

In the opening lines of *Mansus* Milton stresses the fact that his poem is not the only one (*haec quoque*) which Manso has received (1-2).[16] He is extremely well known to the chorus of Apollo (*Manse choro notissime*

---

[12] *Poesie Nomiche*, 304: "Mal discerno Signor, qual più risplende/Per tè, se'l saggio Apollo, o'l fiero Marte" (1-2). Cf. the prose preface to *Mansus* in which Milton had quoted Tasso's praise "Risplende il Manso."

[13] *Poesie Nomiche*, 310: ["Praise in warfare and in learning."]

[14] *Poesie Nomiche*, 310: ["He compares his praise in warfare and in writing."]

[15] *Poesie Nomiche*, 310.

[16] While it is just possible that *haec quoque* means "this as well as other poems of mine," it is much more likely that it means "this as well as other tributes which you have received." See Bush, *Variorum*, 270.

Phoebi [2]) and, like Gallus and Maecenas, has been honored by the god.[17] Milton is echoing Virgil's sixth eclogue in which the *Phoebi chorus* rose up to honor the poet Gallus.[18] Now this chorus of Phoebus has honored Manso through the composition of tributes. This is the *honos* (3) which he has received. And, Milton states, if his own *Musa* proves adequate, Manso will sit among victorious wreaths of ivy and laurel (*Tu quoque si nostrae tantum valet aura Camoenae/victrices hederas inter laurosque sedebis.* [*Mans.* 5-6]). The opening six lines seem to place Milton's Latin tribute among the Italian poems addressed to, and in praise of, Manso. His poem is but one among the many *carmina* which the *Pierides* are singing. The three features: *Pierides*, the *Phoebi chorus* and *lauri* occur in an Italian tribute by a certain Don Vincenzo Toraldo. Here the "figlie di Pierio" are conquered by the Muses. They in turn are surpassed by Manso himself, who receives a new garland and for whom the laurels grow. Indeed it is in Manso that Apollo has renewed the "extinct glories" of his "chorus":

> Restar le figlie di Pierio (à prova
>   Con le Muse cantando) e dome, e vinte,
>   Voi lor vincete, e le palme, onde cinte
>   Fur quelle, à voi tesson ghirlanda nova.
> Sì che ne l'età nostra in voi rinova
>   Le glorie Febo del suo Choro estinte;
>   Per voi crescon gli allori: e in voi distinte
>   Par, che le gratie sue largo il Ciel piove. (1-8) [19]

[The Pierians (singing in competition with the Muses) remained subdued and vanquished. You conquer them [i.e. the Muses] and they are weaving the palms with which they had been girt as a new garland for you. In such a way in our age does Phoebus renew in you the extinct glories of his chorus. For you the laurels grow and it seems that Heaven generously rains down her own graces especially upon you.]

One final noteworthy aspect of lines 1-6 is the reference to Maecenas. Since Gallus and Maecenas, Apollo has deemed no one so worthy of honor as Manso. While the equation with Maecenas is almost inevitable in a poem

---

[17] *Mans.* 3-4: *Quandoquidem ille alium haud aequo est dignatus honore,/post Galli cineres, et Mecaenatis Hetrusci.*

[18] Virgil, *Ecl.* 6.64-66: *Tum canit errantem Permessi ad flumina Gallum/Aonas in montis ut duxerit una sororum,/utque viro Phoebi chorus adsurrexerit omnis.*

[19] *Poesie Nomiche*, 262.

addressed to a great patron, it also occurs in the Italian tributes. Estonne Stordito calls Manso a "nova Mecena e glorioso,"[20] and develops the theme as he prophesies that mount Parnassus will call Manso "Maecenas, whose name will never have an end":

> Vedrò (volgendo gl' anni) il tuo bel crine
>   Cinto di chiari, e gloriosi rai,
>   O magnanimo MANSO, hor ch' appres'hai
>   A giovar vive menti, e pellegrine.
> Mecenate, il cui nome unqua haurà fine,
>   Te chiamerà Parnaso, e tù ben sai,
>   Che nè Apollo obliò, nè Urania mai
>   Di magnanimo cor gratie divine. (1-8)[21]

[As the years roll by, I will see your beautiful hair surrounded by bright and glorious rays, o great-hearted Manso, now that you have learnt how to assist living and foreign minds. Mount Parnassus will call you Maecenas, whose name will never have an end, and you are well aware that neither Apollo nor Urania have ever forgotten the divine graces of a generous heart.]

Milton proceeds to present Manso vis-à-vis his relationship with Tasso and Marino. Then he gradually introduces himself — a "young foreigner" who has come to Italy:

> Tu quoque si nostrae tantum valet aura Camoenae
> victrices hederas inter laurosque sedebis.
> Te pridem magno felix concordia Tasso
> iunxit et aeternis inscripsit nomina chartis.
> Mox tibi dulciloquum non inscia Musa Marinum
> tradidit, ille tuum dici se gaudet alumnum,
> dum canit Assyrios divum prolixus amores;
> mollis et Ausonias stupefecit carmine nymphas. (5-12)

[You too, if the breath of our Camoena is sufficiently strong, will sit among the ivy and laurels of victory. In times past a happy friendship joined you to the mighty Tasso and inscribed your name in his eternal pages. Next the Muse, not without knowledge, entrusted the sweetly-speaking Marino to you; he rejoiced in being called your nursling, while in verbose fashion he sang of the Assyrian love affairs of the gods, and gently with his verse amazed the Ausonian nymphs.]

---

[20] *Poesie Nomiche*, 286.

[21] *Poesie Nomiche*, 287.

....
Ergo ego te Clius et magni nomine Phoebi
Manse pater, iubeo longum salvere per aevum
missus Hyperboreo iuvenis peregrinus ab axe.
Nec tu longinquam bonus aspernabere musam,
quae nuper gelida vix enutrita sub Arcto
imprudens Italas ausa est volitare per urbes. (24-29)

[Therefore, father Manso, in the name of Clio and of mighty Apollo, I, a
young foreigner sent from the Hyperborean skies, wish you a lengthy and
healthy life. You in your goodness will not spurn a muse who has travelled
a long distance, and, having with difficulty found nourishment beneath the
frozen Bear, has recently ventured in her rashness to fly through the cities
of Italy.]

The general thematic and structural progression of Milton's lines bears a
striking resemblance to one of the Italian tributes by a certain Angelita
Scaramuzza:

Il Loda nelle lodi del Tasso, e del Marino

Gloria di Pindo, honor del secol nostro,
   Pregio di Febo e Marte, al cui gentile
   Eccelso nome io riverente humile,
   MANSO, inchino'l pensier, sacro l'inchiostro.
Cedano à voi l'alte corone, e l'ostro,
   Voi, cui la fama oltre a l'estrema Thile
   Porta raccolta in sen d'heroico stile
   Di saver, di valor mirabil mostro.
Voi protettor de l'alta, che Buglione
   Tromba cantò con celebrato grido,
   Voi del plettro dolcissimo d'Adone.
Di me peregrin tratto à questo lido
   Per sì, di veder voi, nobil cagione,
   Gradite il cor divoto, il voler fido.[22]

[*Praise included in the praises of Tasso and Marino*

Glory of Mount Pindus, honor of our age, merit of Phoebus and Mars,
to your noble, sublime name, Manso, I reverently and humbly incline my
thought and consecrate my ink. Let lofty garlands and purple yield to
you, you whose fame a collection [of poems] carries within its heroic

---

[22] *Poesie Nomiche*, 300.

style beyond furthermost Thule — a wonderful prodigy of your wisdom and valor. You were the patron of the lofty trumpet which sang of [Godfrey of] Bouillon with its renowned blare; you were the patron of the very sweet plectrum of *L'Adone*. Accept my devoted heart and loyal desire — I who, as a foreigner, have been brought to this shore in order to see you — a noble reason.]

In both instances Manso is presented as a victor (*victrices hederas inter* [6]/"Cedano à voi l'alte corone" [5]); this is followed by a reference to the renown which he will achieve through the heroic writings of Tasso (7-8)/(9-10). In Milton, Tasso has written Manso's name in his eternal pages (*et aeternis inscripsit nomina chartis* [8]) — a theme which occurs in one of Tasso's tributes to Manso in which he states that Manso's name is inscribed by the gods in beautiful metal or in stone — not only in one thousand pages ("E'l il nome vostro in bel metallo, o in pietra/Scriver si dee, non solo in mille carte." [5-6]).[23] Milton's line is a reference to the fact that Tasso mentioned Manso by name in his *Gerusalemme Conquistata* — a point made in the prose preface to *Mansus*.[24] Scaramuzza too alludes to Tasso, not to the *Gerusalemme Conquistata*, as in Milton, but to the *Gerusalemme Liberata*, the hero of which was Godfrey of Bouillon (hence "Buglione" [9]). In both Milton and Scaramuzza this is followed by an allusion to Marino. In both poems Manso is depicted as Marino's patron: in Milton, Marino is Manso's *alumnus* (10); in Scaramuzza Manso is Milton's "protettor" (9)/(11).[25] More specific is the reference to Marino's Italian poem *L'Adone* (1623) and to the "sweetness" of Marino's style.[26] In Milton, he is *dulciloquum ... Marinum* (9) and *mollis* (12) as he composes *L'Adone* (*dum canit Assyrios divum prolixus amores* [11]);[27] Scaramuzza mentions the "plettro dolcissimo d'Adone" (11). Noteworthy is the subsequent progression of the passages in each poem whereby the speaker introduces himself as a foreigner — a *peregrinus* — who has come to a new land. Milton is a *iuvenis peregrinus* (26) whose *Musa* has ventured to fly *Italas ... per urbes* (29); the speaker of the Italian poem is introduced as "me peregrin tratto à questo lido" (12).

---

[23] *Poesie Nomiche*, 257.

[24] See 120 above.

[25] Line 11, sc. "protettor."

[26] See Mirollo, *Poet of the Marvelous*, 115-164.

[27] Bush, *Variorum*, 271, perceptively states that Marino's "conceits ... are doubtless comprehended in Milton's *dulciloquum* (9) and *mollis* (12)."

Having described himself as a young foreigner, Milton proceeds to defend the literary merits of his native land. To do so, he employs the image of the swan for the poet (30-33), discussed below.[28] It is interesting to note at this point that the swan/poet allegory also occurs in some of the Italian tributes, as the members of the Accademia degli Oziosi are depicted as swans. This seems to give special emphasis to Milton's *nos etiam* (30) as he states that he too (like Manso) has heard swans/poets singing. A certain Ferrante Rovitto, for example, describes the members of the academy as "a band of swans unique and rare in song" ("Schiera di Cigni al canto unica e rara" [4]).[29] Gio. Camillo Cacace expresses his desire to become a member of the academy ("Desidera esser seco nell'Accademia"). He praises Manso. If admitted, he envisages himself as being able to sing as a swan upon the waves: "O se frà quelle in sorte esser mi lice/Potrò cantar anch'io Cigno su l'onde."[30]

Milton's poem itself contains some possible allusions to Manso's academy and its members. Lines 54-69 constitute a mythological passage in which Milton states that Apollo will be said to have dwelt in Manso's abode, even though it was with reluctance that the same god came to king Admetus's farm. When he wished to avoid the noisy cowherds, he retreated to the cave of gentle Chiron and found solace in his music. The significance of this passage and, in particular, of the Manso/Chiron analogy will be discussed in detail below,[31] but at this point it should be noted that Milton's lines contain a number of features which merit consideration in the context of the Italian tributes, and which might support the suggestion that this is in fact an allegorical representation of the Accademia degli Oziosi. The depiction of *otium* in Chiron's *nobile ... antrum* (60) is not without significance in view of the name of Manso's academy. Furthermore, the adjective *nobile* (60) could certainly be applied to the academy, and does indeed occur in one of the tributes, as Tomaso Ciamboli describes his escape from noisy warfare into the "nobil magion" of Manso:

---

[28] For a discussion of the motif in relation to Leland and Ariosto, see 165-178 below.

[29] *Poesie Nomiche*, 288.

[30] *Poesie Nomiche*, 274, lines 12-13. ["O, if I can have the good fortune to be among such men, I too will be able to sing as a swan upon the waves."]

[31] See 149-164 below.

> Però fuggendo a te da le crud' armi
>> Di tai nemici anch'io, dal volgo fuori
>> In sì nobil magion tento ritrarmi.
> Ove l'Otio spargendo ampi sudori
>> Sù i bei campi di gloria al suon de' carmi,
>> Miete palme, e trofei di mille honori.[32]

[Yet I too, by fleeing to you from cruel battle and from such enemies, I try to retire from the populace outside into so noble a dwelling, where leisure, by lavishing toil in abundance upon the beautiful fields of glory to the sound of music, wins palms and trophies of a thousand honors.]

Milton too describes the escape from noise into a noble abode. That element of "otio" explicitly mentioned in the Italian poem is implied in *Mansus* — in the presentation of the traditional features of pastoral *otium* (greenery, a stream, the shade of a tree, and music).

One final point is possible punning on Manso's name. While this feature occurs in Manso's distich (*Anglus/Angelus*), in Bede's passage (*Angli/Angeli*; *Deiri/de ira*; *Aelle/Alleluia*), in line 60 of Milton's poem (*nobile mansueti cessit Chironis in antrum* [60]) and, as discussed below, in the Ovidian source of that passage,[33] it is striking that specific wordplay on Manso's name (and formal title) also occurs in some of the Italian tributes. This is most clearly illustrated by a poem entitled "Lodi espresse nel nome" by Gennaro Grossi — an example of the device on a much more extensive and ingenious level:

> La *MAN SO*vrana, onde'l Monarca Hispano
>> Debellò più d'un campo, e più d'un mostro,
>> Voli' hai, Signor, da ogni tenzon lontano
>> Solitaria à trattar penna, ed inchiostro. (1-4)[34]

[Sir, you wished that that sovereign hand, with the help of which the Spanish Monarch won more than one battle-field and overcame more than one monster, far from every strain, should use the pen and ink in solitude.]

---

[32] *Poesie Nomiche*, 281, lines 9-14.

[33] For the Ovidian connection, see 155-158 below.

[34] *Poesie Nomiche*, 277.

Di tue glorie il gran *MAR, CHE SE*mpre nove
   Piaggie, e Reggie circonda, adduce al Mondo
   Te *DI VILLA*, e Cittade, hor Pane, hor Giove. (12-14)[35]

[The great sea of your glories, which always encircles new shores and palaces,
reveals you to the universe — you who are now Pan of the villa and now
Jupiter of the city.]

The same device is used by Margherita Sarrocchi, who proclaims:

Già mira in te risorti il secol nostro
   Gli antichi honori, e'l tuo gran nome addita
   Di Virtù *MAN SO*vrana altero mostro." (12-14)[36]

   [Already our age admires the ancient honors which have been revived in you,
   and your mighty name indicates your sovereign hand as a proud demonstration
   of your valor.]

Milton proceeds to describe the effect of Apollo's music upon the
world of nature, attributing to his *carmen* the power which is usually
associated with Orpheus: it can thus move river-banks and boulders, cause
cliffs to nod, trees to hurry down mountain-slopes, and lynxes to grow tame
(65-69).[37] Some of the Italian poets had attributed a similar power to Manso's
poetry. Angelo di Costanzo, for example, states:

D'Italia, al suon de' tuoi soavi accenti
   Fioriscono le rive, e i piani, e i monti,
   Versan liquidi argenti i fiumi, e i fonti,
   Stan cheti a udirti i più rabbiosi venti.
E gli augelli, e le fere, e i pesci intenti
   Sono a tuoi carmi sì famosi, e conti.[38]

---

[35] *Poesie Nomiche*, 277.

[36] *Poesie Nomiche*, 303.

[37] *Mans.* 65-69: *Tum neque ripa suo, barathro nec fixa sub imo,/saxa stetere loco, nutat
Trachinia rupes,/nec sentit solitas, immania pondera, silvas,/emotaeque suis properant
de collibus orni,/mulcenturque novo maculosi carmine lynces.*

[38] *Poesie Nomiche*, 257. Borzelli, *Giovan Battista Manso*, 57-58, points out that this
poem was originally dedicated to a certain Ferrante Carafa, Marchese di San Lucido.

[At the sound of your sweet accents the streams and plains and mountains of Italy begin to bloom; clear silver rivers and springs pour forth their waters; the most furious winds are quiet to hear you. And the birds and wild beasts and fish are attentive to your songs so renowned and accomplished.]

But Milton has adapted these motifs to a novel context. Instead of hymning Manso's poetic powers, he proclaims instead the excellence of Apollo, who may in fact function here as a prototype of the speaker himself.[39] Milton, as the young man from the Hyperborean skies belongs to a people beloved of Apollo.[40]

Finally the association of Manso with such gods as Jupiter and Apollo occurs in both *Mansus* and the Italian tributes. Milton says that these gods must have looked with favor on Manso's birth:

Diis dilecte senex, te Iupiter aequus oportet
nascentem, et miti lustrarit lumine Phoebus,
Atlantisque nepos; neque enim nisi carus ab ortu
diis superis poterit magno favisse poetae. (*Mans.* 70-73).

[Old man, beloved of the gods, Jupiter must have been favorable towards you at your birth, and Phoebus and the grandson of Atlas must have looked upon you with kindly glance, for no one, unless he is dear to the gods from his birth, could have shown favor to a mighty poet.]

This general notion of divine favor at Manso's birth can be observed in a poem by Fra. Giulio Carrafa:

Havesti al nascer tuo benigna stella,
    Che placido si rende'l mar, e'l lido,
    E per dritto sentier t'adduce al porto." (9-11)[41]

[You had an auspicious star at your birth, which renders the sea and shore so calm and brings you to the harbor by a direct route.]

The explicit reference to Jupiter and Apollo is to be found in a poem by Gio. Ambrosio Biffi, who sees Manso as a second Jupiter ("un folgorante Giove")

---

[39] Cf. Revard, *The Tangles of Neaera's Hair*, 219: "he has made Apollo's song the poet's song — his own unstoppable song."

[40] Cf. Revard, *The Tangles of Neaera's Hair*, 217.

[41] *Poesie Nomiche*, 261.

brandishing his thunderbolts; simultaneously he is a second Apollo because of the quality of his verse:

> *Il pareggia à Giove, Apollo e à Marte*
>
> Un folgorante Giove il tuo valore
>   Ti rende al balenar, qual'hor s'accinga
>   La fulminante destra à l'arme, e spinga
>   Frà gli eserciti, ò MANSO, alto il furore. (1-4)
>
> ....
>
> La spada al guerreggiar, la Cetra in pace,
>   Fà lieto ribombar qual più riluce
>   Apollo, e Marte in Ciel, te solo in Terra. (12-14)[42]

> [*The comparison with Jupiter, Apollo and Mars*
>
> Your valor renders you a Jove flashing with lightning when your fulminating right hand prepares itself for battle and, o Manso, incites great fury among armies.
>
> ....
>
> Your sword in war, your lyre in peace happily proclaim the great extent to which Apollo and Mars shine in the sky, but you alone on earth.]

Antonio Gallerati likens Manso to Apollo: "Il paragona ad Apollo nell' arme, e nel canto": Manso is a second Apollo on account of his military and literary skill. In fact, both Mars and Apollo adorn him with the palm and laurels of victory.[43] Similarly, in another poem, Gallerati states that Manso has been honored by Apollo and Mars: "Honorato da Apollo, e da Marte."[44]

It is evident that *Mansus* acknowledges certain virtues of Manso which had likewise been extolled by contemporary Italian academicians in the *Poesie di Diversi*. But Milton innovates at the same time as he imitates. In singing the praises of poetry, he enunciates his own poetic plans, reinventing the entire panegyric tradition, as his purported tribute to Manso becomes in effect a quite daringly self-referential "written encomium."

---

[42] *Poesie Nomiche*, 267.

[43] *Poesie Nomiche*, 267: "di palma, e d'alloro/Festeggiandone in Cielo/T'ornaron Marte, e'l gran Signor di Delo." (8-10) ["Mars and the great Lord of Delos in celebration in Heaven adorn you with the palm and the laurel."]

[44] *Poesie Nomiche*, 268.

CHAPTER 10

Mansueti ... Chironis: Manso, the Tame Centaur

If Milton's poem assumes its rightful place in a seventeenth-century academic context, it also looks back to the world of classical mythology. As is so frequently true of Milton's Latin poetry, *Mansus* thus draws upon things "ancient" as well as "modern." That subtle intellectual humor already noted as underlying Milton's response to, and inversion of, Manso's Latin distich manifests itself on a mythological level also, especially in regard to the role played in the poem by the centaur Chiron. It is by means of an analogy between Manso and Chiron that the poem pays a uniquely humorous tribute to a tame host, or to describe him in Milton's own words in the poem, a *mansuetus ... Chiron*. But the role of Chiron is not confined to addressee. On the contrary, it sometimes shifts from addressee to speaker and vice versa. Milton moreover remoulds into a novel contemporary setting traditional features of the Chiron myth, and, in particular, Ovid's versions of that myth. But why should Manso be equated with a hybrid creature?

Chiron was a learned centaur, host and famous foster-father of poets; tutor, educator and even tamer of heroes. It was under his painstaking care that such heroes as Aesculapius, Hercules, Jason, and Achilles were nurtured, educated and instructed in the arts of warfare, wrestling, poetry, music, and song. According to Hesiod,[1] he lived on mount Pelion and was the teacher of Achilles, Jason, Actaeon and others. Hesiod indeed seems to have taken a particular interest in Chiron the educator, as fragmentary evidence suggests that he wrote a work on the subject of Chiron's teachings. Chiron also occurs in Homer, four times in the *Iliad*.[2] And yet Homer seems to have suppressed Chiron's role as teacher and instead to have, in a sense, played up the role of Achilles'

---

[1] Cat, fr 204.87ff.

[2] Two occurrences describe a spear given by Chiron to Peleus, and a spear used by Achilles in the duel with Hector (*Iliad* 16.141-144; 19. 388-391); and two outline Chiron's role as instructor of medicine (*Iliad* 4. 217-219 and 11. 828-832).

other teacher Phoenix, his instructor in warfare and debate, doing so, quite deliberately, Mackie argues, because Chiron and Phoenix together help to reveal different aspects of Achilles' personality.[3] By contrast, other ancient sources, chief among whom are Pindar and Ovid, put particular emphasis upon Chiron's skill as a teacher; some also highlight his essential humanity, his well-disposed attitude towards human nature in general, and, more specifically, his restraining influence upon potentially bellicose heroes (a theme which may not be unrelated to that religious tension between Manso and Milton already noted). In Pindar, *Pythian* 3 Chiron fosters Aesculapius, and teaches him the healing of diseases. Elsewhere in Pindar he is presented as the foster-father of Jason (*Pythian* 4) and of Achilles (*Pythian* 6). Much more vivid details of the Chiron myth, however, are furnished by Ovid, and it is upon Ovid's versions in particular that Milton seems to draw. But while turning back to a world of classical mythology, Milton in fact reworks Ovid in such a way that details of the Chiron story undergo a dramatic transformation as they are adapted to the setting of a seicento Neapolitan academy, its founder, that founder's achievements and, by implication, the speaker's own confidence in the power of the written word to rescue a worthy author from the fires of the funeral pyre and render him immortal. It will be seen then that the Chiron myth is related to the poem's academic context and closely connected to its pervasive theme of literary immortality.

In *Metamorphoses* 2 it is to the cave of Chiron that Apollo brings the infant Aesculapius for tutelage. A few details of the story are of relevance to *Mansus*. One day Apollo is informed by a somewhat gossipy crow that his beloved Coronis has, in his absence, slept with a young Thessalian. Apollo thereby roused to anger, seizes his weapons and pierces Coronis' breast. She struggles to pull out the arrow, and informs him that she is pregnant with his (Apollo's) child. Now, she says, two will die for the price of one. Apollo repents of his anger all too late. In panic he tries to apply his healing art, but all to no avail. When Coronis is on the pyre about to be consumed by the flames, Apollo does not permit his unborn son to be reduced to ashes, but snatches him from the flames and from his mother's womb, and carries him to the cave of Chiron the centaur:

---

[3] C.J. Mackie, "Achilles' Teachers: Chiron and Phoenix in the *Iliad*," *G&R* 44.1 (1997), 1-10.

> non tulit in cineres labi sua Phoebus eosdem
> semina, sed natum flammis uteroque parentis
> eripuit, geminique tulit Chironis in antrum.
> (Ovid, *Metamorphoses* 2. 628-630)

[Phoebus did not allow his own seed to fall into the same ashes, but snatched his son from the flames and the womb of his parent and brought him into the cave of the twin-form Chiron.]

Chiron is delighted with the honor and responsibility of looking after the son of a god:

> semifer interea divinae stirpis alumno
> laetus erat mixtoque oneri gaudebat honore.
> (Ovid, *Metamorphoses* 2. 633-634)

[Meanwhile the half-beast was pleased in the nursling of divine stock and rejoiced in the admixture of responsibility and honor.]

It is hardly a coincidence that two aspects of the Ovidian terminology used to describe Chiron's hospitable reception of Aesculapius recur in Milton's account of another host and educator,[4] Manso, who had received into his care the poet Marino:

> Mox tibi dulciloquum non inscia Musa Marinum
> tradidit; ille tuum dici se gaudet alumnum,
> dum canit Assyrios divum prolixus amores,
> mollis et Ausonias stupefecit carmine nymphas.
> (*Mansus* 9-12)

[Next the Muse, not without knowledge, entrusted the sweetly-speaking Marino to you; he rejoiced in being called your nursling, while in verbose fashion he sang of the Assyrian love affairs of the gods, and gently with his verse amazed the Ausonian nymphs.]

In *Mansus*, the Muse is performing a role similar to that of Ovid's Apollo, entrusting an *alumnus* (Marino/Aesculapius) to Manso/Chiron for fostering:

---

4 As noted by Low, "*Mansus*," 115.

OVID					
APOLLO		**AESCULAPIUS**		**CHIRON**	who rejoiced in his nursling: *alumno/laetus... gaudebat*
	entrusts		to		
MILTON					
MUSE		**MARINO**		**MANSO**	Marino rejoiced in being called Manso's nursling: *ille tuum dici se gaudet alumnum*

But Milton has inverted the Ovidian original by transferring the emotion of joy from the agent (Chiron) to the recipient (Marino) of the tutelage. Thus that sweetly-speaking master of the baroque, that prolix poet rejoices in being called the ward of Manso. An honor indeed. And inversion is a key element of Milton's reworking of this particular myth. In Ovid, Apollo does not permit his own son to "fall into the same ashes" (*in cineres labi ... eosdem* [*Met.* 2. 628]). Perhaps this has some bearing upon the end of Milton's poem as the speaker envisages his own surrendering to ashes, to the power of death (*annorumque satur cineri sua iura relinquam* [86]), but proceeds nonetheless to envisage himself being rescued or snatched from the forces of oblivion and remembered by a weeping friend who would create a marble bust of him. He even imagines transcending his earthly existence. It should also be noted at this point that the Ovidian line-ending *Chironis in antrum* (*Met* 2. 630) will occur at *Mansus* 60.

In Ovid, just when all seems well, Chiron's own daughter, who possesses the gift of prophecy, suddenly appears. She looks upon the young Aesculapius and predicts his destiny: he will have the ability to restore those who are already dead, but one day even he will incur the ill-favor of the gods because of this very skill; hence from an immortal god he will be reduced to a corpse, but later will be resurrected to divine status. She then turns to address her father, Chiron, and predicts his agonising death through an arrow poisoned by the blood of the Hydra:

> Tu quoque, care pater, nunc immortalis et aevis
> omnibus ut maneas nascendi lege creatus,
> posse mori cupies, tum cum cruciabere dirae
> sanguine serpentis per saucia membra recepto;
> teque ex aeterno patientem numina mortis
> efficient triplicesque deae tua fila resolvent.
>
> (Ovid, *Metamorphoses* 2.649-654)

[You too, dear father, now immortal and created by the conditions of birth to remain for all eternity, you too will long to be able to die, at the moment when you are tortured by the blood of the dread serpent permeating your wounded limbs; and the gods will reduce you from an immortal, causing you to suffer death, and the threefold goddesses will unloose the threads of your destiny.]

The accidental death of Chiron alluded to here receives even fuller treatment by Ovid at *Fasti* 5.379-414. There in the course of his twelve labors the hero Hercules reaches mount Pelion, the home of Chiron, where he receives a hospitable welcome from Chiron and his pupil Achilles. Overcome with wonder, Chiron handles Hercules' weapons, but accidentally drops onto his foot one of Hercules' arrows poisoned by the blood of the Hydra. In spite of panic attempts to find a remedy through the application of every possible herb, Chiron is unable to recover and subsequently dies. In reward for his good offices on earth, however, the gods transfer him to the sky where he is transformed into the constellation Centaurus (3 May; evening rising 15 April).

That Milton was familiar with the story of Chiron's death is evident from a reference in his earlier Latin poem *In Obitum Procancellarii Medici*, an elegy on the Cambridge Vice-chancellor Dr John Gostlin. There, arguing for the inevitability of death,[5] Milton states that if medical skill could overcome death, Chiron (named by reference to his mother, the nymph Philyra) would not have been injured as a result of the arrow smeared with the Hydra's blood:

> laesisset et nec te Philyreie
> sagitta echidnae perlita sanguine.
> (Milton, *In Obitum Procancellarii Medici*, 25-26)

---

[5] For a discussion of the poem, see Estelle Haan, "Milton and Two Italian Humanists: Some Hitherto Unnoticed Neo-Latin Echoes in *In Obitum Procancellarii Medici* and *In Obitum Praesulis Eliensis*," *N&Q*, n.s. 22.2 (June, 1997), 176-181. There I suggest *inter alia* that Milton's poem echoes Politian's *Elegia Sexta*, which however concerns a doctor who is still alive. That, I argue, is precisely the point as Milton picks up and inverts features of Politian's elegy, assuming an entirely different perspective by presenting a doctor whose skill in repelling death and in upsetting the laws of fate did not go unpunished, as was the case in Politian. Rather, from the opening lines of the poem the reader is made aware of the inevitability of death — this time the doctor himself has become its victim — a fact which is conveyed by a skilful tour de force whereby the very privileges enjoyed by Antonio, the subject of Politian's poem, are transformed into a series of warnings, and by the emphatic assertion that the laws of fate must be obeyed and that death is inevitable. The reader is thereby enabled to view the skills of Dr Gostlin from an ironic standpoint.

[nor would the arrow smeared with the blood of the Lernaean hydra have injured you, son of Philyra.]

Milton's phraseology (*sanguis* and *echidna*) seems to echo Ovid, *Fasti* 5.405: *sanguine Centauri Lernaeae sanguis echidnae.*[6] In Milton, Gostlin, like Ovid's Chiron, though skilled in medicine, could not withstand the force of death.[7] But where medicine fails, poetry succeeds, and such perhaps is the point of *Mansus*. For Milton's poem conveys the immortalising power of the written word. Thus in a reworking of the motifs of death and rebirth implicit in Ovid in the physical realism of Chiron's painful death followed by the eventuality of his glorious catasterism, Manso as Chiron will, it is implied, suffer no such fate; on the contrary, in a passage that conveys an ability to transcend death itself, Milton states that wherever Tasso and Marino win fame so will Manso be immortalised:

> Fortunate senex, ergo quacunque per orbem
> Torquati decus et nomen celebrabitur ingens,
> claraque perpetui succrescet fama Marini,
> tu quoque in ora frequens venies plausumque virorum,
> et parili carpes iter immortale volatu.
> (*Mans.* 49-53)

[And so, fortunate old man, wherever through the world is celebrated the glory and huge name of Torquato, and wherever increases the radiant fame of the immortal Marino, you too will frequently be on the lips and in the applause of men, and with equal flight will you pluck the journey of immortality.]

While a related metronymic *Phillyrides* (of Chiron) occurs in Virgil[8] and Propertius,[9] it is in Ovid, that he is referred to as *Philyreius* [*heros*].[10] And

---

[6] Milton's combination of *sagitta* and *perlita* finds a parallel in Carolus Stephanus's account of the incident in his *Dictionarium Historicum, Geographicum, Poeticum* (Geneva, 1621). See D.T. Starnes and E.W. Talbert, *Classical Myth and Legend in Renaissance Dictionaries* (Univ. of North Carolina Press: Chapel Hill, 1955), 235.

[7] Instead, Milton states (37-40), Persephone snapped the threads of his life, angry in seeing him rescue so many from the black jaws of death by his skill and potent medicine. Medicine can rescue others from death but not the skilled doctor himself. Cf. *Ep. Dam.*, where Milton makes a rather similar point. As Thyrsis, he had imagined Damon (Diodati) discussing his herbs and healing arts, but then laments: *Ah pereant herbae, pereant artesque medentum/gramina, postquam ipsi nil profecere magistro* (153-154). In a letter to Diodati (*CM* 12, 24) Milton had praised his addressee as one who *illam medicinae tyrannicam nactus arcem.*

[8] *Georgics* 3.550.

[9] Propertius, 2.1.60. Cf. Hesiod, *Theog.* 1002; Apollonius of Rhodes, *Arg.* 1.554.

this is precisely the phrase used by Milton of Chiron at *Elegia Quarta* 27. There recounting his own gratitude towards his tutor Thomas Young, he compares him to a whole range of famous classical instructors of heroes. Among these is the "Philyran hero," Chiron, tutor of Achilles:

> qualis Amyntorides, qualis Philyreius heros
> Myrmidonum regi, talis et ille mihi.
>> (*Elegia Quarta* 27-28)
>
> [What the son of Amyntor, what the heroic son of Philyra were to the king of the Myrmidons, such is he to me.]

There are however several other indications that it is Ovid's account of Chiron in the *Fasti* in particular that may have inspired the passage in *Mansus*. Milton seems to pick up and invert aspects of the Ovidian passage, thereby suggesting a series of semi-humorous parallels between Manso and Chiron.

Mansus also contains an <u>explicit</u> reference to Chiron. This occurs in 59-64 as Milton describes Apollo's retreat to Chiron's cave. There amid woodland pastures and shades, overcome by the persuasions of his friend, through song he finds alleviation for the hardships of his exile:

> Tantum ubi clamosos placuit vitare bubulcos,
> nobile mansueti cessit *Chironis in antrum*,
> irriguos inter saltus frondosaque tecta
> Peneium prope rivum. Ibi saepe sub ilice nigra
> ad citharae strepitum blanda prece victus amici
> exilii duros lenibat voce labores.
>> (*Mans.* 59-64)

> [But when he wished to avoid the noisy herdsmen, he withdrew into the noble cave of the gentle Chiron amid the well-watered meadows and the leafy dwellings beside the river Peneus. There beneath the dark oak, vanquished by the winsome pleading of his friend he would often alleviate the harsh toils of exile with his voice to the accompaniment of the resounding lyre.]

The verbal parallel with Ovid is obvious.[11] Striking however is the role of Apollo in Milton's poem, who does not simply entrust a ward to Chiron, as

---

10 *Metamorphoses* 2.676; *Fasti* 5.391.

11 Commentators also note a similar line-ending at Valerius Flaccus, *Arg.* 1.407 (Cf. Douglas Bush, *Variorum*, 276), but similarities do not go beyond this. Unmentioned by scholars however is a possible neo-Latin parallel provided by Politian's *Praefatio* to his first book of *Sylvae*. See Estelle Haan, "John Milton Among the Neo-Latinists: Three Notes on *Mansus*," *N & Q*, n.s. 22.2 (June 1997), 172-176 at 174-175, where I point out that the phrase *Chironis ad antrum* occurs as Politian describes the withdrawal of

in Ovid, *Metamorphoses*, but who actually visits Chiron's cave of his own accord and sojourns there. Lacking classical precedent, the visit of Apollo here seems to be an innovation on the part of Milton. The point is noted by John Carey,[12] who however does not venture to posit any motivation for what he terms Milton's "invention." Douglas Bush suggests that Milton may have invented the visit on the strength of Chiron being the tutor of Aesculapius and Achilles.[13] While this is possible, it is not unreasonable to suggest that this inclusion of Apollo as guest and even pupil of the centaur Chiron is quite deliberate, and that in so doing the speaker is thereby drawing a double analogy: between Chiron and Manso and (quite daringly) between Apollo and himself![14] Milton as a second Apollo need not surprise the reader of a poem which, as noted above, outlines *inter alia* his own poetical aspirations and his ambitions to compose an *Arthuriad*, and represents poetry itself as bestowing immortality upon both subject and poet. If so, Milton is substituting Apollo for what in traditional accounts should be Hercules or Achilles — a substitution which would be appropriate in the given context of *Mansus* as a poem about poetry itself, and more specifically as the expression of one poet's gratitude for a "written encomium" composed by another.

---

the Argonauts to the cave of Chiron: *Conveniunt Minyae gemini Chironis ad antrum,/qua fugit obliquo garrula lympha pede,/quaque ingens platanus genialibus excubat umbris;/explicat hic faciles rustica mensa dapes./Crescit fronde torus, vernant in flore capilli;/sed viret herculeis populus alba comis.* (5-10) (Text: Angelo Ambrogini Poliziano, *Prose Volgari Inedite e Poesie Latine e Greche Edite e Inedite*, ed. Isidore del Lungo [Hildesheim, New York, 1976]). Besides the verbal similarity, both passages associate the cave with a river; both mention a tree which provides shade; both convey the luxurious growth and vegetation of the scene. The *Praefatio* proceeds to describe the power of Orpheus's music and its effect upon the world of nature (13-20). It is striking that Milton's description of the cave is followed by a passage which conveys the Orphic powers of Apollo's music (*Mans*. 62-69). On a more general level, it should be remarked that the *Praefatio* is a preface to *Manto*, the first book of Politian's *Sylvae*; *Mansus* is among the miscellaneous verse to which Milton gave the heading *Sylvarum Liber*. It is tempting to see in Milton's Latinised term *Mansus* a subtle allusion to Politian's *Manto*. Perhaps, as in the phrase *mansueti ... Chironis* (60), he is playing once again on Manso's name.

[12] Carey, ed., *Milton: Complete Shorter Poems*, 266.

[13] Bush, *Variorum*, 276.

[14] This identification may even underlie lines 24-25 of *Mansus* where Milton had wished Manso a long and healthy life in the name of Clio and Phoebus: *Ergo ego te Clius et magni nomine Phoebi/Manse pater, iubeo longum salvere per aevum.* My point is anticipated by Revard, *Milton and the Tangles of Neaera's Hair*, 219: "Clearly Milton thinks of Apollo's visit to Chiron in the vale of Tempe as parallel to his own visit to evergreen springtime Naples, the garden of Italy, and to Manso's villa."

On a reading of Milton's lines, the application of the adjective *mansuetus* to the centaur Chiron may seem surprising. Why should this hybrid creature (half-man/half-horse) be described as "tame" or "gentle"?[15] Perhaps the answer lies partly in the fact that in *Fasti* 5, as Ian Brookes has noted,[16] Ovid actually suppresses Chiron's hybrid nature in order to let us sympathize with him as a human. Thus he is described as a *iustus senex* (*F.* 5.384), who through the power of music can impose some form of restraint upon the warlike instincts of Achilles (*ille manus olim missuras Hectora leto/creditur in lyricis detinuisse modis.* [*F.* 5. 385-386]). And this is a remarkable achievement. Under Chiron, the hands of Achilles, destined to kill Hector in brutal combat, are "detained in the strains of the lyre." Such is the calming effect of Chiron's instruction.[17] But there may be another reason for Milton's choice of the adjective *mansuetus*. It is likely that this is intended as a pun on Manso's name,[18] a device which, as noted above, finds a parallel in contemporary Italian poems in Manso's honor. Moreover unnoticed by commentators on *Mansus* is a strikingly similar neo-Latin pun provided by Milton's Florentine friend and fellow-academician Jacopo Gaddi. In his *De Scriptoribus Non Ecclesiasticis* published in 1648 Gaddi would describe Manso as *Mansus mansuetus*[19] — a phrase suggested perhaps from his reading of *Mansus*,[20] and which in any case lends credence to the possibility that Milton's *mansueti ... Chironis* contains an implicit pun on Manso's name. Thus through witty

---

[15] It is interesting to note that the attribute "Mansuetudine" was among the virtues applied to Tasso by Manso in his *Vita di Torquato Tasso*, 259. See 182 below.

[16] "The Death of Chiron: Ovid, *Fasti* 5.379-414," *CQ* 44.2 (1994), 444-450.

[17] The same point is made by Statius at *Silvae* 2. 1.88-89: *tenero sic blandus Achilli/ semifer Haemonium vincebat Pelea Chiron*, and at 5.3.93-94: *quique tubas acres lituosque audire volentem/Aeaciden alio frangebat carmine Chiron.*

[18] Just as perhaps *manse tuae* in line 1 is a possible anagram of *mansuetae*. Cf. Milton's punning on Salzilli's name (*Salsillus* is the Latinized form) at *Ad Salsillum* 41: *adusque curvi salsa regna Portumni* discussed at 87, 97-98 above.

[19] Jacopo Gaddi, praising Manso's *Erocallia*, states at *De Scriptoribus*, 120: *In partibus a me lustratis Herocalliae videtur omnigena fere doctrina et eruditio breviter apteque contexta, in qua rationum et argumentationum vis ac robur excellit. Siquidem nullus forsitan Graecus, Latinus, etruscus adeo solide, graviter, docte, adeo luculenter et copiose egit de Amore, cuius Definitiones, vel potius descriptiones mancas, superfluas, indoctas, valide, ac sapienter reiicit, exploditque Mansus mansuetus et modestus maximus disceptator, qui solidis fundamentis innixus Theol. ac Philos. praesertim Peripateticae revocat ad principia et divisiones rerum stabiles sua placita.*

[20] For links between Milton and Gaddi, see 10-15 above.

wordplay Manso is humorously equated with Chiron. And, as Santini has
shown,[21] wordplay is an inherent feature of the Ovidian passage. For
example, in the occurrence of the noun *manus* at 385-386, 395-396 and
409, Ovid cleverly puns on the derivation of the name Chiron from the
Greek χείρ meaning "hand." Perhaps he is also playing on the twofold
meaning of *manus* as "hand"//"armed force/corps of soldiers," with Chiron
in a sense restraining Achilles' potential army. Through the punning phrase
mansueti ... Chironis Milton is thus developing a device present in the
Ovidian original. Indeed is there a possible echo of *manus* (hence Chiron /
χείρ /"hand") in Manso's own name (or its Latinized equivalent *Mansus*)?
Chiron had a restraining effect upon the *manus* of Achilles; in a not
dissimilar way Manso may have had to impose restraint upon the
potentially bellicose Milton, all too ready to voice his opinions about
religion. Milton refers to the cave of *mansueti ... Chironis* as a *nobile ...
antrum* (60). This too is not without possible punning undertones — this
time an allusion perhaps to the *Collegio di Nobili* founded by Manso;
furthermore the subsequent lines describing a retreat into what is in effect
pastoral *otium* may, as noted above, indirectly refer either to the title of
Manso's academy, the Accademia degli Oziosi, or more generally to
Manso's own villa. Milton's Chiron, the centaur, is a gentle teacher
instructing his protégés, his members. Like his Ovidian counterpart, he is
"a responsible teacher of the peaceful arts."[22] In founding this academy
Manso has played host to countless *litterati*, and has revealed himself to
be a responsible teacher. Other humanising Ovidian tactics, noted by
Brookes, are the reference to Chiron as *senex* (384); when Chiron is
wounded, Achilles stands as though before his own father – this would be
the sort of grief he would feel if his father Peleus were to die:

> stabat, ut ante patrem, lacrimis perfusus Achilles;
> sic flendus Peleus, si moreretur erat.
>
> (Ovid, *Fasti* 5. 407-408)
>
> [Achilles stood, as though before his father, drenched with tears. Thus
> would Peleus have to be lamented if he were to die]

As if to highlight this quasi-filial bond, at 412 Achilles actually addresses
him as *care ... pater*, as he kisses his hands and begs him not to die:

---

[21] C. Santini, "Lettura Strutturale ed Etimologia in un Cataterismo dei *Fasti*,"
Materiali e Contributi per la Storia della Narrativa Greco-Latina 1 (1976), 49-56.

[22] Brookes, "The Death of Chiron," 446.

> oscula saepe dedit, dixit quoque saepe iacenti
> "vive, precor, nec me, care, relinque, pater."
> (Ovid, *Fasti* 5.411-412)

[Frequently he gave kisses and frequently he said to him as he lay there: "Live, I beg thee, and, dear father, do not leave me."]

As Brookes rightly points out, Ovid is cleverly anticipating the moment when Priam will kiss the hands of Achilles, killer of his son.[23]

Chiron as *senex* and *pater* finds a striking parallel in the role of Manso in Milton's poem, who, as noted above, is equated with Chiron in that punning phrase *mansueti ... Chironis*. But Milton uses the noun *senex* of Manso twice in his poem. In line 49 Milton addresses him in the phrase *fortunate senex*, an echo of the address to Tityrus in Virgil's first *Eclogue*,[24] envied by Meliboeus for his ability to relax in pastoral *otium*; at 70 Manso is *diis dilecte senex*. Even more striking is Milton's presentation of Manso as a second father figure. In a sense, that paternal surrogacy inherent in Ovid and implied by Achilles in his address to the dying Chiron as *care pater* is adopted by Milton. This seems to work on both an explicit and implicit level in *Mansus*: 1) explicitly, through addressing Manso as *Manse pater* (25), and 2) implicitly, through verbal and thematic echoes of Milton's own Latin poem *Ad Patrem*, that poem to a father, who was in effect presented as an excellent educator, thanked by Milton for enabling him to acquire an ideal education including Latin, Greek, French, Italian, Hebrew etc.[25] For the youthful poet sojourning in Naples the elderly Manso is perhaps a father figure and in his own way, like Milton senior, a committed educator of poets. In *Ad Patrem*, Milton père did not despise poets or encourage his son to seek the path towards materialism. *Manse pater* parallels such stock phrases as *pater optime* (*Ad Pat* [6]) and *care pater* (*Ad Pat* [111]). But there are also some noteworthy verbal and thematic echoes of *Ad Patrem* in *Mansus*.[26] At *Mansus* 6 Milton states that if his own Muse has sufficient breath, Manso will sit among the ivy and laurels of victory:

---

[23] Brookes, "The Death of Chiron," 448.

[24] Virgil, *Ecl.* 1.47: *Fortunate senex, ergo te tua rura manebunt.*

[25] See Estelle Haan, "John Milton's *Ad Patrem* and Hugo Grotius's *In Natalem Patris*," *N&Q* forthcoming.

[26] For a general survey of points of contact between the two poems, see Revard, *Milton and the Tangles of Neaera's Hair*, 215-217.

victrices hederas inter laurosque sedebis

(*Mansus* 6)

[You will sit among the ivy and laurels of victory]

This is an almost verbatim repetition of a line from *Ad Patrem* describing Milton's own envisaged position as one day sitting among laurels and ivy:

Ergo ego iam doctae pars quamlibet ima catervae
victrices hederas inter laurosque sedebo

(*Ad Patrem* 101-102)

[Therefore I, now a part, albeit a lowly part, of the learned throng, will sit among the ivy and laurels of victory.]

Other possible verbal parallels exist: at *Mansus* 30 Milton aims to justify the literary merits of his native land. The British, like the Italians, have their poets (*nos etiam* ...); at 38 "we too worship Phoebus" (*nos etiam colimus Phoebum.*) This phrase may echo *Ad Patrem* 30-32 (*nos etiam ... ibimus*) used there to convey the envisaged experiences in Heaven at the end of time; Milton develops the phraseology of *nos etiam* in *Mansus* to make it contrast with *Tu quoque* at 5 and 52. *Ergo ego* in *Mansus* 24, as the speaker wishes the Italian Manso a long life, finds a parallel in *Ad Patrem* 101 as the speaker imagines some form of poetic longevity for himself. That *Mansus* is picking up and even inverting motifs from *Ad Patrem* is possible from such shared concepts and themes as the role of the Pierians,[27] the subject-matter of heroic poetry,[28] the Orphic power of music,[29] the addressee as nurturer of poets,[30] the role of Apollo,[31] and the notion of some form of immortality after death as concluding the poem(s). In *Ad Patrem* Milton addresses his poems in the hope that they survive the funeral pyre of their master:

---

[27] *Ad Patrem* opens with the speaker's desire for the Pierian springs *Pierios ... fontes* (1) to suffuse his lips; *Mansus* opens with the *Pierides* (2) singing this song for Manso.

[28] *Heroumque actus, imitandaque gesta canebat* (*Ad Patrem* [46]) becomes in *Mansus* part of the speaker's possible epic song (*magnanimos heroas* [83]).

[29] *Ad Patrem* 52-55; *Mansus* 65-69.

[30] Milton père enabled his son to devote himself to poetry: *Phoebaeo lateri comitem sinis ire beatum* (76); Manso was the friend and patron of Tasso and Marino, the latter of whom is described as his *alumnus* (10).

[31] In *Ad Patrem* 64-66 the elder and younger Milton share the god Apollo, who has given *altera dona mihi, ... altera dona parenti* (65); in *Mansus* Apollo is worshipped by the British and in this instance is the recipient, rather than the bestower, of gifts: *nos etiam colimus Phoebum, nos munera Phoebo ... misimus* (38-41).

> Et vos, o nostri, iuvenilia carmina, lusus,
> si modo perpetuos sperare audebitis annos,
> et domini superesse rogo, lucemque tueri
> nec spisso rapient oblivia nigra sub Orco,
> forsitan has laudes decantatumque parentis
> nomen ad exemplum sero servabitis aevo.
>
> (*Ad Patrem* 115-120)

[And you, o pastimes of mine, youthful verses, if only you dare to hope for years of eternity and to survive your master's pyre and to gaze upon the light, and if dark oblivion does not snatch you down beneath crowded Orcus, perhaps you will preserve as an example to a later age these praises and the name of a parent which I have hereby sung.]

It is as though the poems can be snatched from the burning pyre of their creator (perhaps rescued by a willing hand as Aesculapius was from the womb of Coronis already on the pyre) and preserve his father's name for all eternity. In *Mansus* Manso has been able to do precisely this by writing biographies of Tasso and Marino and thereby making them immortal:

> ... cupis integros rapere Orco,
> qua potes, atque avidas Parcarum eludere leges:
> amborum genus et varia sub sorte peractam
> describis vitam moresque et dona Minervae
>
> (*Mansus* 18-21).

[You wished to snatch them intact from Orcus, as far as you were able, and to make sport of the greedy laws of the Parcae: you described the race of both, their lives completed under varying fortunes, their characters, and gifts of Minerva.]

By the end of *Mansus* Milton inverts the whole as he envisages immortality for <u>himself</u>. Although his own remains may be in urn, he will transcend the bounds of his earthly existence, reach the heavens, look down and applaud himself after death. It is evident that *Mansus* contains some general parallels with *Ad Patrem* and other more specific echoes, and that Manso is being presented as a second father figure, as both *senex* and *pater* and as an ideal educator (as indeed was Chiron). All of this would seem to suggest perhaps that Manso knew *Ad Patrem*, (which is usually dated to the early 1630s,[32] and in any case generally accepted as predating *Mansus*). One could go further than this by arguing that such echoes would suggest that Manso had actually read *Ad Patrem* in manuscript (or perhaps heard Milton recite it in a Neapolitan Academy

---

[32] For a summary of respective arguments for the dating of *Ad Patrem*, see Carey, ed., *Milton: Complete Shorter Poems*, 153-154.

[the Oziosi perhaps?]) and was intended to see the parallel between himself and the elder Milton. Knowledge of the poem would seem to be deemed necessary if Manso was intended to pick up these flattering compliments.

There are other parallels between Chiron and Manso. Both show friendship and hospitality towards their newly-arrived guest. In Pindar, Chiron had been described as having "a friendly disposition towards men": νόον ἔχοντ' ἀνδρῶν φίλον.[33] Manso likewise is the friendly host of heroes. In the prose *argumentum* to *Mansus* he is described as *Tassi amicissimus* and the addressee of Tasso's *Dialogue on Friendship*.[34] This theme is picked up in the poem proper — in Manso's *pietas* for the shade of his deceased *amicus* Marino (*nec manes pietas tua cara fefellit amici.* [15]), in Chiron's gentle persuasion as he urges Apollo to relax and soothe the hardships of exile through music (*ad citharae strepitum blanda prece victus amici* [63]); in Milton's wish to have such a life-long friend as Manso (*o mihi si mea sors talem concedat amicum* [78]). The host/guest motif, so prominent in the poem, is likewise highlighted in the *argumentum* where Milton states that Manso showed him the greatest kindness when he was staying in Naples, and that "that guest before leaving the city sent him this poem so that he should not reveal himself to be ungrateful."[35] Chiron received the *iuvenis* Hercules hospitably: *excipit hospitio iuvenem Philyreius heros* (*F.* 5.391). Milton, like Hercules, is a *iuvenis*: a *iuvenis peregrinus* (26). In both instances the host's dwelling is a source of relaxation for his guest. As noted above, it is likely that the description of the playing of the lyre and of the orphic effect of *carmen* recalls the delights of Italian academies such as Manso's *Oziosi*.[36] The orphic powers of *carmen* are highlighted in 65-69 as it causes river-banks and boulders to move, cliffs to nod, trees to rush down their slopes, and even spotted lynxes to grow tame as they listen to the unusual music: *mulcenturque novo maculosi carmine lynces* (69). While the effects of the orphic power of music are quite conventional, this last point of spotted lynxes soothed by strange/unfamiliar music is by comparison less common. Bush

---

[33] *Pythian* 3.5.

[34] *Ad quem Torquati Tassi dialogus extat de Amicitia scriptus; erat enim Tassi amicissimus.*

[35] *Ad hunc itaque hospes ille antequam ab ea urbe discederet, ut ne ingratum se ostenderet, hoc carmen misit.*

[36] By contrast, Marjorie H. Nicolson has argued that Milton's description of hell in the opening of *Paradise Lost* was influenced by a visit to the Phlegraean Fields, west of Naples and near Manso's villa. See her "Milton and the Phlegraean fields," *UTQ* 7 (1938), 500-513.

compares Virgil, *Eclogue* 8.3: *stupefactae carmine lynces*; *Aeneid* 1.323: *maculosae tegmine lyncis*; Mantuan, *Eclogue* 6. 27: *maculosaque tergora lyncis*.[37] But there may well be a topical reason for choosing lynxes at this point as there existed in Rome at this time an Accademia Nazionale dei Lincei, an academy of the "Lynxes," of which Galileo had been a member, famed for their wholly exclusive devotion to mathematical and physical researches. The nature of this academy is well summarised by Masson:

> In calling themselves "the Lynxes," the mathematicians and physical philosophers of Italy had selected a happy symbol. It was as if they proclaimed that it was in *their* constitution still to see when it might be dark to others, and that *their* occupation of penetrating the recesses of nature, seizing facts that eluded the common search, and holding them as if in permanent excruciation within the fangs of their definite relations of magnitude, weight, and number, might be carried on when poets were asleep, metaphysicians jaded, painters poor and meretricious, and orators without employment.[38]

Perhaps the point of Milton's reference is that the power of the unfamiliar music (*novo ... carmine* [69]) produced by Apollo (or by participants of Manso's own Academy [Milton perhaps included?]) is such that it could miraculously win over even the mathematicians and physicists of the "[Academy of the] Lynxes." Thus the Accademia degli Oziosi can charm and outwit even the Accademia Nazionale dei Lincei!

By the end of the poem Milton has turned the Ovidian situation upon its head. In the closing lines it is *he*, not Manso/Chiron who seems to undergo a virtual catasterism. Assuming the stance perhaps of Ovid's dying Chiron, he longs for someone to stand dutifully before his bed with weeping eyes (*ille mihi lecto madidis adstaret ocellis,/adstanti sat erit si dicam sim tibi curae* [*Mans.* 87-88]). This wish may suggest the weeping Achilles in Ovid, who stood in tears before the dying Chiron as though before his very father (*stabat ut ante patrem lacrimis perfusus Achilles* [*Fasti* 5. 407]). Now perhaps he imagines for himself a fate not unlike that of Chiron, as he ascends into the heavens, looks down upon all that is earthly and smiles, suffused with a radiant light.[39] The gods rewarded

---

[37] Bush, *Variorum*, 277.

[38] *Life*, I, 165.

[39] Lines 94-100 seem to echo Petrarch's *Epistola ad Amicum Transalpinum*. Cf. Estelle Haan, "John Milton Among the Neo-Latinists," at 175-176. There I suggest that the positioning of *videbo* and *serenum* at the end of lines 97 and 98 respectively could be seen as an inversion of Petrarch's *Pes Italam calcabit humum, purumque serenum/laetius his oculis, et sidera nostra videbo*. (*Petrarche Opera* [Basel, 1554], II, 1369). Other points of contact exist. Both express the wish to possess "so great" or

Chiron for his virtues by transforming him into the constellation Centaurus.[40] If, according to Manso's tribute, Milton actually lacks the *pietas* necessary for him to be admitted into the angelic ranks, then perhaps, like Ovid's Chiron, he will be allocated a particular region of the universe (*secreti ... aliqua mundi de parte* [97]), but with one important difference: in having to applaud his own qualities (*plaudam mihi* [100]), he will undergo a catasterism that is in fact self-imposed.

"such" a "friend" (*tanti...amici* [90]/*talem...amicum* [78]) who will weep (*lacrimantis* [90]/*madidis...ocellis* [87]); the very fact of having such a person will be a source of consolation (*solamen ... erit* [89-90]) or sufficient in itself (*sat erit* [88]); the specific role of the friend is to see to the burial of the speaker (*manibusque sepulchro invectum ... piis* [91-92]/*ille meos artus ... curaret parva componi molliter urna* [89-90]), who will thereby rest in peace (*longum requiescere* [94]/*secura pace quiescam* [93]). Underlying both poems is the contrast between youth and old age. Petrarch reminisces on the faded beauties of his youth (*iamque haec puerilia retro/linquimus, ad metam rapimur properantibus annis* [14-15]) and describes himself as a *senex* (28) as opposed to his youthful addressee (27-28). The theme recurs in an inverted form in *Mansus* for here it is the speaker who is the *iuvenis* — a *iuvenis peregrinus* (26) — while the addressee is the *senex* (49 & 70). One further point of contact between the two poems is the theme of everlasting fame with a reference to *virtus* and an ascent to the heavens. Petrarch longs for immortality and predicts that *Virtus* of her own accord will ascend to the *aethera*: *clara quidem longos Virtus ventura sub annos/viribus ipsa suis sublimis ad aethera surget/non aliena petens inopis suffragia linguae* (59-61). Milton envisages his own ascent *in aethera* — an ascent which is the reward for *ignea virtus*. Finally, the very theme of Petrarch's title (*Epistola ad Amicum Transalpinum*) — as read by Milton — would suit *Mansus* quite well since the latter is a tribute to an Italian paid by an British neo-Latinist who has himself crossed the Alps.

[40] Ovid, *Fasti*, 5.412-413: *nona dies aderat, cum tu, iustissime Chiron,/bis septem stellis corpora cinctus eras.*

CHAPTER 11

Milton, Ariosto, and the Singing Swan

Whether as *Angelus* or as the constellation Chiron, the "pagan" *Anglus* can achieve some form of immortality after death — through the bonds of *amicitia*, through memory, but most importantly through the written word. For *Mansus* is in many respects a celebration of the immortalising power of literature. And one of the ways in which this is achieved is through the image of the swan, and through the theme of biography (or indeed autobiography) as a methodology in tune with the divine. A poem about poetry itself, *Mansus* reveals an Englishman who is confidently optimistic not only about his own powers as a poet, but also about the poetic merits of his native land. The speaker is self-consciously aware of the cold northern climes from which he has travelled to sunny Italy. Although he is a *iuvenis peregrinus* (26), unlike Manso the *senex*, and although he admires the beauty and culture of Italy, Milton proudly acknowledges the fact that England too is not without her own poets. He defends the literary merits of his own country, and in so doing, he employs the symbol of poet as swan:

> Nos etiam in nostro modulantes flumine cygnos
> credimus obscuras noctis sensisse per umbras,
> qua Thamesis late puris argenteus urnis
> Oceani glaucos perfundit gurgite crines.
> Quin et in has quondam pervenit Tityrus oras. (30-34)

> [We too believe that we have heard swans singing in our river amid the dark shadows of night, where the silver Thames with her pure urns soaks her green hair in the ocean's current. Moreover Tityrus once reached these shores.]

It is interesting to note that discussion of the swan is included by Giuseppe Battista among topics debated by the Accademia degli Oziosi during Manso's lifetime.[1] Thus the academy considered such intellectually

---

[1] Giuseppe Battista, *Le Giornate Accademiche* (Venice, 1673).

challenging questions as: "Why does the dying swan sing?"[2] "Why does Horace call swans *purpurei*?"[3] Indeed Horace in *Odes* 2.20 had created an analogy between the poet and the swan and had linked both to the theme of immortality.[4] The theme recurs in Spenser[5] and Ben Jonson,[6] and also in neo-Latin literature, most strikingly in the *Synchrisis Cygnorum et Poetarum* and *Cygnea Cantio* by the sixteenth-century British antiquarian John Leland — poems which, as I have argued elsewhere, may in themselves underlie Milton's self-presentation in *Mansus*.[7] Renaissance

---

[2] Battista, *Le Giornate*, pt 3, 170.

[3] Battista, *Le Giornate*, 182. Cf. H. Schoonhoven, "Purple Swans and Purple Snow," *Mnem.*, series 4, 31 (1978), 200-203. This point is noted by Freeman, "Milton's Roman Connection," 91, 102.

[4] Cf. Horace, *Odes* 2.20.1-5: *Non usitata nec tenui ferar/pinna biformis per liquidum aethera/vates neque in terris morabor/longius invidiaque maior/urbis relinquam* and lines 17-24: *me Colchus et qui dissimulat metum/Marsae cohortis Dacus et ultimi/ noscent Geloni, me peritus/discet Hiber Rhodanique potor./Absint inani funere neniae/luctusque turpes et querimoniae;/conpesce clamorem ac sepulcri/mitte supervacuos honores.* Cf. in a general sense Ennius: *volito vivus per ora virum.*

[5] Spenser uses the Thames/swan symbol at *Prothalamion* 11: "Along the shoare of silver streaming Themmes;" 37-38: "With that I saw two Swannes of goodly hewe/Come softly swimming downe the Lee."

[6] Ben Jonson, viii. 392 (of Shakespeare): "Sweet Swan of Avon! what a sight it were/To see thee in our waters yet appeare,/And make those flights upon the bankes of Thames,/That did so take Eliza, and our James!"

[7] See Estelle Haan, "John Milton Among the Neo-Latinists," 173-174. The *Synchrisis Cygnorum et Poetarum*, as its title suggests, draws parallels between the swan and the poet: the swan is white in body, the poet is white in heart; the swan loves icy rivers, the poet loves his own spring. Both sing a song in springtime and seek the cool shade in the heat of summer. Leland's much lengthier poem, *Cygnea Cantio*, likewise employs the swan/poet allegory. The speaker introduces himself as a white swan reared by the river Thames, who was impelled by an ardent desire to travel upon the river and survey local beauty spots and sites as he swam upstream. This is followed by a catalogue of many landmarks in the Thames valley. The poem concludes with a song of farewell as the speaker envisages himself as a dying swan, leaving the river banks behind him, finding his abode in the heavens and wishing that posterity will remember him. Leland's poem, like *Mansus*, is in the first person. Common to both is the notion of nourishment followed by the speaker's desire to set out on a journey. In Leland, the swan mentions the nourishment which he has received, and expresses his wish to travel (9-20); Milton alludes to a Muse which has scarcely been nourished beneath the frozen Bear (28), yet which nevertheless has ventured to fly through the cities of Italy (*imprudens Italas ausa est volitare per urbes* [29]). The choice of the noun *Musa* as subject and, more specifically, the depiction of her arrival in Italy may moreover echo and invert one of Leland's shorter poems entitled *Commigratio bonarum literarum in Britanniam*: *Cana bonas passim cantavit fama Camaenas/Alpinas nunquam transiliisse nives./Ut*

emblematic literature also makes use of the analogy. For example, Piero Valeriano's *emblematum* or "hieroglyphic" on *Gloriae calcar* states as its theme that poets share with swans a longing for glory, favor and praise: they contend for the praises of Zephyr. Alciato states that, since each was cherished by Apollo, the poet and the swan share parallel glory.[8] Similarly, Ruscelli states that poets resemble swans, and cites Ariosto as evidence of this:

> Et il divino Ariosto con molta leggiadria scrive, che i cigni bianchi son quelli che togliono dall' acqua di Lete cioè dall'oblivione e dalla morte, i nomi delle persone illustri.[9]

> [And the divine Ariosto writes with much elegance that white swans are those who remove from the water of Lethe, that is to say, from oblivion and from death, the names of illustrious persons.]

Ruscelli's reference is in fact to Ariosto, *Orlando Furioso*, cantos 34-35, which, as argued below, seem to contain a range of hitherto unnoticed parallels with *Mansus*.

Before analysing these points of contact, however, it is important to assess to some degree the role of Ariosto in the formulation of Milton's poetic career.[10] One of the paradoxes of his Italian journey is that although

---

Pandionias facundia liquit Athenas,/ venit ad Italicos Musa polita lares./Fronte tamen salva dicam nunc, audiat ipsa/ Roma licet, Musas transiliisse nives./Nam penitus toto divisis orbe Britannis/tersa Camoena dedit, verba rotunda loqui./Illa vetus linguis florebat Roma duabus,/ at linguis gaudet terra Britanna tribus. (Text: *Principum ac Illustrium Aliquot et Eruditorum in Anglia Virorum Encomia, Trophaeo, Genethliaca et Epithalamia a Ioanne Lelando Antiquario Conscripta* [London, 1589]. Milton's depiction of swans on the Thames (lines 30-33) is in general accord with the statement made in the prose dedication of *Cygnea Cantio: Tamesim nemo ignorat cygnorum et altorem et cultorem esse maximum*. The river plays an important role in the poem proper as it carries the swan in its current (132-134). Both poems conclude with the speakers' ascent to, and arrival in, Heaven.

[8] Motto: *Insignia Poetarum*: Picture: a shield charged with a swan hangs by a ribbon from the branch of a leafless tree in front of a marsh. Rushes and other swans are in the marsh waters. Epigram: *Gentiles clypeos sunt qui in Iovis alite gestant;/ sunt quibus aut serpens aut leo signa ferunt./Dira sed haec vatum fugiant animalia ceras,/doctaque sustineant stemmata pulcher olor./Hic Phoebo sacer, et nostrae regionis alumnus,/rex olim veteres servat adhuc titulos* (Andreas Alciatus, *The Latin Emblems I: Index Emblematicus*, ed Peter M. Daly [Toronto, 1985], 183: Emblem 184: Padua, 1621).

[9] Ieronimo Ruscelli, *Delle Imprese Illustri* (Venice, 1580), 153. Cf. Robert J. Clements, "The Cult of the Poet in Renaissance Emblem literature," *PMLA*, 59 (1944), 673-685 at 684.

[10] See, in general, Di Cesare, xx-xxii.

it is for his learned *Latin* poems that Milton is remembered in the surviving
minutes of Italian academies, his experiences in Italy, and more precisely,
the favorable reception which he met with in the Italian academies,
strengthened his belief in the validity of the *vernacular* as a medium, and
indeed enhanced his awareness of his own place within a great English, as
well as Italian, literary tradition. For the academies of seventeenth-century
Italy were obsessed with the purification and improvement of the mother
tongue. As illustrated above, Milton while in Florence showed a keen
interest in, for example, Buonmattei's forthcoming treatise *Della Lingua
Toscana* and even asked for the inclusion of a guide to correct
pronunciation for foreigners.[11] In Naples too, especially in the company of
Manso, nurturer of Italian poets and himself celebrated for his vernacular
writings, Milton had ample opportunity to observe or participate in debates
on the importance of the vernacular and also in discussions of the works of
such great Italian poets as Petrarch, Dante and Ariosto.

In any case, it is evident that Milton's Italian journey was partially
responsible for that increased confidence with which he might now at last
contemplate the composition of a great work — a work through which he
might earn immortality. And it is no accident that this desire is first
enunciated in *Mansus*. Milton clearly expresses his own hopes of fame and
poetic immortality as he delineates his plan to compose a chivalric epic, an
Arthuriad, a magnum opus:

> si quando indigenas revocabo in carmina reges,
> Arcturumque etiam sub terris bella moventem;
> aut dicam invictae sociali foedere mensae,
> magnanimos heroas, et (o modo spiritus adsit!)
> frangam Saxonicas Britonum sub Marte phalanges
> (*Mans.* 80-84)

> [if ever I recall into poetry our native kings, and Arthur waging wars
> even beneath the earth, or if I speak of the great-souled heroes of the
> table rendered invincible by a bond of fellowship, and (if only the breath
> of inspiration be present) break the Saxon phalanxes in a British war]

It is likely that he sees himself here as following in the footsteps of
Ariosto, and of course Spenser, to whom indeed there is a possible allusion
(albeit indirectly) in *Mansus*.[12] This confidence is also reflected to some

---

[11] See 18 above.

[12] It has long been accepted by commentators that *Mansus* 34: *quin et in has quondam
pervenit Tityrus oras* constitutes an allusion to Chaucer (via Spenser). Bush,
Variorum, ad loc, describes the line as "Milton's earliest reference to Spenser's
Shepheardes Calender," and accepts that Milton is referring to Chaucer under the

degree in a much-quoted passage from *The Reason of Church Government*:

> ... I began thus farre to assent both to them [*Italian litterati*] and divers of my friends here at home, and not lesse to an inward prompting which now grew daily upon me, that by labour and intent study (which I take to be my portion in this life) joyn'd with the strong propensity of nature, I might perhaps leave something so written to aftertimes, as they should not willingly let it die ... [13]

There is further evidence however that the precedent of Ariosto in particular may ultimately have contributed in a very particular way to Milton's decision. In the *Reason of Church Government* Milton explicitly states that in choosing to write his epic in the vernacular, as opposed to Latin, he is actually following in Ariosto's footsteps:

> These thoughts at once possest me, and these other. That if I were certain to write as men buy Leases, for three lives and downward, there ought no regard be sooner had, then to Gods glory by the honour and instruction of my country. For which cause, and not only for that I knew it would be hard to arrive at the second rank among the Latines, I apply'd my selfe to that resolution which Ariosto follow'd against the perswasions of Bembo, to fix all the industry and art I could unite to the adorning of my native tongue; not to make verbal curiosities the end, that were a toylsom vanity, but to be an interpreter and relater of the best and sagest things among mine own Citizens throughout this Iland in the mother dialect. That what the geatest and choycest wits of Athens, Rome, or modern Italy, and those Hebrews of old did for their country, I in my proportion with this over and above of being a Christian, might doe for mine: not caring to be once nam'd abroad, though perhaps I could attaine to that, but content with these British Ilands as my world...[14]

While aware that the use of the English language will automatically mean a reduction in the extent of his audience, Milton consciously follows the example of Ariosto, who ignored the dissuasions of Bembo and wrote his epic in the vernacular. Implicitly however he echoes features from Sir John Harington's *Life* of Ariosto,[15] which was appended to Harington's

---

name of Tityrus. Spenser uses the name Tityrus for Chaucer at *The Shepheardes Calender*, *Februarie* 92, *June* 81 and *December* 4.

[13] *CM* 3, 236.

[14] *CM* 3, 236-237.

[15] John Harington, *The Life of Ariosto Briefly and Compendiously Gathered Out of Sundrie Italian Writers* (London, 1591).

translation of the *Orlando Furioso* (London, 1591), and in so doing, he applies them to his own personal experience. There is conclusive evidence moreover that Milton knew the Harington edition, for in *Of Reformation* (1641) he offers a comment on and translation of *Orlando Furioso* 34. 72:

> Ariosto of Ferrara, after both these [Dante and Petrarch] in time, but equal in fame, following the scope of his poem in a difficult knot how to restore Orlando, his chief hero, to his lost senses, brings Astolfo, the English knight, up into the moon, where St John, as he feigns, met him. Cant. 34:

> And to be short at last his guid him brings
> Into a goodly valley, where he sees
> A mighty masse of things strangely confus'd,
> Things that on earth were lost, or were abus'd,[16]

This is virtually identical to Harington's version:

> But to be short at last his guide him brings
> Unto a goodlie vallie, where he sees,
> A mightie masse of things straungely confused,
> Things that on earth were lost, or were abused.[17]

Milton continues:

> And amongst these so abused things listen what he met withal, under the conduct of the Evangelist:

> Then past he to a flowry mountain greene,
> Which once smelt sweet, now stinks as odiously:
> This was that gift (if you the truth will have)
> That Constantine to good Sylvestro gave.

Again this draws quite heavily upon Harington's version:

> Then by a fayre green mountain he did passe,
> That once smelt sweet, but now it stinks perdye,
> This was that gift (be't said without offence)
> That Constantin gave Silvester long since.[18]

---

[16] *CM* 3, 27

[17] Text: *Orlando Furioso* (London, 1591), 286. All translations of the *Orlando Furioso* are those of Harington from this edition. It was thought until recently that the marginalia "questo libro duo volte ho letto, Sept. 21, 1642" at the end of Canto 46 in a copy of the Harington 1591 edition were actually in Milton's hand. This has been refuted by Roy Flannagan in "Reflections on Milton and Ariosto," *EMLS* 2.3 (1996), 4, 1-16 at 1.

Harington's *Life* describes *inter alia* Ariosto's decision:

> [Ariosto] determined, as it should seeme, to make some Poem, finding his strength to serve him to it, and though he could have accomplished it very wel in Latine, yet he chose rather his native tongue, either because he thought he could not attaine to the highest place of praise, the same being before occupied by diverse, and specially Virgill and Ovid, or because he found it best agreed with his matter and with the time, or because he had a desire (as most men have) to enrich their owne language with such writings, as may make it in more account with other nations: but the first of these was the true cause indeed, for when Bembo would have disswaded him from writing Italian, alledging that he should winne more praise by writing Latine: his answere was, that he had rather be one of the principal and chiefe Thuscan writers, then scarce the second or third among the Latines.[19]

Harington speaks of Ariosto's desire to "enrich [his] owne language"; Milton applies this to himself in his explicit wish for "the adorning of my native tongue." Both convey the difficulty of arriving at even second rank among "the Latines."[20] Finally, both extracts mention the Ariosto/Bembo incident and again Milton applies the whole to his own experience as he follows Ariosto in his decision in favor of the vernacular.

But links between Ariosto and Milton work on another hitherto unnoticed level. *Mansus*'s unifying theme of the fame and immortality of poetry and, in particular, the associated role of swans, may owe a particular debt to *Orlando Furioso*, cantos 34-35. This possibility is strengthened by the fact that it was precisely a part of canto 34 that Milton translated in *Of Reformation*. Surely this provides unusually conclusive evidence of his knowledge (undoubtedly first- as well as second-hand) of that precise section of Ariosto's *Orlando Furioso*?[21] At Canto 34 Astolfo,

---

[18] Harington, *Orlando Furioso*, 287.

[19] Harington, *Orlando Furioso*, 416-417.

[20] Milton's phrase "to arrive at the second rank among the Latines" clearly echoes Harington's statement that Ariosto "had rather be one of the principal and chiefe Thuscan writers, then scarce the second or third among the Latines." There is some doubt as to what period of Latin literature is represented by "the Latines." Merritt Y. Hughes in *John Milton: Paradise Regained, The Minor Poems and Samson Agonistes* (New York, 1937), xix-xx, suggests that Milton is referring to Renaissance Latin poets. It is also possible however that he is alluding to Latin poets of the classical period. Cf. his use of the phrase in the *History of Britain*: "I might also produce example, as Diodorus among the Greeks, Livie and others of the Latines ..." (*CM* 10, 3).

[21] For this reason, subsequent quotations from the *Orlando Furioso* will include both the Italian original and Harington's free translation.

after a visit to hell, travels to the Earthly Paradise where he meets St John the Evangelist (54-67); in the company of St John, he visits the moon in order to regain Orlando's lost wits (68-92). As Canto 35 begins, Ariosto praises the immortalising power of poets. Astolfo and St John catch sight of an old man who keeps coming to the river Lethe with a pile of name-plates, filling his lap with these and then dropping them into the river of oblivion (10-13). Crows and vultures and other birds of prey flock to the river: some grasp the name-plates in their beaks; others snatch them in their talons; but unable to hold on to the plaques, they let them drop into the river. Among these birds however are two white swans who do in fact manage to bring back in their beaks the name-plates which fall to them. In this way the swans recover a few at least, rescuing them from the river, contrary to the evil intentions of the old man who would have consigned each and every one of them to oblivion. Swimming and flying, these sacred swans reach a hill-top on which there is a shrine. The place is dedicated to Immortality. A beautiful Nymph takes the names from the swans' beaks and affixes them to a statue on a pillar in the middle of the shrine, consecrating them to all eternity. Astolfo in amazement questions St John about the significance of all this. John tells him that the role of the old man is similar to the ravaging forces of Time upon earth; crows and vultures here parallel panderers and sycophants on earth; most significantly, swans parallel poets. Thus, as the swans carry the plaques to the shrine, so, John explains, poets rescue men of worth from oblivion. He proceeds to extol the power of the written word, refers to ancient biographers who were able to enhance and immortalise their subjects, and concludes by stating that before he was taken up onto the mountain he too, during his earthly existence, was a writer, and recorded details of the life and person of Christ.

The theme of biography (and sometimes even autobiography), whether in prose or in verse, and of its ability to confer immortality upon its subject is central to a full understanding of *Mansus*. Indeed a close reading of the poem reveals several possible points of contact with the Ariosto episode.

It is hardly a coincidence that swan imagery is prominent in Ariosto, *Orlando Furioso* 35. 14ff. There, distinguished from the other birds "Fra tanti augelli,"[22] are two white swans "duo cigni soli." These do not snatch away the name-plates for their own ends nor do they allow them to fall into the waters of Lethe, but instead take pains to preserve them from oblivion:

---

[22] All quotations are from *Ludovico Ariosto: Orlando Furioso*, ed. Remo Cesarini (*Classici Italiani*, 27: Torino, 1962).

"che vengon lieti riportando in bocca/sicuramente il nome che lor tocca."
(35. 14). St John proceeds to equate these swans with poets.

> "Ma come i cigni che cantando lieti
> rendeno salve le medaglie al tempio,
> così gli uomini degni da' poeti
> son tolti da l'oblio, più che morte empio.
> Oh bene accorti principi e discreti,
> che seguite di Cesare l'esempio,
> e gli scrittor vi fate amici, donde
> non avete a temer di Lete l'onde!" (35.22)

> [But as the swanns that here still flying are,
>   With written names, unto that sacred port,
>   So there historians learnd, and Poets rare,
>   Preserve them in cleare fame, and good report;
>   O happie Princes, whose foresight and care,
>   Can win the love of writers in such sort,
>   As Cesar did, so as you need not dread
>   The lake of Lethe after ye be dead.][23]

In addition to the virtually explicit swan/poet allegory of *Mansus*
30-34, a bird metaphor seems to underlie Milton's depiction of the
nurturing (*gelida vix enutrita sub Arcto* [28]) and subsequent flight of his
own Muse (*imprudens Italas ausa est volitare per urbes* [29]).[24]
Renaissance emblems had stated that swans and poets were alike because
both are sacred to Apollo. This is evident in the Alciato emblem quoted
above. It is interesting to note that at *Mansus* 38 Milton highlights his
reverence for Apollo (*nos etiam colimus Phoebum*).[25] *Nos etiam* (38)
parallels *nos etiam* (30) used there in the specific context of the speaker's
awareness of his own native swans. Now in his professed reverence for
Apollo, Milton seems to take his place among these elevated birds. It is a

---

[23] Translation: John Harington, *Orlando Furiosto* (London, 1591).

[24] The notion of nourishment followed by flight occurs in Leland's *Cygnea Cantio*. See
Haan, "John Milton among the neo-Latinists" cited at note 7 above. Cf. Milton's
description of himself in *Ad Salsillum* as an *alumnus* of London who has left his "nest"
and has come to Italy (9-16). Milton's self-portraiture as an *alumnus* from a local
region echoes perhaps Alciato's description of the swan as *nostrae regionis alumnus*.
On bird imagery associated with Milton's poetic descriptions of his Italian journey, see
2 above.

[25] He continues: *nos munera Phoebo/flaventes spicas et lutea mala canistris/
halantemque crocum (perhibet nisi vana vetustas)/misimus et lectas Druidum de gente
choreas* (*Mans.* 38-41). For an excellent discussion of Milton and Apollo, cf. Revard,
Milton and The Tangles of Neaera's Hair, 205-236.

pride that is national at the same time as it is personal. Ariosto makes the point that poets and swans are rare; both however preserve the names of the great for all eternity.[26]

The immortalising power of literature is indeed another linking theme between Milton and Ariosto. This works on a number of levels in *Mansus*. In the prose preface to the poem Milton draws attention to the fact that Manso's name has been immortalised by the writings of Tasso. In the poem proper Milton alludes to the fact that Tasso has inscribed Manso's name "in his eternal pages" (*aeternis inscripsit nomina chartis* [8]). In terms of the Ariosto episode, Manso's own name-plate has, as it were, been rescued from the waters of Lethe. Later, Milton prophesies that wherever through the world the glory and huge name of Tasso are celebrated (*ergo quacunque per orbem/Torquati decus et nomen celebrabitur ingens* [49-50]) and wherever Marino wins acclaim (*claraque perpetui succrescet fama Marini* [50]), so will Manso receive applause, and will pluck an immortal journey in a flight like theirs (*tu quoque in ora frequens venies plausumque virorum,/et parili carpes iter immortale volatu.* [52-53]). The reference to an "immortal journey" may be significant in view of the fact that it was to *Immortality* that the shrine in Ariosto was dedicated. And the favor seems to be a reciprocal one, for Manso in his own way has seen to it that the name-plates of Marino and Tasso have been rescued from oblivion. He has achieved his wish to snatch both Tasso and Marino from Orcus through biography. Milton states that in doing so, Manso rivals Herodotus:

> ...   cupis integros rapere Orco,
> qua potes, atque avidas Parcarum eludere leges:
> amborum genus et varia sub sorte peractam
> describis vitam moresque et dona Minervae
> aemulus illius Mycalen qui natus ad altam
> rettulit Aeolii vitam facundus Homeri.   (18-23)

> [You wished to snatch them intact from Orcus, as far as you were able, and to make sport of the greedy laws of the Parcae: you described the race of both, their lives completed under varying fortunes, their characters, and gifts of Minerva, emulating that man born by the lofty Mycale, who eloquently related the life of Aolian Homer.]

---

[26] " Son, come i cigni, anco i poeti rari,/poeti che non sian del nome indegni;/sì perché il ciel degli uomini preclari/non pate mai che troppa copia regni,/sì per gran colpa dei signori avari/che lascian mendicare i sacri ingegni;/che le virtù premendo, et esaltando/i vizii, caccian le buone arti in bando." (35. 23)

The language is emphatic: the phrase *cupis ... rapere* conveying an eager and forceful attempt to rescue great men from Orcus. Such is the power of biography to "elude the greedy laws of the *Parcae*." The phraseology of Milton's *amborum genus et vitam ...* (20-21) implies that Manso composed two *Vitae*: one of Tasso, another of Marino. Manso's *Vita di Torquato Tasso* was, as noted above, published at Venice in 1621, and probably the object of much discussion between Manso and Milton. Manso's ms life of Marino[27] has not survived. Manso had also assisted the Venetian Giovanni Francesco Loredano, founder of the great Accademia degli Incogniti, with his biography of Marino, published in Venice in 1633 and hence accessible to Milton during his sojourn.[28] Loredano had indeed emphasised the ability of biography to immortalise its subject "Le vite de gli huomini illustri sono le scorte della posterità."[29] Thus Marino's name, he had stated, would be able to live for all eternity.[30] In Ariosto, too, it is precisely on account of the literary skill of biographers that great men can win immortality: heroes have been clever in befriending talented poets, who have the power and ability to augment and enhance their deeds by writing eloquently and floridly about them (35.22). St John states that writers are responsible for conferring renown upon heroes: poets and biographers alike can enhance and augment the deeds and characters of those whom they immortalise through their writings — thus Aeneas was not so pious, Achilles not so brave, Hector not so fierce as the reputations which they subsequently achieved; instead, they owe these to their *scrittori* (35. 25). Similarly the accepted characters of Augustus, Nero and Agamemnon are largely the product of those who have written about them. St John continues by professing his personal affection for writers. In his

---

[27] See Michele Manfredi, *Giovanni Battista Manso nella Vita e nelle Opere* (Naples, 1919), 259.

[28] *Vita del Cavalier Marino di Gio. Francesco Loredano Nobile Veneto* (Venice, 1633). For the help which Manso gave to Loredano in his *Vita* of Marino, see Nardo, "Academic Interludes," 211, a help surprisingly unacknowledged by Loredano in the prefatory epistle to the *Vita*, who, however, does at least allude to Manso among those whose villas provided "a harbor for the shipwrecked [Marino]," 5: "Le Case de' Duchi di Bisacci, di Bonino, e del Marchese di Villa furono il porto de' suoi naufragi per lo spatio di tre anni."

[29] Loredano, *Vita del Cavalier Marino*, 1

[30] Loredano, *Vita del Cavalier Marino*, 29-30: "Il suo nome però viverà con l'Eternità de gli Anni, e con la duratione de' secoli. La morte non hà giurisdittione sovra le memorie di coloro, che hanno eternati se stessi nelle carte ... I Marmi e' Bronzi caderanno nell' oblio sepolti dalla propria antichità. Il Marino viverà ad onta del tempo e de gli anni."

own earthly life he was a biographer of sorts, and has thereby acquired something which neither Time nor Death can take away from him: he praised Christ and earned for him the reward of great fortune.[31] Similarly it could be argued that Tasso has rescued Manso's own name by including it in his "eternal pages." Perhaps too Milton can be a swan preserving the name of Manso. He promises Manso the ivy and laurels of victory, if the breath of his [Milton's] Muse is sufficiently powerful (*si nostrae tantum valet aura Camoenae* [5]). And powerful indeed is that Muse. As noted above, Milton announces his own intention to compose a chivalric epic (78-84), and conveys his wish that he too may possess such a friend as Manso, who would know how to adorn poets ("the men of Phoebus"). Perhaps his desire is not only for a dutiful friend, but also for a writer who would adorn him (*decorasse* [79]) in an eloquent biography. Posterity was certainly to grant Milton his desire.

In some respects Milton in introducing himself to Manso as a young foreigner, a *iuvenis peregrinus* (26) who has been "sent from the northern skies" (*missus Hyperboreo ... ab axe* [26]),[32] parallels Ariosto's Astolfo, who had been described in similar terms. Thus at *Orlando Furioso* 34.55 John addresses him as one who has come from "the northern hemisphere" ("venuto sei da l'Artico emisperio") to the earthly paradise ("nel terrestre paradiso").[33] But there is one important and ironic point of contrast. St John acknowledges that Astolfo has come to him through religious motivation 34.56: "la santa fé." Milton, on the other hand, while certainly a northerner who has obviously come for the sake of learning (*animi causa*), seems not to have been able to show that necessary tact when religion was discussed. So from Manso's point of view at least, perhaps the young Milton lacks the *pietas* of the young Astolfo.

But if Milton then is not quite an Astolfo, can Manso himself be a second John the Evangelist? There are indeed some parallels. Firstly both are described as old men and as hosts to the newly-arrived youths from the north. Manso is addressed as *senex* (49; 70), and later Milton prays that he may be blessed with Aeson's eternal youth and that his locks may never

---

[31] "Gli scrittori amo, e fo il debito mio;/ch'al vostro mondo fui scrittore anch'io./E sopra tutti altri io feci acquisto/che non mi può levar tempo né morte:/e ben convenne al mio lodato Cristo/rendermi guidardon di sì gran sorte." (35. 28-29)

[32] At line 37 Milton refers to the British as suffering *brumalem ... Booten*. See in general Z.S. Fink, "Milton and the Theory of Climatic Influence," *MLQ* 2 (1941), 67-80; Revard, *Milton and the Tangles of Neaera's Hair*, 215-218.

[33] *Orlando Furioso*, 34.55: "O baron, che per voler divino/sei nel terrestre paradiso asceso;/come che né la causa del camino,/né il fin del tuo desir da te sia inteso,/pur credi che non senza alto misterio/venuto sei da l'Artico emisperio."

fall from his brow (76). In Ariosto, St John is described as a *vecchio* (34.54). Noteworthy is Astolfo's first sighting of him. In the gleaming hallway of his happy abode the old man goes to meet Astolfo. He is wearing a scarlet mantle; he has white hair and a white beard reaching down to his chest. He is so venerable that he seems to be one of the elect of Paradise:

> Nel lucente vestibulo di quella
> felice casa un vecchio al duca occorre,
> che'l manto ha rosso, e bianca la gonnella,
> che l'un può al latte, e l'altro al minio opporre.
> I crini ha bianchi, e bianca la mascella
> di folta barba ch'al petto discorre;
> et è sì venerabile nel viso,
> ch'un degli eletti par del paradiso.

(34. 54)

> [Now while the Duke his eyes with wonder fed,
>   Behold a fayre old man in th' entrie stood,
>   Whose gown was white, but yet his iacket red,
>   The tone as snow, the tother lookt as blood,
>   His beard was long and white, so was his hed,
>   His count'naunce was so grave, his grace so good,
>   A man thereby might at first sight suspect
>   He was a saint, and one of Gods elect.]

Astolfo is amazed to discover that this old man is indeed John (34. 57-58). For the young Milton, arrival in Italy is undoubtedly the equivalent of reaching an earthly paradise. Manso, a noble and venerable *senex*, is not unlike Ariosto's St John. Thus he enjoys the beauties of a peaceful abode and is likewise associated with an ideal paradise, far removed from troubles and pain — a place of repose which has a mitigating effect upon its inhabitants. St John, like Manso, is a scrupulous host. Thus Astolfo receives food and rest and all possible hospitality at the hands of the old man:

> Poi ch'a natura il duca aventuroso
> satisfece di quel che se le debbe,
> come col cibo, così col riposo,
> che tutti e tutti I commodi quivi ebbe;
> lasciando già l'Aurora il vecchio sposo. (34. 61)

> [Now when the Duke his nature satisfied,
>   With meat and drinke, and with his due repose,
>   (For that were lodgings fayre, and all beside
>   That needfull for mans use, man can suppose)
>   He getts up earlie in the morning tyde.]

Like Manso, St John is a biographer. As noted above, he tells Astolfo that
he loves writers and that when he was on earth he wrote the deeds of
Christ (34. 28-29). Manso too has immortalised subjects through his *Vitae*.
And perhaps this is Milton's wish: he too longs to have a writer who will
immortalise his name.

Such immortality is indeed possible. Ariosto erroneously follows a
tradition wholly unsubstantiated by biblical sources, that St John, like
Enoch and Elias, did not die, but was assumed into heaven ("quivi fu
assunto" [34. 59]). Perhaps by the end of *Mansus* another John is
envisaging, albeit semi-humorously, such an honor for himself. And it is
here that the wheel has come full circle: the *Anglus* has become not only
Manso's *angelus* but Ariosto's ev*ANGEL*ist.

CHAPTER 12

Amicitia and Biography

Immortality in *Mansus* can be achieved not only in Heaven, but also on earth through the power of biography. Milton's poem constitutes in effect an encomium of a contemporary biographer Manso, who in writing his *vitae* of Tasso and Marino, is presented as a second Herodotus (18-23), but more than that: for Manso is not only biographer, but also friend of the poets whose lives he documents. The themes of *amicitia* and biography are so closely intertwined in the poem that they become virtually inseparable. Manso, after all, was *Tassi amicissimus*. Perhaps too Milton's longing for an *amicus*, a longing expressed so poignantly in the poem's conclusion, can also be read as a wish for a biographer of his own, for someone like Manso who could in fact assume both roles. In other words, Milton dares to hope to become a second Tasso or Marino immortalised by *talis* ... *amicus* (78). The possibility of this analogy, or at least of an analogy between Milton and the Tasso described by Manso, is strengthened by the fact that *Mansus* seems to contain a number of hitherto unnoticed points of contact with the *Vita di Torquato Tasso Scritta da Giovanni Battista Manso Napolitano* (Venice, 1621), a work to which, along with that now lost ms. life of Marino, Milton undoubtedly refers at *Mans.* 20-21: *amborum genus et varia sub sorte peractam/describis vitam moresque et dona Minervae*, and which in its turn assumes a not insignificant place within the poem's complex intertextual background. As before, Milton's skill lies in subtle echo and witty inversion.

In the prose *argumentum* to *Mansus* Milton in signalling the relationship between Manso and Tasso highlights three facts: 1) that Tasso addressed his *Dialogue on Friendship* to Manso (*ad quem Torquati Tassi dialogus extat de Amicitia scriptus*); 2) that Manso was a great friend of Tasso (*erat enim Tassi amicissimus*); 3) that in the *Gerusalemme Conquistata* Tasso actually praised Manso by name (*ab quo etiam inter Campaniae principes celebratur in illo poemate cui titulus Gerusalemme Conquistata, lib 20*: "Fra cavalier magnanimi e cortesi/Risplende il

Manso"). It is hardly a coincidence that these are precisely the three points singled out in the opening pages of Manso's *Vita*. Manso is described as:

> stretto amico del Tasso, come i suoi versi, e le prose in molti luoghi, e spetialmente la *Gerusalemme*, e'l *Dialogo dell' Amicitia*, ch' egli intitolò *il Manso*, feciono fede ....[1]

> [a close friend of Tasso, as his verse and prose in many passages and especially the *Gerusalemme* and the *Dialogue on Friendship* which he entitled *Il Manso* testify ...]

Later in the work Manso describes in greater detail the nature of their *amicitia*, stating that the very title of Tasso's *Dialogue*: *Il Manso overe Dell' Amicitia Dialogo* reflected "quasi per forma della vera amicitia, ch'haveva in lui per molti anni e per molte pruove fedelissima sperimentata."[2] That Milton thought highly of the bond of *amicitia* is evident in, for example, that letter to Charles Diodati written in the autumn of 1637, in which he had advocated that friendship should not depend on letters and greetings (*non enim in epistolarum ac salutationum monumentis veram verti amicitiam volo*), but should rest in the deep roots of the mind (*sed altis animi radicibus niti utrinque ac sustinere se*); it should moreover be sincere and free from all blame and suspicion (*coeptam sinceris et sanctis rationibus, etiamsi mutua cessarent officia, per omnem tamen vitam suspicione et culpa vacare*).[3]

Manso's *Vita* had stated that Tasso was a loyal observer of the sacred laws of friendship ("Quindi è ch'egli fù così leale osservatore delle sacre leggi dell' Amicitia") and that he exemplified these by his deeds and also by his *Dialogue* on the subject. He was in short a "fidelissimo amico."[4] As noted above, the theme of *amicitia* recurs on three specific occasions in *Mansus* (lines 15, 63 and 78).

Both the *Vita* and *Mansus* emphasise the world-wide fame of Tasso's writings. Thus Milton had confidently predicted immortality (*iter immortale* [53]) for Manso himself wherever through the world is celebrated the glory and mighty name of Tasso (*quacumque per orbem/Torquati decus et nomen celebrabitur ingens* [49-50]). A similar

---

[1] Manso, *Vita di Torquato Tasso*, 4. Italics are mine. Cf. 138, 192.

[2] Manso, *Vita d Torquato Tasso*, 210.

[3] *CM* 12, 24.

[4] Manso, *Vita di Torquato Tasso*, 243.

point was made in the introduction of the *Vita* as Tasso's fame is not confined to Italy but is celebrated through "tutto'l mondo."[5]

But fame is possible in other respects also. The richly mythological lines 54-60 of *Mansus* may assume additional significance when read in the context of the *Vita*. Milton proclaims that it will be said that Cynthius (Apollo) dwelt of his own accord in Manso's home (*Dicetur tum sponte tuos habitasse penates/Cynthius* [54-55]). Milton's choice of Cynthius here, combined with the contracted perfect infinitive *habitasse* may punningly allude to the fact that in the *Vita* it was Cardinal *Cynthio* who actually came to visit *Tasso* — on that occasion to give the dying poet a papal blessing:

> In tanto risaputo il Cardinal Cinthio da' Medici, che a Torquato rimanevan poche hore di vita, andò a visitarlo, e a recargli in nome del Pontefice la sua santa benedittione, la qual non suole, se non à Cardinali e a persone di grandissimo affare à questo modo concedere.[6]

> [Cardinal Cyhthio de Medici who in the knowledge that for Tasso there remained only a few hours of his life, came to visit him and bore in the name of the Pope his holy blessing, which is not usually granted except to Cardinals and to persons of very great affairs.]

Milton's lines continue by contrasting Apollo's voluntary visit to Manso's home with his reluctant visit, when in exile, to the abode of Admetus, referred to patronymically as "the son of Pheres" (*at non sponte tamen idem et regis adivit/rura Pheretiadae caelo fugitivus Apollo* [56-57]). Could this bear some relation to Manso's fanciful account of the exiled Tasso assuming the disguise of a shepherd in order to visit his sister? Manso had actually compared Tasso's disguise to that assumed by Apollo

---

[5] Manso, *Vita di Torquato Tasso*, 1-2: "Ma le cose ch'egli e in versi e in prosa scrisse sono già per se stesse celebri divenute e saranno si com' io credo immortali percioche col volo della sua penna medesima hanno immantenente corsa e ripiena non solamente l'Italia dove sono state con tanta cupidità tante volte trascritte e ristampate, ma tutto'l mondo altresì non essendo quasi lingua alcuna, perbarbara e straniera ch'ella sia nella quale state non sieno l'opere di lui da eccellentissimi autori trasportate e con lode universale rilette ..."

[6] Manso, *Vita di Torquato Tasso*, 230-231.

when he shepherded the herds of Admetus.[7] Milton states that when Apollo wished to avoid the noisy cowherds, he withdrew into the noble cave of the gentle (*mansuetus*) Chiron. According to Manso, "mansuetudine" was one of Tasso's key qualities ("Da questa così profonda humiltà di Torquato se gli ingenerò nell' animo un' incredibile Mansuetudine").[8]

As the poem nears its conclusion Milton imagines a deathbed scene — his own:[9]

> tandem ubi non tacitae permensus tempora vitae
> annorumque satur cineri sua iura relinquam,
> ille mihi lecto madidis adstaret ocellis,
> adstanti sat erit si dicam "sim tibi curae";
> ille meos artus liventi morte solutos
> curaret parva componi molliter urna.
> Forsitan et nostros ducat de marmore vultus,
> nectens aut Paphia myrti aut Parnasside lauri
> fronde comas. At ego secura pace quiescam.
>
> *(Mans.* 85-93)

[Then at last when I have measured forth the span of a life not silent, and in the fullness of years have bequeathed to the ashes the due that is theirs, he would stand before my bed with soaking eyes. It will be enough if I say to him as he stands there "Take me into your care." He would see to it that my limbs loosened by livid death were placed in a small urn. And perhaps he would depict my face in marble, binding my hair with Paphian myrtle or Parnassian laurel, but I will rest safely in peace.]

When viewed in the context of the *Vita*, the envisaged friend as recipient of the poet's final words and weeping before his bed seems to find a parallel in Cardinal Cynthio himself. According to Manso, it was the

---

[7] Manso, *Vita di Torquato Tasso*, 82: "Quivi tra per lo disagio e per l'indispositione non prendendo molto sono e crescendo gli i malanconosi sospetti, pensò di travestirsi per più celatamente andare in habitato di pastore, onde nel mattino sù l'alba, richiesto a' suoi hosti un loro vestimento, e havutolo in cambio del suo che lasciò loro molto migliore; e forse sovvenendogli d'Apollo qual' hora nello stesso habito guidava gli armenti d'Ameto, se ne rivestì e si pose la via tra' piedi."

[8] Manso, *Vita di Torquato Tasso*, 259. Cf. 260: "La qual sofferenza hebbe in tutto il rimanente della sua vita con animo così mansueto, che per molto che stato fosse perseguitato, e lacerato, e nell' operationi, e ne gli scritti da suoi gavillatori, egli non pure non volle giammai, ne vendetta, ne gastigamento prendere in fatti, mà ne meno si dolse à parola d'alcun di loro."

[9] For imaginary funerals, cf. Revard, *Milton and the Tangles of Neaera's Hair*, 220-223.

Cardinal who received Tasso's final wishes, after which he took his farewell with tears in his eyes, while other bystanders likewise wept.[10] When Tasso was asked what would he like as his epitaph, he had smiled, replying that a single plain stone would be enough ("Sorisse Torquato e disse che alla sua fossa bastarebbe una sola tavola per coverchio");[11] Milton states that it will be enough (*sat erit* [88]) to entrust himself to the care of his friend, who would place his ashes in a small urn (*parva ... urna* [90]). Tasso's burial was without ceremony in the church of St Onuphrius beneath a simple stone.[12] Cardinal Cynthio had proposed to erect a great monument in Tasso's memory, but was prevented from doing so. Then ten years later Manso came to Rome and visited Tasso's remains, but discovered to his dismay that there was no memorial in the church. It was Manso who eventually prevailed upon the brothers to have the simple inscription *Hic iacet Torquatus Tassus* engraved in marble.[13]

Finally, Milton's wish that his friend might perhaps depict his countenance in marble, binding his hair with myrtle or laurel is noteworthy in view of the fact that the frontispiece to the *Vita* depicts Tasso adorned with a laurel wreath, while in the biography proper Manso describes in some detail how in 1551 Tasso went to Rome to receive a "laurel crown" from the pope, and was acclaimed in a triumphal procession throughout the city.[14] The theme recurs, albeit in a symbolic sense, in Manso's description

[10] Manso, *Vita di Torquato Tasso*, 232-233: "E così fù fatto: percioche chiedendogli il Cardinal commiato, e retinendo à fatica le lagrime, le quali nell' uscir della stanza, egli e tutti gli altri circostanti sparsero per gli occhi copiosamente."

[11] Manso, *Vita di Torquato Tasso*, 228.

[12] Manso, *Vita di Torquato Tasso*, 233-234: "Fù adunque nella medesima sera il corpo di Torquato, com'egli morendo havea detto, nella stessa Chiesa di Santo Onofrio con private essequie condotto, e sotto un semplice, e picciol marmo seppellito, pensando il Cardinal Cinthio di dovervi quanto prima un magnifico e splendido sepolcro innalzare."

[13] Manso, *Vita di Torquato Tasso*, 234: "In modo che essendo ito di là dieci anni Gio. Battista Manso in Roma nella sedia vacante dopò la morte di Clemente VIII e andando à vistar l'ossa del morto amico, nè ritrovando nè in quella Chiesa memoria veruna, procurò di fargli alcuna honorevole sepoltura ... La onde appena potette il Manso ottener da' Frati di far sù lo stesso marmo scolpir solamente *Hic iacet Torquatus Tassus*." Cf. Marino's sonnet to Manso entitled "Tomba del Tasso Amico del Marchese" at *Poesie Nomiche*, 269, in which Manso is described as visiting Tasso's urn while Tasso himself dwells in heavenly Parnassus. For an interesting discussion of the closing lines of *Mansus* in the light of this sonnet, cf. Revard, *Milton and the Tangles of Neaera's Hair*, 221-222.

[14] Manso, *Vita di Torquato Tasso*, 223: "Entrato poscia in Palaggio a bacir le mani de' Cardinali Cinthio, e Pietro, e, con amendue, i piedi del Papa, gli fù da lui con lieto e benigno volto detto; c'haveva determinato, ch'egli con la sua virtù honorasse la corona dell' alloro quant' essa havea per l'addietro gl' altri honorato. Egli per queste parole

of Tasso's deathbed scene, where Tasso contemplates heavenly happiness as the divine analogy of his earthly coronation: "dicendo che questa era quella coronatione, le quale era venuto assai volentieri a prendere in Roma."[15] In *Mansus* the two themes are ingeniously fused as the earthly iconographical representation of the laureate Milton finds a heavenly parallel in the *praemia certa bonorum* (94).

By the end of *Mansus* Milton, the *iuvenis*, has grown old. Perhaps he imagines himself as a *senex*, as another Manso or Tasso who has achieved his literary ambitions; perhaps too as a great man who deserves a worthy biographer to perpetuate his name. But at the same time as both poet and biographer himself, he has taken his place among the *scrittori*. In composing his own one hundred-line verse-biography, as it were, of Manso, he too has inscribed Manso's name "in his eternal pages." The traveller from the north, not without his own form of *pietas*, the poet, the biographer — all are united in the closing lines of the poem. That quest for the Idea of the Good (τοῦ καλοῦ ἰδέαν) may at last be realised in the acknowledgement that an *ignea virtus* (96) can serve as a personal passport to a very different realm, whereby the earthly paradise of Italy can be exchanged for the celestial paradise that is Heaven.

---

bacìò di nuovo i piedi a Clemente: e dall'hora in poi s'attese a far l'apparecchiamento grande, e magnifico non solamente nel palagio papale, dove Torquato albergava, e nel Campidoglio, dove coronar si doveva, ma per tutti i luoghi della Città, per gli quali la trionfal pompa haveva a passare."

[15] Manso, *Vita di Torquato Tasso*, 231.

APPENDIX

Milton's Latin poems of the Italian Journey
Text and Facing Translation

Ad Salsillum poetam Romanum aegrotantem.
Scazontes.

O Musa gressum quae volens trahis claudum
Vulcanioque tarda gaudes incessu
nec sentis illud in loco minus gratum
quam cum decentes flava Dëiope suras
alternat aureum ante Iunonis lectum,   5
adesdum et haec s'is verba pauca Salsillo
refer, camoena nostra cui tantum est cordi
quamque ille magnis praetulit immerito divis.
Haec ergo alumnus ille Londini Milto,
diebus hisce qui suum linquens nidum   10
polique tractum (pessimus ubi ventorum,
insanientis impotensque pulmonis
pernix anhela sub Ioue exercet flabra),
venit feraces Itali soli ad glebas
visum superba cognitas urbes fama   15
virosque doctaeque indolem iuventutis;
tibi optat idem hic fausta multa, Salsille,
habitumque fesso corpori penitus sanum,
cui nunc profunda bilis infestat renes
praecordiisque fixa damnosum spirat,   20
nec id pepercit impia quod tu Romano
tam cultus ore Lesbium condis melos.
O dulce divum munus, o Salus, Hebes
germana, tuque Phoebe, morborum terror
Pythone caeso, sive tu magis Paean   25
libenter audis, hic tuus sacerdos est!
Querceta Fauni vosque rore vinoso
colles benigni, mitis Evandri sedes,
siquid salubre vallibus frondet vestris
levamen aegro ferte certatim vati.   30
Sic ille caris redditus rursum musis
vicina dulci prata mulcebit cantu.
Ipse inter atros emirabitur lucos
Numa ubi beatum degit otium aeternum,
suam reclivis semper Aegeriam spectans;   35
tumidusque et ipse Tibris hinc delinitus
spei favebit annuae colonorum,
nec in sepulchris ibit obsessum reges
nimium sinistro laxus irruens loro,
sed frena melius temperabit undarum   40
adusque curvi salsa regna Portumni.

To Salzilli, a poet of Rome, when he was sick:[1]
Scazontes

O Muse, who willingly drag a limping foot, and in your sluggishness rejoice in the gait of Vulcan, without realising that in its place this is less pleasing than when golden Deiopea with her seemly ankles dances before the golden couch of Juno: be present, and carry, if you will, these few words to Salzilli, to whose heart my poetry is so dear, and which he preferred, quite undeservedly to the mighty gods; carry therefore these words spoken by that nursling of London, Milton, who recently left his own nest and region of the heavens (where the worst of winds, powerless to control its madly heaving lungs, swiftly puffs its panting blasts beneath the sky), and came to the fertile clods of Italian soil in order to see cities known by proud reputation, and the men and genius of its learned youth. This same Milton wishes you, Salzilli, many good fortunes and thoroughly good health for your weary body. Now an overflow of bile assails your kidneys and, implanted in your stomach, breathes its deadly breath; lacking respect, it does not spare the fact that you so elegantly fashion the song of Lesbos upon Roman lips.

O sweet gift of the gods, o Health, sister of Hebe, and you, Phoebus — or whether you more willingly attend under the name of Paean —, terror of diseases ever since your slaughter of Python, this man is your priest! Oak-groves of Faunus, and you, hills abundant in the dew of grapes, abode of the gentle Evander, if any health-giving plant blooms in your valleys, bring it eagerly to your sick bard. In this way, restored once more to his dear muses, he will soothe the neighboring meadows with his sweet song. Numa himself will be amazed when amid the dark groves he spends a blessed eternity of rest as he reclines, forever gazing upon his own Egeria, and the swollen Tiber himself, charmed by the strains, will favor the yearly hope of the farmers, and will not seek to besiege kings in their tombs by rushing along with the left rein too slack, but he will keep the reins of his waves under control all the way to the salty kingdom of the curved Portumnus.

---

[1] All translations are mine.

Ad Leonoram Romae canentem

Angelus unicuique suus (sic credite gentes)
    obtigit aethereis ales ab ordinibus.
Quid mirum, Leonora, tibi si gloria maior,
    nam tua praesentem vox sonat ipsa Deum!
Aut Deus, aut vacui certe mens tertia caeli   5
    per tua secreto guttura serpit agens;
serpit agens, facilisque docet mortalia corda
    sensim immortali assuescere posse sono.
Quod si cuncta quidem Deus est per cunctaque fusus,
    in te una loquitur; cetera mutus habet.   10

Ad eandem

Altera Torquatum cepit Leonora poetam,
    cuius ab insano cessit amore furens.
Ah miser ille tuo quanto felicius aevo
    perditus, et propter te, Leonora, foret!
Et te Pieria sensisset voce canentem   5
    aurea maternae fila movere lyrae,
quamvis Dircaeo torsisset lumina Pentheo
    saevior aut totus desipuisset iners,
tu tamen errantes caeca vertigine sensus
    voce eadem poteras composuisse tua,   10
et poteras aegro spirans sub corde quietem
    flexanimo cantu restituisse sibi.

Ad eandem

Credula quid liquidam Sirena Neapoli iactas,
    claraque Parthenopes fana Achelöiados,
litoreamque tua defunctam naiada ripa
    corpora Chalcidico sacra dedisse rogo?
Illa quidem vivitque et amoena Tibridis unda   5
    mutavit rauci murmura Pausilipi.
Illic Romulidum studiis ornata secundis,
    atque homines cantu detinet atque deos.

To Leonora singing at Rome

Each person (believe this o peoples) has been allotted a winged angel from the celestial ranks. What wonder then if, Leonora, you have a greater glory, for your very voice proclaims the presence of God. Either God or certainly the third mind has left an empty space in the sky and secretly progresses, coiling its way through your throat. Coiling its way, it progresses, and easily teaches hearts that are mortal gradually how to grow accustomed to a sound that is immortal. For if God is indeed all things and is diffused through all things, it is in you alone that he speaks, while holding everything else in silence.

To the same

Another Leonora captivated the poet Torquato, who became mad on account of his insane love for her. Ah how much more happily would that poor man have been ruined in your life-time and on your account, Leonora! And had he heard you singing with your Pierian voice and heard the strumming of the golden strings of your mother's lyre, even though he had rolled his eyes more savagely than Dircaean Pentheus or had been utterly dull and senseless, still, through your voice you could have calmed those senses reeling in their blind wanderings, and breathing repose into the depths of his troubled heart, through your soul-moving song, you could have restored him to himself.

To the same

Why, credulous Naples, do you boast of your clear-voiced Siren and of the famous shrine of Achelous's daughter, Parthenope, and that when she, a naiad of the shore, died on your coasts, you placed her sacred body upon a Chalcidian pyre? In actual fact, she is alive and has changed the murmurs of the hoarse Posillipo for the pleasant waters of the Tiber. There, honored by the favorable enthusiasm of Roman audiences, she captivates both men and gods with her song.

Mansus

Ioannes Baptista Mansus Marchio Villensis vir ingenii laude tum
literarum studio nec non et bellica virtute apud Italos clarus in
primis est. Ad quem Torquati Tassi dialogus exstat de Amicitia
scriptus; erat enim Tassi amicissimus, ab quo etiam inter
Campaniae principes celebratur in illo poemate cui titulus
Gerusalemme conquistata, lib 20:

> Fra cavalier magnanimi, e cortesi
> Risplende il Manso ――――

Is auctorem Neapoli commorantem summa benevolentia
prosecutus est multaque ei detulit humanitatis officia. Ad hunc
itaque hospes ille, antequam ab ea urbe discederet, ut ne
ingratum se ostenderet, hoc carmen misit.

Haec quoque Manse tuae meditantur carmina laudi
Pierides, tibi Manse choro notissime Phoebi,
quandoquidem ille alium haud aequo est dignatus honore,
post Galli cineres et Mecaenatis Hetrusci.
Tu quoque, si nostrae tantum valet aura Camoenae,   5
victrices hederas inter laurosque sedebis.
Te pridem magno felix concordia Tasso
iunxit et aeternis inscripsit nomina chartis.
Mox tibi dulciloquum non inscia Musa Marinum
tradidit: ille tuum dici se gaudet alumnum   10
dum canit Assyrios divum prolixus amores,
mollis et Ausonias stupefecit carmine nymphas.
Ille itidem moriens tibi soli debita vates
ossa tibi soli supremaque vota reliquit.
Nec manes pietas tua cara fefellit amici: 15
vidimus arridentem operoso ex aere poetam.
Nec satis hoc visum est in utrumque, et nec pia cessant
officia in tumulo, cupis integros rapere Orco,
qua potes, atque avidas Parcarum eludere leges:
amborum genus et varia sub sorte peractam   20
describis vitam moresque et dona Minervae
aemulus illius Mycalen qui natus ad altam
rettulit Aeolii vitam facundus Homeri.
Ergo ego te Clius et magni nomine Phoebi,
Manse pater, iubeo longum salvere per aevum,   25
missus Hyperboreo iuvenis peregrinus ab axe.
Nec tu longinquam bonus aspernabere musam,
quae nuper gelida vix enutrita sub Arcto
imprudens Italas ausa est volitare per urbes.
Nos etiam in nostro modulantes flumine cygnos   30
credimus obscuras noctis sensisse per umbras,
qua Thamesis late puris argenteus urnis
oceani glaucos perfundit gurgite crines.
Quin et in has quondam pervenit Tityrus oras.

Manso

Giovanni Battista Manso, Marquis of Villa, is a man particularly
famous among Italians for the glory of his genius and his literary
studies, and also his bravery in war. Addressed to whom there
exists a dialogue of Torquato Tasso on Friendship, for he was a
great friend of Tasso, by whom he is also celebrated among the
princes of Campania in that poem which is entitled *Gerusalemme Conquistata*, bk. 20.
  "Among great-hearted and magnanimous courtiers
  Manso is resplendent — "
When the author was delaying in Naples he tended him with the
greatest kindness and conferred on him many humane services.
And so that guest before leaving that city sent him this poem in
order that he might not appear ungrateful.

These songs also, Manso, do the Pierans compose in your
praise: for you, Manso, well known to the chorus of Phoebus,
since it has deemed no one else worthy of equal honor since the
death of Gallus and of the Etruscan Maecenas. You too, if the
breath of our Camoena is sufficiently strong, will sit among the
ivy and laurels of victory.
  In times past a happy friendship joined you to the mighty
Tasso and inscribed your name in his eternal pages. Next the
Muse, not without knowledge, entrusted the sweetly-speaking
Marino to you; he rejoiced in being called your nursling, while in
verbose fashion he sang of the Assyrian love affairs of the gods,
and gently with his verse amazed the Ausonian nymphs. Indeed
that bard, as he died, entrusted his bones to you alone, to you
alone his final wishes. And your caring sense of duty did not fail
your friend's spirit: we have seen the poet smiling from well-
wrought bronze. But it did not seem to you that this was
sufficient for either of them, nor did your dutiful services cease
at the tomb. You wished to snatch them intact from Orcus, as
far as you were able, and to make sport of the greedy laws of the
Parcae: you described the race of both, their lives completed
under varying fortunes, their characters, and gifts of Minerva,
emulating that man born by the lofty Mycale, who eloquently
related the life of Aolian Homer. Therefore, father Manso, in the
name of Clio and of mighty Apollo, I, a young foreigner sent
from the Hyperborean skies, wish you a lengthy and healthy life.
You in your goodness will not spurn a muse who has travelled a
long distance, and, having with difficulty found nourishment
beneath the frozen Bear, has recently ventured in her rashness to
fly through the cities of Italy. We too believe that we have heard
swans singing in our river amid the dark shadows of night,
where the silver Thames with her pure urns soaks her green hair
in the ocean's current. Moreover Tityrus once reached these
shores.

Sed neque nos genus incultum nec inutile Phoebo,   35
qua plaga septeno mundi sulcata Trione
brumalem patitur longa sub nocte Booten.
Nos etiam colimus Phoebum, nos munera Phoebo
flaventes spicas et lutea mala canistris
halantemque crocum (perhibet nisi vana vetustas)   40
misimus et lectas Druidum de gente choreas.
(Gens Druides antiqua sacris operata deorum
heroum laudes imitandaque gesta canebant);
hinc quoties festo cingunt altaria cantu
Delo in herbosa Graiae de more puellae   45
carminibus laetis memorant Corineida Loxo,
fatidicamque Upin cum flavicoma Hecaerge
nuda Caledonio variatas pectora fuco.
Fortunate senex, ergo quacunque per orbem
Torquati decus et nomen celebrabitur ingens,   50
claraque perpetui succrescet fama Marini,
tu quoque in ora frequens venies plausumque virorum,
et parili carpes iter immortale volatu.
Dicetur tum sponte tuos habitasse penates
Cynthius, et famulas venisse ad limina musas;   55
at non sponte domum tamen idem et regis adivit
rura Pheretiadae caelo fugitivus Apollo;
ille licet magnum Alciden susceperat hospes.
Tantum ubi clamosos placuit vitare bubulcos,
nobile mansueti cessit Chironis in antrum,   60
irriguos inter saltus frondosaque tecta
Peneium prope riuum; ibi saepe sub ilice nigra
ad citharae strepitum blanda prece victus amici
exilii duros lenibat voce labores.
Tum neque ripa suo, barathro nec fixa sub imo   65
saxa stetere loco; nutat Trachinia rupes,
nec sentit solitas, immania pondera, silvas,
emotaeque suis properant de collibus orni,
mulcenturque novo maculosi carmine lynces.
Diis dilecte senex, te Iupiter aequus oportet   70
nascentem, et miti lustrarit lumine Phoebus
Atlantisque nepos; neque enim nisi carus ab ortu
diis superis poterit magno favisse poetae.
Hinc longaeva tibi lento sub flore senectus
vernat, et Aesonios lucratur vivida fusos,   75
nondum deciduos servans tibi frontis honores
ingeniumque vigens et adultum mentis acumen.

But we, who endure the wintry Bootes for the night's length in that region of the universe furrowed by his seven-fold wagon, we are a people neither uncultured nor useless to Phoebus. We too worship Phoebus, we have sent Phoebus gifts: yellow ears of grain and golden apples in baskets and the fragrant crocus (unless ancient lore be spoken in vain), and choirs chosen from the Druid race. (The Druids, an ancient race, were well-versed in the rites of the gods — they used to sing the glories of heroes and their exploits worthy of imitation). Hence as often as Greek girls upon grassy Delos circled the altars in festive song according to custom, they relate in happy verses Luxo, daughter of Corineus, and prophetic Upis, together with golden-haired Hecaerge, all of whose bare breasts are colored with Caledonian paint.

And so, fortunate old man, wherever through the world is celebrated the glory and huge name of Torquato, and wherever increases the radiant fame of the immortal Marino, you too will frequently be on the lips and in the applause of men, and with equal flight will you pluck the journey of immortality. Then will it be said that Cynthius dwelt of his own free will in your home, and that the muses came as servants to your threshold; but it was not of his own free will that that same Apollo, a fugitive from heaven, approached the home and the farm of the royal son of Pheres, even though the latter had hospitably received the mighty Hercules. But when he wished to avoid the noisy herdsmen, he withdrew into the noble cave of the gentle Chiron amid the well-watered meadows and the leafy dwellings beside the river Peneus. There beneath the dark oak, vanquished by the winsome pleading of his friend he would often alleviate the harsh toils of exile with his voice to the accompaniment of the resounding lyre. Thereupon neither river-banks nor boulders lodged in the lowest abyss remained in their places; the Trachinian cliff nodded and could not feel the customary weight of its forests, and mountain ashes were dislodged and hastened down the hills, while spotted lynxes were soothed by the unfamiliar music.

Old man, beloved of the gods, Jupiter must have been favorable towards you at your birth, and Phoebus and the grandson of Atlas must have looked upon you with kindly glance, for no one, unless he is dear to the gods from his birth, could have shown favor to a mighty poet. Hence your old age is spring-like with late blossom and vigorously acquires the spindles of Aeson, preserving the glory of your brow not yet fallen, your intellect alive, and the sharpness of your mind mature.

O mihi si mea sors talem concedat amicum
Phoebaeos decorasse viros qui tam bene norit,
si quando indigenas revocabo in carmina reges,   80
Arcturumque etiam sub terris bella moventem,
aut dicam invictae sociali foedere mensae,
magnanimos heroas, et (o modo spiritus adsit)
frangam Saxonicas Britonum sub Marte phalanges,
tandem ubi non tacitae permensus tempora vitae   85
annorumque satur cineri sua iura relinquam,
ille mihi lecto madidis adstaret ocellis,
adstanti sat erit si dicam "sim tibi curae";
ille meos artus liventi morte solutos
curaret parva componi molliter urna.   90
Forsitan et nostros ducat de marmore vultus,
nectens aut Paphia myrti aut Parnasside lauri
fronde comas. At ego secura pace quiescam.
Tum quoque, si qua fides, si praemia certa bonorum,
ipse ego caelicolum semotus in aethera divum,   95
quo labor et mens pura vehunt, atque ignea virtus
secreti haec aliqua mundi de parte videbo
(quantum fata sinunt) et tota mente serenum
ridens purpureo suffundar lumine vultus
et simul aethereo plaudam mihi laetus Olympo.   100

Oh, if my fate would grant me such a friend who knows so well how to adorn the followers of Phoebus, if ever I recall into poetry our native kings, and Arthur waging wars even beneath the earth, or if I speak of the great-souled heroes of the table rendered invincible by a bond of fellowship, and (if only the breath of inspiration be present) break the Saxon phalanxes in a British war, then at last when I have measured forth the span of a life not silent, and in the fullness of years have bequeathed to the ashes the due that is theirs, he would stand before my bed with soaking eyes. It will be enough if I say to him as he stands there "Take me into your care". He would see to it that my limbs loosened by livid death were placed in a small urn. And perhaps he would depict my face in marble, binding my hair with Paphian myrtle or Parnassian laurel, but I will rest safely in peace. Then also, if faith exists anywhere, if there are fixed rewards for the virtuous, I myself, removed into the ethereal regions of the heaven-dwelling gods, whither toil and a pure mind and fiery virtue conduct one, will behold these things from some region of a secluded universe (as far as the fates permit) and with utter serenity of mind, as I smile, my face will be suffused with a radiant light while at the same time in joy I will applaud myself on ethereal Olympus.

BIBLIOGRAPHY

1 MANUSCRIPTS

Florence: Biblioteca Marucelliana

Ms A.36, ff. 11^r - 142^v Anton Francesco Gori: notes on the Accademia degli Apatisti: its membership and practices.

Florence: Biblioteca Riccardiana

Cod. Riccardiano 1949, 85^r - 88^r *Ordini del Simposio*: statutes for the symposia of the Accademia degli Affidati of S. Miniato.

Florence: Biblioteca Nazionale Centrale

Magliabecchiana Ms cl. VII 356	*Poesie di Diversi non Ancora Stampate Raccolte da Piu Manuscritti 1650*
Magliabecchiana Ms cl. IX 60	Minutes of Svogliati meetings (July-September, 1638) (ff. 46^v - 48); minutes of Svogliati meetings of March 1639 (ff. 52-52^v)
Magliabecchiana Ms cl. XXIV 57	includes Giovanni Salzilli, *Sonetto in Lode di Giulio da Montevecchio* on his *Scorneide*, and the *Scorneide del Signor Conte Giulio di Montevecchio* (f. 80ff.)
Ms cl. II, IV 17	Domenico Poltri, *Poesie*; 214^r - 219^r: *Poesie di Alcuni Accademici Apatisti*
Ms cl. VI 94	Iacopo Gaddi, *Esercitazioni Retoriche*
Ms cl. VI 163	*Statuti dell' Accademia degli Svogliati*
Ms cl. VI 694	*Iacobi Gaddii Carmina*
Ms cl. VI 696	*Iacobi Gaddii Patricii Fiorentini Carminum Libri Duo*
Ms cl. VII 357	includes compositions by Francesco Rovai
Ms cl. VII 391	includes lecture by Antonio Malatesti to the Apatisti (on some verses of Petrarch)
Ms cl. VII 623	*Poesie di Alcuni Accademici Apatisti*
Ms cl. VII 697	*Poeticus Hortus ab Iacopo Gaddio non Alienis Flosculis Gemmatus*
Ms cl. VII 698	*Esemplare a Stampa dei Carmi di Jacopo Gaddi*
Ms cl. VII 699	*Annotationes ex Martiale et Aliis Poetis Epigrammaticis Depromptae* (by Jacopo Gaddi)

London: British Museum

BM Add. MS 5016 ff. 5 and 71   Two undated Greek leters from Charles Diodati to John Milton

2   MILTON: EDITIONS/COMMENTARIES

Poems of Mr. John Milton, Both English and Latin, Compos'd at Several Times (London, 1645).

Poems Upon Several Occasions, English, Italian and Latin, ed Thomas Warton (London, 1785).

Latin and Italian Poems of Milton Translated Into English Verse, by Wiliam Cowper (London, 1808).

The Poems of John Milton, ed. Thomas Keightley (London, 1859).

The Poetical Works of John Milton, ed. David Masson (London, 1874), 3 vols.

The Latin Poems of John Milton, ed. Walter MacKellar (*Cornell Studies in English*, vol. 15 [New Haven, 1930]).

The Works of John Milton, ed. Frank A. Patterson, *et al* (New York: Columbia University Press, 1931-1940) 18 vols.

John Milton: Paradise Regained, The Minor Poems and Samson Agonistes, ed. Merritt Y. Hughes, (New York, 1937).

John Milton: Complete Shorter Poems, ed. John Carey, (Longman: London and New York, 1971; 2nd revised ed., 1997).

A Variorum Commentary on the Poems of John Milton: Vol. I: The Latin and Greek Poems, ed. Douglas Bush (New York, 1970).

3.   OTHER TEXTS AND ANTHOLOGIES

ALCIATUS, ANDREAS, *The Latin Emblems I: Index Emblematicus*, ed Peter M. Daly (Toronto, 1985).

Applausi Poetici alle Glorie della Signora Leonora Baroni, ed. Vincenzo Costazuti (Rome, 1639).

ARIOSTO, LUDOVICO, *Orlando Furioso*, ed. Remo Cesarini (*Classici Italiani*, 27: Torino, 1962).

BEDE, *Ecclesiastical History of the English People*, eds. B. Colgrave & R.A.B. Mynors (Oxford, 1969).

BUONMATTEI, BENEDETTO, "Sopra l'Ozio," *Prose Fiorentine Raccolte dallo Smarrito Accademico della Crusca*, ed. Carlo Dati (Florence, 1716-1745).

Carmina Illustrium Poetarum Italorum, ed. G.G. Bottari (Florence, 1719-1726).

CATULLUS, *The Poems*, ed. Kenneth Quinn (London, 1970; 2nd ed. 1973; rpt. Bristol Classical Press, 1996).

CHAUCER, GEOFFREY, *Works*, ed. F.N. Robinson (London, 1957).

CHIABRERA, GABRIELLO, *Canzonette, Rime Varie, Dialoghi*, ed. Luigi Negri (Torino, 1964).

COLTELLINI, AGOSTINO, *Endecasillabi Fidentiani d'Ostilio Contalgeni Accademico Apatista* (Florence, 1641).

DATI, CARLO, *Delle Lodi del Commendatore Cassiano del Pozzo* (Florence, 1664).

_____, *Discorso dell' Obbligio di Ben Parlare La Propria Lingua di C. D. con la Declinazioni de' Verbi de Benedetto Buommattei* (Florence, 1657).

_____, *Lettera a Filaleti di Timauro Antiate della Vera Storia della Cicloide e della Famosissima Esperienza dell' Argento Vivo* (Florence, 1663).

_____ , *Prose Fiorentine Raccolte dallo Smarrito Accademico della Crusca*, (Florence, 1661), vol. 1.

_____ , *Veglie Inedite*, ed. F. Grazzini (Florence, 1814).

DE PIETRI, FRANCESCO, *I Problemi Accademici overe Le Piu Famose Questioni Proposte nell' Illustrissima Accademia degli Oziosi di Napoli* (Naples, 1642).

EVELYN, JOHN, *Diary*, ed. E.S. de Beer (Oxford, 1955).

FIORETTI, BENEDETTO, *Osservazioni di Creanza* (Florence, 1675).

FONTANI, FRANCESCO, *Elogio di Carlo Roberto Dati Recitato Nella Reale Accademia Fiorentina nell' Adunanza del di 30. Di Settembre 1790 dall' Abate Francesco Fontani Bibliotecario della Riccardiana* (Florence, 1794).

GADDI, JACOPO, *Adlocutiones et Elogia, Exemplaria, Cabalistica, Oratoria, Mixta Sepulcralia* (Florence, 1636).

_____ , *Corollarium Poeticum, scil. Poematia, Notae, Explicationes Allegoricae Olim Conscriptae* (Florence, 1636).

_____ , *De Scriptoribus non Ecclesiasticis, Graecis, Latinis, Italicis Primorum Graduum in Quinque Theatris, scilicet, Philosophico, Poetico, Historico, Oratorico, Critico*, 2 vol. (Florence, 1648).

_____ , *Elogia Historica Tum Soluta Cum Vincta Numeris Oratione Perscripta et Notis Illustrata* (Florence, 1637).

_____ , *Poematum Libri Duo* (Patavii, 1628)

GARUFFI, GIUSEPPE MALATESTA, *Italia Accademica* (Rimini, 1689).

GORI, ANTON FRANCESCO, *Discorso Recitato nella Celebre Accademia degli Apatisti* (Florence, 1754).

GROTIUS, HUGO, *Poemata Collecta* (Leiden, 1617).

HARINGTON, JOHN, *Orlando Furioso in English Heroical Verse* (London, 1591).

HEINSIUS, NICOLAS, *Poemata* (Lugd. Batav., 1653).

HORACE, *The Odes*, ed. Kenneth Quinn (Macmillan, 1980; rpt. Nelson, 1992).

JONSON, BEN, *Poems*, ed. Ian Donaldson (Oxford, 1975).

Le Glorie degli Incogniti O vero Gli Huomini Illustri dell' Accademia de' Signori Incogniti di Venetia (Venice, 1647).

LELAND, JOHN, *Cygnea Cantio* (London, 1658).

_____ , *Principum ac Illustrium Aliquot et Eruditorum in Anglia Virorum Encomia, Trophaeo, Genethliaca et Epithalamia a Ioanne Lelando Antiquario Conscripta* (London, 1589).

LETI, GREGORIO, *L'Itala Regnante* (Valenza, 1676).

LOREDANO, FRANCESCO, *Discorsi Accademici: Accedemia degli Incogniti* (Venice, 1635).

_____ , *Vita del Cavalier Marino di Gio. Francesco Loredano Nobile Veneto* (Venice, 1633).

MANSO, GIOVANNI BATTISTA, *Erocallia ovvero dell' Amore e della Bellezza* (Venice, 1628).

_____ , *Poesie Nomiche, ... Divise in Rime Amorose, Sacre, e Morali*, ed. A. Berardelli (Venice, 1635).

_____ , *Vita di Torquato Tasso* (Venice, 1621).

_____ , *Vita, Virtù e Miracoli Principali di S. Patricia Vergine* (Naples, 1611).

MANTUAN, BAPTISTA, *Eclogues*, ed. W.P. Mustard (Baltimore, 1911).

MARULLUS, MICHAEL, *Carmina*, ed. A. Perosa (Zurich, 1951).

MAUGARS, ANDRÉ, *Response Faite à un Curieux Sur Le Sentiment de la Musique d'Italie, Escrite à Rome le Premier Octobre 1639*, ed. Ernest Thoinan (Paris, 1865).

PETRARCH, FRANCESCO, *Opera* (Basel, 1554).

PIAZZA, BARTOLOMEO, *Eusevologio Romano* (Rome, 1690)

Poesie de' Signori Accademici Fantastici di Roma (Rome, 1637).

POLIZIANO, ANGELO AMBROGINI, *Prose Volgari Inedite e Poesie Latine e Greche Edite e Inedite*, ed. Isidore del Lungo (Hildesheim, New York, 1976).

RILLI, JACOPO, *Notizie Letterarie ed Istoriche agli Uomini Illustri dell' Accademia Fiorentina* (Florence, 1700).

ROVAI, FRANCESCO, *Poesie*, ed. N. Rovai (Florence, 1652).

RUSCELLI, IERONIMO, *Delle Imprese Illustri* (Venice, 1580).

SALVINI, A.M., *Discorsi Accademici ... Sopra Alcuni Dubbi Proposti nell' Accademia degli Apatisti* (Florence, 1695)

SALVINI, SALVINO, *Fasti Consolari dell' Accademia Fiorentina* (Florence, 1717).

STEPHANUS, CAROLUS, *Dictionarium Historicum, Geographicum, Poeticum* (Geneva, 1621).

STIGLIANI, TOMASO, *Lettere* (Rome, 1664).

TASSO, TORQUATO, *Il Manso, overe Dell' Amicitia Dialogo del Sig. Torquato Tasso al Molte Illustre Sig. Giovanni Battista Manso* (Naples, 1596).

TIBULLUS, *Elegies* I, ed. P. Murgatroyd (Bristol Classical Press, 1980).

4   WORKS OF REFERENCE

BOSWELL, J.C., *Milton's Library* (New York and London, 1975).

CAMPBELL, GORDON, *A Milton Chronology* (Macmillan, London; St Martin's Press, New York, 1997)

COOPER, LANE, *A Concordance to the Latin, Greek, and Italian Poems of John Milton* (Halle, 1923).

COSENZA, M.E., *Biographical and Bibliographical Dictionary of the Humanists and of the World of Classical Scholarship in Italy, 1300-1800* (Boston, 1962), 5 vols.

Dictionary of National Biography (London, 1885-1901), 22 vols.

Dizionario Biografico degli Italiani (Rome, 1960-)

FRENCH, J.M., *The Life Records of John Milton*, 5 vols. (Rutgers Studies in English, no. 7 [1949-1958])

Grande Dizionario della Lingua Italiana (Turin, 1981).

LOCKWOOD, L. E., *Lexicon to the English Poetical Works of John Milton* (New York, 1907).

MAZZATINTI, G. ed., *Inventari dei Manoscritti delle Biblioteche d'Italia*, (Florence, 1890-).

SADIE, STANLEY, ed., *The New Grove Dictionary of Music and Musicians* (6th ed.) (London, 1980), 20 vols.

5   SECONDARY LITERATURE

ADEMOLLO, ALESSANDRO, *I Teatri di Roma nel Secolo Decimo-settimo* (Rome, 1888).
_____, *La Bell' Adriana ed Altre Virtuose del Suo Tempo alla Corte de Mantova* (Citta di Castello: Lapi, 1888).
_____, *La Leonora di Milton e di Clemente IX* (Milan, 1885).
ALLODOLI, ETTORE, *Giovanni Milton e l'Italia* (Prato, 1907).
ANDREINI, GUIDI, *La Vita e l'Opera di Carlo Roberto Dati* (Milan, 1963).
ARTHOS, JOHN, *Milton and the Italian Cities* (London, 1968).
BENVENUTI, EDOARDO, *Agostino Coltellini e l'Accademia degli Apatisti a Firenze nel Secolo XVII* (Pistoia, 1910).
BISHOP, W.H., "Maugars' Response Faite à un Curieux sur le Sentiment de la Musique d'Italie," *Journal of the Viola da Gamba Society of America* 8 (1971), 5-17.
BLACK, JOHN, *Life of Torquato Tasso* (Edinburgh, 1810).
BORZELLI, ANGELO, *Giovan Battista Manso* (Naples, 1916).
BRADNER, LEICESTER, "Milton's *Epitaphium Damonis*," *Times Literary Supplement* 18 Aug. 1932, 581.
BRAND, C.P., *Torquato Tasso: A Study of the Poet and of His Contribution to English Literature* (Cambridge, 1965)
BROOKES, IAN, "The Death of Chiron: Ovid, *Fasti* 5.379-414," *Classical Quarterly* 44.2 (1994), 444-450.
BROWN, CEDRIC, *John Milton: A Literary Life* (Macmillan, 1995).
BUSH, DOUGLAS, "The Date of Milton's *Ad Patrem*," *Modern Philology* 61 (1963-64), 204-208.
BYARD, MARGARET, "Adventurous Song: Milton and the Music of Rome," *Milton in Italy: Contexts, Images, Contradictions*, ed. M.A. Di Cesare (Binghamton, 1991), 305-328.
CAMPBELL, GORDON, "Francini's Permesso," *Milton Quarterly* 15 (1981), 122-133.
_____, "Milton's Spanish," *Milton Quarterly* (1997), 127-132.
CAREY, JOHN, "The Date of Milton's Italian Poems," *Review of English Studies*, n.s. 14 (1963), 383-386.
CHAMBERS, D.S.,"The Earlier 'Academies' in Italy" in D.S. Chambers & F. Quiviger eds., *Italian Academies of the Sixteenth Century* (Warburg Institute: London, 1995), 1-14.
CHAMBERS, D.S. & QUIVIGER, F., eds., *Italian Academies of the Sixteenth Century* (Warburg Institute: London, 1995)
CHANEY, EDWARD, *The Grand Tour and the Great Rebellion* (Geneva, 1985).
CIARDI, R.P., "A Knot of Words and Things: Some Clues for Interpreting the *Imprese* of Academies and Academicians," *Italian Academies of the Sixteenth Century*, eds. Chambers, D.S. & Quiviger, F. (Warburg Institute: London, 1995), 37-66.
CLARK, D.C., *John Milton at St Paul's School* (New York, 1948; rpt. Hamden, 1964).
CLAVERING, ROSE and SHAWCROSS, JOHN, "Milton's European Itinerary and His Return Home," *Studies in English Literature* 5 (1965), 49-59.
CLEMENTS, R.J., "The Cult of the Poet in Renaissance Emblem Literature," *Publications of the Modern Language Association of America*, 59 (1944), 673-685.
COCHRANE, E.W., *Tradition and Enlightenment in the Tuscan Academies 1690-1800* (Chicago, 1961).

CONDEE, R.W., "*Mansus* and the Panegyric tradition," *Studies in the Renaissance* 15 (1968), 174-192.

——————, "Ovid's Exile and Milton's Rustication," *Philological Quarterly* 37 (1958), 498-502.

——————, *Structure in Milton's Poetry: From the Foundation to the Pinnacles* (Pennsylvania, 1974).

DE FILIPPIS, Michele, *Anecdotes in Manso's Life of Tasso and Their Sources* (Berkeley, 1936).

——————, "Milton and Manso: Cups or Books?" *Publications of the Modern Language Association of America* 51 (1936), 745-756.

DEMARAY, HANNAH, "Milton's Perfect Paradise and the Landscapes of Italy," *Milton Quarterly* 8 (1974), 33-41.

DI CESARE, M.A., ed., *Milton in Italy: Contexts, Images, Contradictions* (Medieval and Renaissance Texts and Studies, vol. 19 [Binghamton, 1991]).

DORIAN, D.C., "Milton's *Epitaphium Damonis*, Lines 181-97," *Publications of the Modern Language Association of America* 54 (1939), 612-613.

——————, *The English Diodatis* (New Brunswick, 1950).

FABRICIUS, J.A., *Conspectus Thesauri Literariae Italiae* (Hamburg, 1749).

FEHL, PHILLIP, "Poetry and the Entry of the Fine Arts into England: *Ut Pictura Poesis*," in *The Age of Milton: Backgrounds to Seventeenth-Century Literature*, ed. C.A. Patrides and R.B. Waddington (Manchester, 1980), 273-306.

FIELD, A., *The Origins of the Platonic Academy of Florence* (Princeton, 1988).

FINK, Z.S., "Milton and the Theory of Climatic Influence," *Modern Language Quarterly* 2 (1941), 67-80.

FINNEY, G.L., "Chorus in Samson Agonistes," *Publications of the Modern Language Association of America* 58 (1943), 649-664.

FLANNAGAN, ROY, "Reflections on Milton and Ariosto," *Early Modern Literary Studies* 2.3 (1996), 4, 1-16.

FLETCHER, H.F., "Milton's *Apologus* and its Mantuan Model," *Journal of English and Germanic Philology* 55 (1956), 230-233.

——————, "The Seventeenth-Century Separate Printing of Milton's *Epitaphium Damonis*," *JEGP* 61 (1962), 788-796.

FORSYTH, NEIL, "Of Man's First Dis," *Milton in Italy: Contexts, Images, Contradictions*, ed. M.A. Di Cesare (Binghamton, 1991), 345-369.

FREEMAN, J.A., "Milton's Roman Connection: Giovanni Salzilli," *Milton Studies* 19 (1984), 87-104.

FRYE, ROLAND, *Milton's Imagery and the Visual Arts: Iconographic Tradition in the Epic Poems* (Princeton, 1978).

HAAN, ESTELLE, "John Milton's *Ad Patrem* and Hugo Grotius's *In Natalem Patris*," *Notes and Queries*, n.s. forthcoming.

——————, "John Milton Among the Neo-Latinists: Three Notes on *Mansus*," *Notes and Queries*, n.s. 22.2 (June 1997), 172-176.

——————, *John Milton's Latin Poetry: Some Neo-Latin and Vernacular Contexts* (Ph.D. thesis, The Queen's University of Belfast, 1987).

——————, "Milton and Two Italian Humanists: Some Hitherto Unnoticed Neo-Latin Echoes in *In Obitum Procancellarii Medici* and *In Obitum Praesulis Eliensis*," *Notes and Queries*, n.s. 22.2 (June, 1997), 176-181.

_____, "Milton's Latin Poetry and Vida," *Humanistica Lovaniensia: Journal of Neo-Latin Studies* 44 (1995), 282-304.

_____, "Milton's *Naturam non Pati Senium* and Hakewill" *Medievalia et Humanistica*, n.s. 24 (1997), 147-167.

_____, "Milton, Manso, and Ovid's Chiron," *Classical and Modern Literature* 17.3 (1997), 251-264.

_____, "Milton, Manso and the Fruit of That Forbidden Tree," *Medievalia et Humanistica*, n.s. 25 forthcoming 1998.

_____, "*Written encomiums*: Milton's Latin Poetry in its Italian Context," *Milton in Italy: Contexts, Images, Contradictions*, ed. M.A. Di Cesare (Binghamton, 1991), 521-547.

HALE, J.K., *Milton's Languages: The Impact of Multilingualism on Style* (Cambridge, 1997).

HAMMOND, FREDERICK, *Music and Spectacle in Baroque Rome: Barberini Patronage Under Urban VIII* (London, 1994).

HANFORD, J.H., *A Milton Handbook* (New York, 1946).

_____, *John Milton Englishman* (New York, 1949).

HANKINS, J., "The Myth of the Platonic Academy of Florence," *Renaissance Quarterly* 44 (1991), 427-475.

HARRIS, NEIL, "Galileo as Symbol: the "Tuscan artist" in *Paradise Lost*," *Annali dell' Istituto e Museo di Storia della Scienza di Firenze* 10 (1985), 3-29.

HENINGER, S.K., *Touches of Sweet Harmony: Pythagorean Cosmology and Renaissance Poetics* (California, 1974).

HILL, J.S., "Poet-Priest: Vocational Tension in Milton's Early Development," *Milton Studies* 8 (1975), 41-69.

HORWOOD, A.J., ed., *A Common-place Book of John Milton, and a Latin Essay and Latin Verses Presumed to be by Milton* (Camden Society, London, n.s. 16, 1877).

HUBBARD, EDITH, *Notes and Queries*, n.s. 8 (1961), 171-172.

LAZZERI, ALLESSANDRO, *Intellettuali e Consenso nella Toscana del Seicento: L'Accademia degli Apatisti* (Milan, 1983).

LEEDHAM-GREEN, E.S., *Books in Cambridge Inventories: Book-lists From Vice-Chancellors' Court Probate Inventories in the Tudor and Stuart Periods* (Cambridge, 1986).

_____, *Private Libraries in Renaissance England* (*Medieval and Renaissance Texts and Studies* [New York, Binghamton, 1994]).

LOW, ANTHONY, "*Mansus*: In Its Context," *Milton Studies* 19 (1984), 105-126.

MCCOLLEY, D.K., "Edenic Iconography: *Paradise Lost* and the Mosaics of San Marco," *Milton in Italy: Contexts, Images, Contradictions*, ed. M.A. Di Cesare (Binghamton, 1991), 197-214.

_____, "Tongues of Men and Angels: *Ad Leonoram Romae Canentem*," *Milton Studies* 19 (1984), 127-147.

MACKIE, C.J., "Achilles' Teachers: Chiron and Phoenix in the *Iliad*," *Greece and Rome* 44.1 (1997), 1-10.

MANFREDI, MICHELE, *Giovanni Battista Manso nella Vita e nelle Opere* (Naples, 1919)

MASSON, DAVID, *The Life of John Milton: Narrated in Connexion with the Political, Ecclesiastical, and Literary History of his Time* (Cambridge, 1859-94), 6 vols.

MAYLENDER, MICHELE, *Storia delle Accademie d'Italia* (Bologna, 1926-1930) 5 vols.

MILLER, LEO, "Milton's *patriis cicutis,*" *Notes and Queries*, n.s. 28 (1981), 41-42.

_____, "Milton and Holstenius Reconsidered," *Milton in Italy: Contexts, Images, Contradictions,* ed. M.A. Di Cesare (Binghamton, 1991), 573-587.

MIROLLO, J.V., *The Poet of the Marvelous: Giambattista Marino* (New York, 1963).

MONTAGU, JENNIFER, *An Index of Emblems of the Italian Academies* (Warburg Institute, 1988).

NARDO, A.K., "Academic Interludes in *Paradise Lost,*" *Milton Studies* 27 (1991), 209-241.

_____, "Milton and the Academic Sonnet," *Milton in Italy: Contexts, Images, Contradictions,* ed. M.A. Di Cesare (Binghamton, 1991), 489-503.

NEGRI, G., *Istoria degli Scrittori Fiorentini* (Ferrara, 1722).

NICOLSON, M. H., "Milton and the Phlegraean Fields," *University of Toronto Quarterly* 7 (1938), 500-513.

OBERHELMAN, S.M. and MULRYAN, JOHN, "Milton's Use of Classical Meters in the *Sylvarum Liber,*" *Modern Philology* 81 (1983), 131-145.

O' CONNELL, MICHAEL, "Milton and the Art of Italy: A Revisionist View," *Milton in Italy: Contexts, Images, Contradictions,* ed. M.A. Di Cesare (Binghamton, 1991), 215-236.

PADIGLIONE, CARLO, *Le Leggi dell' Accademia degli Oziosi in Napoli Ritrovate nella Biblioteca Brancacciana* (Naples, 1878).

PARKER, W.R., Milton: *A Biography* (Oxford, 1968) 2 vols; rev. ed. by Campbell, Gordon (Oxford, 1996).

_____,"Milton and the News of Charles Diodati's Death," *Modern Language Notes* 72 (1957), 486-488.

_____, "Notes on the Chronology of Milton's Latin Poems," in A. Williams, ed., *A Tribute to George Coffin Taylor* (Carolina, 1955), 113-131

PRINCE, F.T., *The Italian Element in Milton's Verse* (Oxford, 1954).

REBORA, PIERO, "Milton a Firenze," *Nuova Antologia* 88 (1953), rpt. in *Interpretazioni Anglo-Italiane: Saggi e Ricerche* (Adriatica editrice, 1961), 139-157.

REVARD, S.P.,"Milton and Chiabrera," *Milton in Italy: Contexts, Images, Contradictions,* ed. M.A. Di Cesare (Binghamton, 1991), 505-520.

_____, *Milton and the Tangles of Neaera's Hair* (Missouri, 1997)

RICHEK, ROSLYN, "Thomas Randolph's Salting (1627): its Text, and John Milton's Sixth *Prolusion* as Another Salting," *English Literary Renaissance* 12 (1982), 102-131.

RICKS, CHRISTOPHER, *Milton's Grand Style* (Oxford, 1963).

ROSEN, EDWARD, "A friend of John Milton: Valerio Chimentelli," *Bulletin of the New York Public Library* 57 (1953), 159-174

SANTINI, C., "Lettura Strutturale ed Etimologia in un Cataterismo dei *Fasti,*" *Materiali e Contributi per la Storia della Narrativa Greco-Latina* 1 (1976), 49-56.

SCHLEINER, LOUISE, "Milton, G.B. Doni and the Dating of Doni's Works," *Milton Quarterly* 16 (1982), 36-42

SCHOONHOVEN, H., "Purple Swans and Purple Snow," *Mnemosyne*, series 4, 31 (1978), 200-203.

SCHUYLER, EUGENE, "Milton's Leonora," *Nation* 47 (18 October, 1888), 310-312.

SEARS, DONALD, "*La Tina*: the Country Sonnets of Antonio Malatesti as Dedicated to Mr. John Milton, Englishman," *Milton Studies* 13 (1979), 275-317.

SHAWCROSS, J.T., "*Epitaphium Damonis*: lines 9-13 and the Date of Composition," *Modern Language Notes* 71 (1956), 322-324.

──────, *John Milton: The Self and the World* (Lexington, 1993)

──────, "The Date of Milton's *Ad Patrem*," *Notes and Queries*, n.s. 6 (1959), 358-359.

──────, "The Date of the Separate Edition of Milton's *Epitaphium Damonis*," *Studies in Bibliography* 18 (1965), 262-265.

SIRLUCK, E., *Milton Studies in Honour of Harris Francis Fletcher* (Urbana, 1961).

SMART, J. S., "Milton in Rome," *Modern Language Review* 8 (1913), 91-92.

STARNES, D.T. and TALBERT, E.W., *Classical Myth and Legend in Renaissance Dictionaries* (Univ. of North Carolina Press: Chapel Hill, 1955).

STOYE, J.W., *English Travellers Abroad, 1604-1667* (London, 1952).

TREIP, MINDELE, "Celestial Patronage: Allegorical Ceiling Cycles of the 1630s and the Iconography of Milton's Muse," *Milton in Italy: Contexts, Images, Contradictions*, ed. M.A. Di Cesare (Binghamton, 1991), 237-279.

──────, *Descend from Heav'n Urania: Milton's Paradise Lost and Raphael's Cycle in the Stanza della Segnatura*, English Literary Studies 35 (University of Victoria, 1985).

VIVIANI, ALBERTO, *Gabriello Chiabrera* (Rome, 1938).

WALKER, J.C., *Historical Memoir on Italian Tragedy* (London, 1799).

WEST, R.H., *Milton and the Angels* (Athens, 1955).

WILLIAMS, F.B., *Index of Dedications and Commendatory Verse In English Books Before 1649* (London, 1962).

INDEX NOMINUM

www.ingramcontent.com/pod-product-compliance
Lightning Source LLC
Chambersburg PA
CBHW080924100426
42812CB00007B/2364

* 9 7 8 0 8 7 1 6 9 8 8 6 5 *